IMAGES
of America

DANVILLE REVISITED

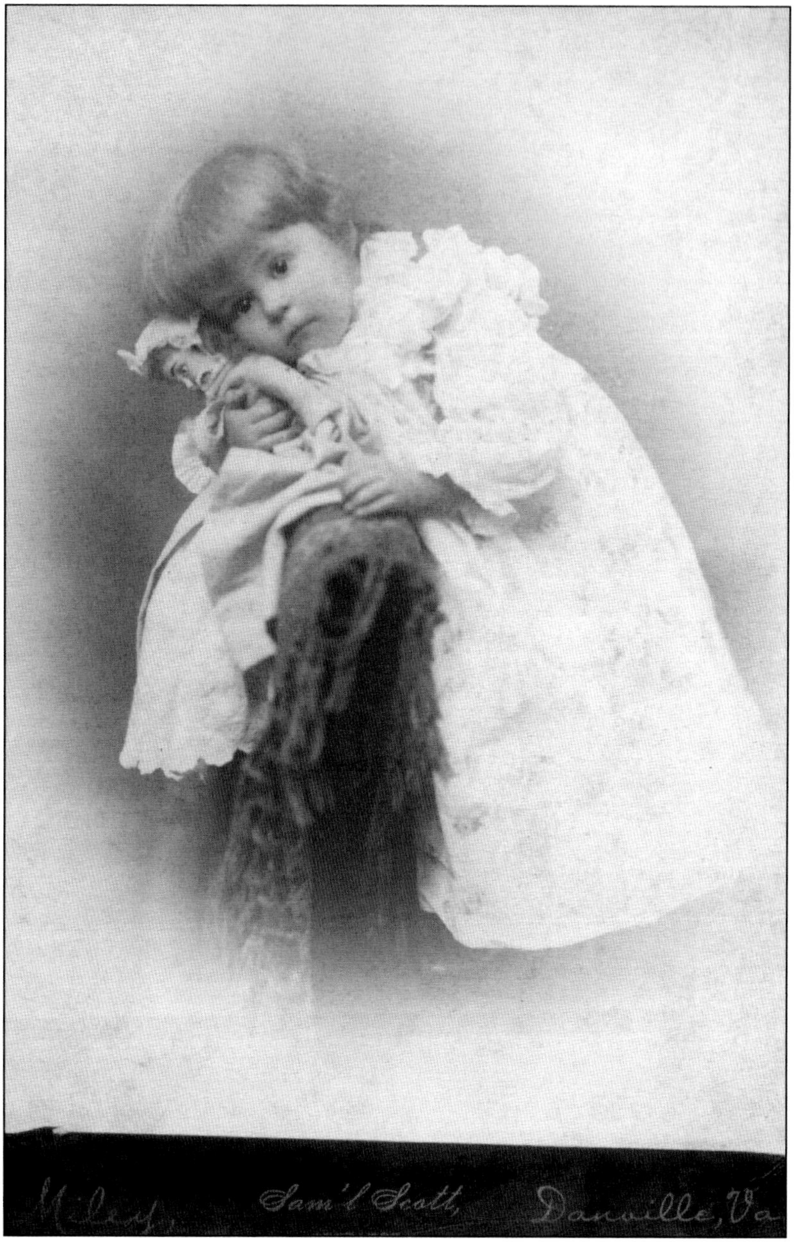

Photographer Michael Miley captured the childhood innocence of Cobbie Marie Vaughan posing with her doll. Miley worked in Danville from 1887 to 1889; he then moved to Lexington, Virginia, where he experimented with a color photography process for which he received a patent. Miley produced some of the earliest color photographic prints in the United States. (Photograph by Michael Miley; courtesy of the Danville Museum of Fine Arts and History.)

ON THE COVER: During World War I, Danville women volunteered with the same patriotic fervor as the servicemen who went off to war. Pictured at the Red Cross canteen in Danville's railroad yard is one of ten companies marshaled by Fannie Fitzgerald Martin, a member of Calvary Methodist Church. In Danville, some 375,000 people benefited from supplies and medical assistance provided by the local canteen. (Photograph by Leon Taylor; courtesy of Clara Fountain.)

IMAGES
of America

DANVILLE REVISITED

Clara G. Fountain and Gary Grant

ARCADIA
PUBLISHING

ISBN 978-1-4671-2001-2

Published by Arcadia Publishing
Charleston, South Carolina

Printed in the United States of America

Library of Congress Control Number: 2013930701

For all general information, please contact Arcadia Publishing:
Telephone 843-853-2070
Fax 843-853-0044
E-mail sales@arcadiapublishing.com
For customer service and orders:
Toll-Free 1-888-313-2665

Visit us on the Internet at www.arcadiapublishing.com

To Leon N. Taylor (1882–1937) and to George Eastman and his Eastman Kodak Company (1888–2012)

Contents

ACKNOWLEDGMENTS

The authors wish to thank all the people and organizations who have contributed to this work. Special thanks go to our editor, Lissie Cain, and the staff of Arcadia Publishing for their many helpful suggestions. We appreciate those who have offered their encouragement and who have given us many tidbits of local history during this eight-month project.

The authors in particular wish to thank the following, who gave us permission to use their photographs and provided us with facts and anecdotes about the subjects of their images: Peggy Adkins, Mildred M. Alvarez, Averett University Archives, Lyn Benefield, Wayne Brumfield, Edith F. Burns, Linda M. Burns, Susan H. Burns, Stavros Calos, Steve Calos, Allen B. Carter, Jane Carter, Cindy Castle, Mike Compson, Patsi Compton, Michael Craddock, Stuart Craig, Jeanette Cruz, Joan W. Daniel, Danville Historical Society, Danville Museum of Fine Arts and History, Danville Public Library, Richard T. Davis, Elaine Day, Kim Demont, Laurie Calos Dishman, Margaret Winn Dryden, Danville fire chief David Eagle, Charles Easley III, Claudia C. Easley, Mary Gail Easley, Judy Edmonds, Zoe Edmunds, Marc Fountain, Martha Fowlkes, Earle Garrett III, William H. Garrett, Sue B. Glidewell, Meredith W. Gravely, James Green, Travis Hackworth, Carol Handy, Dot Handy, Jan Grant Harris, Dr. Edwin Harvie Jr., Lou Hendricks, Diannia Hudgins, Sonja Ingram, Lula Jeffers, William E. Land, Wanda Landrum, Langhorne House, Johnny Laramore, Dan Latham, Sarah Latham, Harry Lea, C.B. Maddox, John P. Maurakis, Patricia Maurakis, Lawrence McFall, Carolyn W. Miles, Judy Mills, Betty Lou Montgomery, Thelma B. Motley, Mount Vernon United Methodist Church, National Tobacco-Textile Museum, Mike Owen, PIP Printing, Danielle Pritchett, Emma Rich, Ruby Lee Rich, Bobby Ricketts, Danny Ricketts, Lee Robertson, Glenn Scarboro, Schoolfield Museum & Cultural Center, Jonathan Scollo, Terry Shadrick, Dee Smith, Carol Strange, Charlton Strange, Leon Townsend, Arnold Turner, Virginia State Chamber of Commerce, Virginia State Library (Library of Virginia), VA-NC Piedmont Genealogical Society, Patrick Wasley, Lee Wayland, Joan Waynick, Joyce Wilburn, Carl Williams, Christina Williams, Mike Williams, Geraldine Wilson, and Carson Womack.

Unless otherwise noted, all images appear courtesy of Clara Fountain.

INTRODUCTION

In May 2012, Clara Fountain purchased a box of Danville photographs from the estate sale of Judge William E. Land sponsored by Joan Daniel of Simpson Realty and The Attic Hound. Most of the photographs were taken by Leon N. Taylor, a North Danville native who photographed people, buildings, and events in the city from around 1900 to the 1930s. Several of his prints captured scenes previously believed to be lost to the passage of time. Fountain became so intrigued by their importance to the collective memory of Danville that she showed them to fellow local historian Gary Grant, and they resolved to publish Taylor's photographs and make them available to present-day residents of Danville.

Since the subject matter of the more than 100 prints was widely disparate, the next step was to figure out a theme that could connect them. The idea of paying homage to Danville's photographers, who visually recorded the city's past, provided the logical thread of continuity for this volume. Other works about Danville's history have looked at the city chronologically. The authors of this book, however, chose to revisit Danville by organizing the study from a fresh perspective.

Over the course of more than 150 years of photography in this area, fellow Danvillians have gone about their daily routines—raising their families, attending local churches, playing and working. Yet those who worked as photographers, recording the living history around them, have remained almost invisible to that history—always behind the camera, only rarely in the frame. The authors wish to bring long overdue attention to these individuals who preserved such vivid insights into their times.

Using city directories at the Danville Public Library, the authors began a search to record all local photography studios listed from 1879 to 2010. The library did not own an entire run of directories, thus some names may not have been discovered, and for this, the authors apologize. With phone calls and personal entreaties, the authors continued their hopeful quest of obtaining at least one photograph from each of Danville's professional photographers. Fountain and Grant soon realized that they would be lucky to find photographs taken by one-third of the more than 120 Danville photographers. Needing to add more images to this book, the authors extended their search to include images from private photographers whose pursuit of the art ranked them with professionals.

This book provides a glimpse into the lives of both ordinary citizens and public figures. Early scenes of Main Street show the uphill expansion of local businesses, which followed an ancient Indian trail. Images of other streets—such as Patton, Green, Holbrook, West and North Main Streets—reveal the development of the city as it benefited from the tobacco and textile magnates who built mansions along what is now called Millionaires Row. Some photographs show the emergence of public transportation.

To fully appreciate the visual heritage left to Danville by the professionals who stepped outside their studios and took photographs of the city and all its energy, one might benefit from a few facts about the evolution of photography.

Photography began in 1839 with Frenchman Louis Daguerre, who created a permanent positive image on a silver-plated sheet of copper. To protect the fragile picture, Daguerre positioned it under a sheet of glass inside a folding leather case. This "daguerreotype" procedure rapidly spread across the globe, becoming especially popular in the United States. Hamilton Smith, an Ohio photographer, invented the tintype, an image captured on a thin sheet of iron that could be trimmed to fit small frames. Both of these processes produced only one positive image.

Soon, photographic innovators perfected a process to produce multiple prints on coated paper from negative images on wet glass. The first photographs created using this method were called *cartes de visite* (CDV) and were the size of business cards, with images fixed onto small cardboard backings. Later, when customers desired prints slightly larger than the CDV, the market responded with the cabinet card. For those unable to afford oil portraits or painted miniatures, the advent of photography as a means to capture family members' likenesses was exciting, affordable, and almost instantaneous.

According to local historian Danny Ricketts, Danville had a photography studio as early as 1851. A letter in Ricketts' possession written by William C. Shelton states, "On reaching Danville I concluded to have my likeness taken. I therefore remained in that place 'til it could be done . . . and for which I paid $3.00 and to tavern for horse 25 cents to barber nine cents."

The first professional photographer to advertise a studio in Danville was Eugene N. Medernach, who moved to the United States from France. Medernach came to Danville in the 1860s and opened a studio on Main Street, near the 1851 covered bridge. As the earliest local photographer to record images other than portraits, Medernach captured Main Street's downtown on glass negatives in 1878, including two images that were included in *Winding Through Time*, a commemorative book published for Danville's 1993 bicentennial. A similar Medernach image is reproduced in this book.

It is difficult to locate the exact sites of the earliest area studios, which existed before Danville assigned street numbers. Yet by the 1880s, specific, numbered addresses became more common. Anthony H. Blunt opened the Blunt Art Palace in 1879 at 46 Main Street. By 1886, he had moved to 317 Main Street, on the second floor of the Waddill Building. Succeeding Blunt in this studio were Michael Miley, Samuel Scott, Frank A. Kroneberger, Charles W. Eutsler and his brother William E. Eutsler, Oliver W. Cole, and Phillip W. Dunford.

Over the years, several photographers and businesses had studios at 421 Main Street, including Alfonso D. Rice, Frank H. Richardson, Letcher H. Brown, and the Danville Photograph Gallery. By 1917, a different Danville Gallery occupied a studio at 427 Main Street, followed by John J. Hitchcock, his son J. Raymond Hitchcock, and Polivios Zazopoulis. W.G.R. Frayser had a studio at 236 Main Street, and Leon Taylor opened his own studio in 1914 at 563 Main Street.

In North Danville, John R. Shelkett advertised a studio at 410 North Main Street from 1898 to 1907. When he left Danville and moved to South Carolina, Shelkett worked as a photographer in Greenville from 1917 until his death in 1921. William S. Brown took over Shelkett's studio on North Main Street.

In 1921, Henry Boyd operated a studio at 655 High Street. Jesse G. Seay and his father maintained the only studio in Schoolfield, which was located above the cotton mill's cloth store. Of course, many other photographers practiced in Danville, but these are among the early ones who worked outside of their homes in professional studios.

The authors wish to express thanks to the many photographers who recorded our city's history. Their valuable work has given us a visual sense of our past, including the faces of many individuals (and their clothing and accessories), exteriors and interiors of homes and buildings, and the different types of architecture in our city.

With George Eastman's invention of roll film in 1883, photography became available to everyone, not just those trained at a studio. Eastman and his Eastman Kodak Company products enjoyed exceptional popularity for over 100 years. Early in the 21st century, the masses embraced newer digital photographic technology, which mostly swept away its film predecessor.

One

People

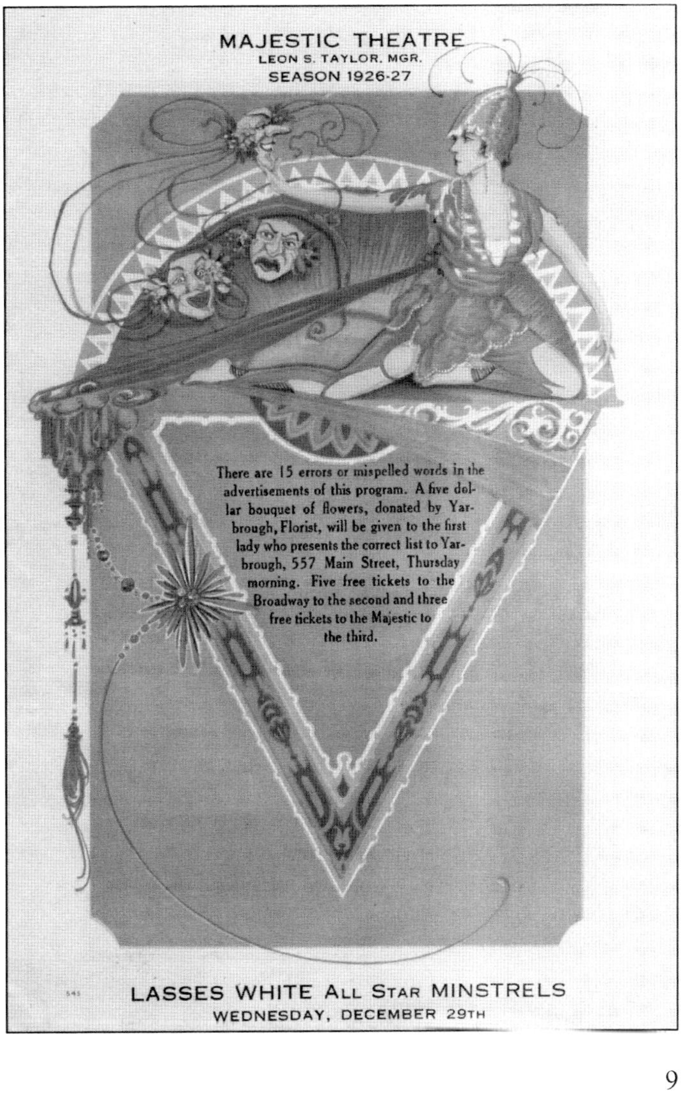

Leon N. Taylor was the first professional photographer to chronicle the daily history of Danville, which he did for about 30 years. Taylor maintained a studio at 563 Main Street, uphill from the Majestic Theater (later the Virginia), where he played the piano for silent movies. This 1926 program included a puzzle containing 15 errors (including Taylor's middle initial) and was intended to lure winners to the minstrel show. (Courtesy of the Danville Historical Society.)

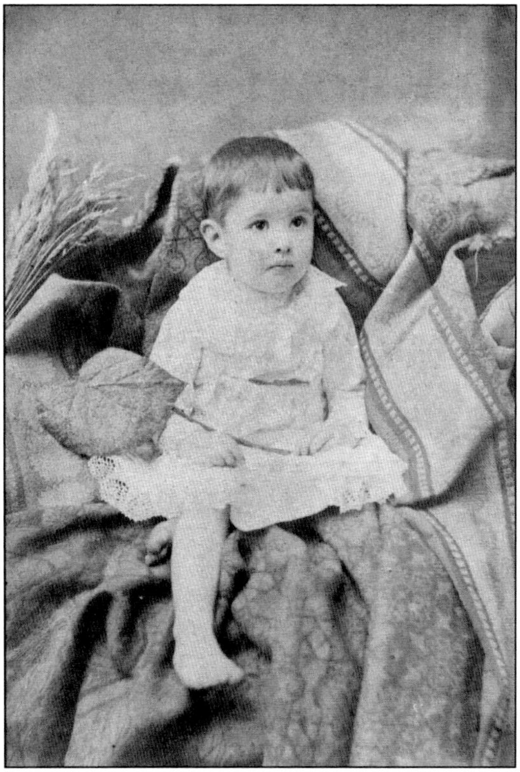

Leon Norvell Taylor, seen here at age three, was born on April 28, 1882, in North Danville. The son of Katherine Yardy and George W. Taylor, Leon was Danville's leading photographer from the early 1900s until the 1930s. Among North Danville's first families, the Taylors lived at 1002 North Main Street and helped establish Calvary Methodist Church, where they remained loyal members. (Courtesy of William E. Land.)

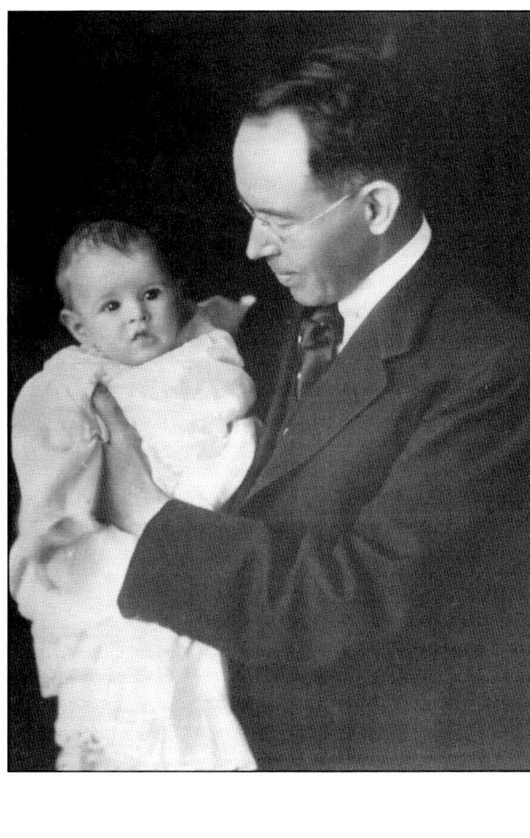

In this 1917 image, taken 35 years after the photograph above, Leon Taylor holds his newly born son, Leon Jr. Leon Sr.'s brother Clinton G. Taylor worked with him (they specialized in children's portraits), and Leon's wife, Margaret Pierce Taylor, worked as their clerk. Margaret worked in the Taylor studio until Leon's death in 1937; thereafter, she worked as a clerk at the studio of Raymond Hitchcock. (Courtesy of William E. Land.)

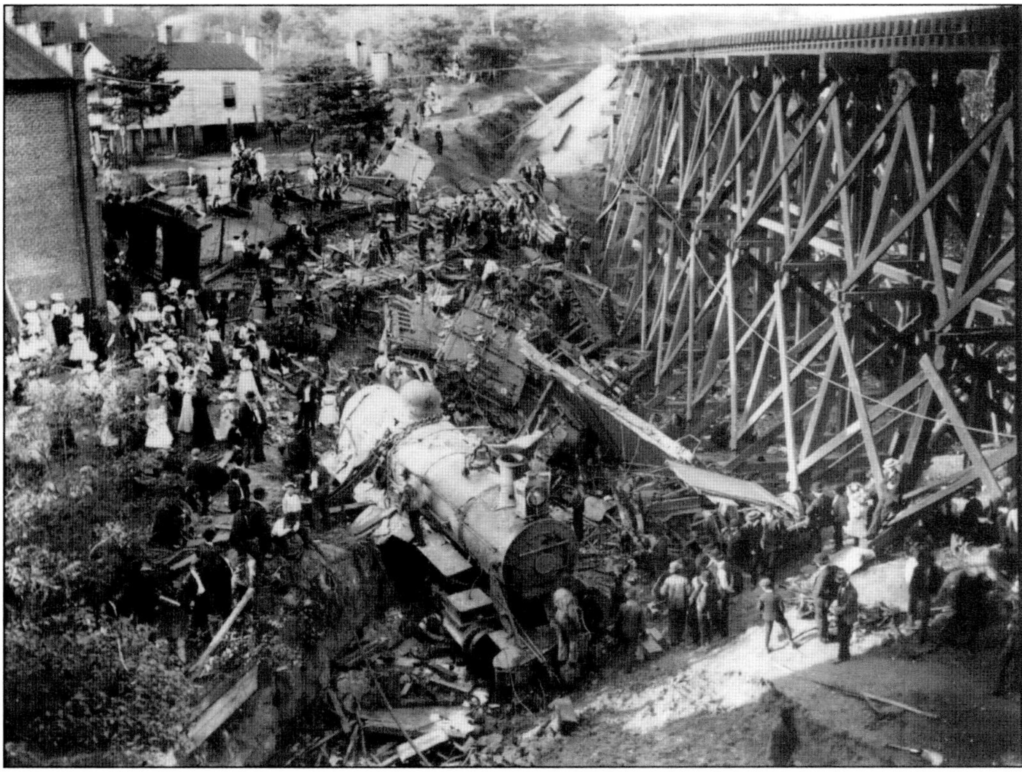

Most everyone who has heard of the Wreck of the Old 97 has seen these two photographs, but not many know who took them. Leon Taylor's series of photographs of the 1903 train wreck in Danville remain its official photographic canon. Taylor's images, recorded as negatives onto glass plates, allowed multiple prints from each. (Photograph by Leon Taylor.)

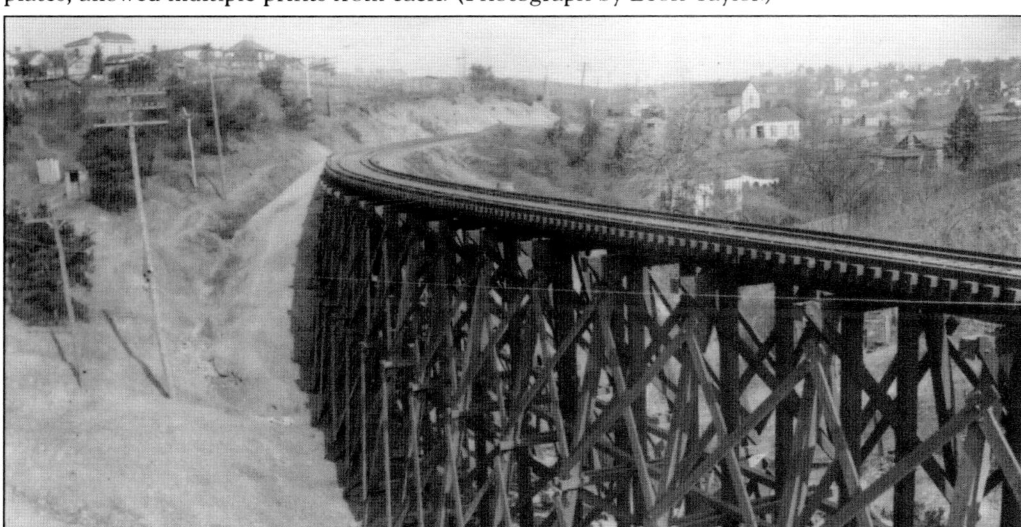

Taylor photographed the Stillhouse Trestle from the rooftop of one of the Riverside Cotton Mills buildings that was nearly struck by engine No. 1102 (the "Old 97") as the famous mail train crashed into the ravine below. This image, also printed from a glass negative, showed the descending grade of the tracks from Lima towards the Dan River. (Photograph by Leon Taylor.)

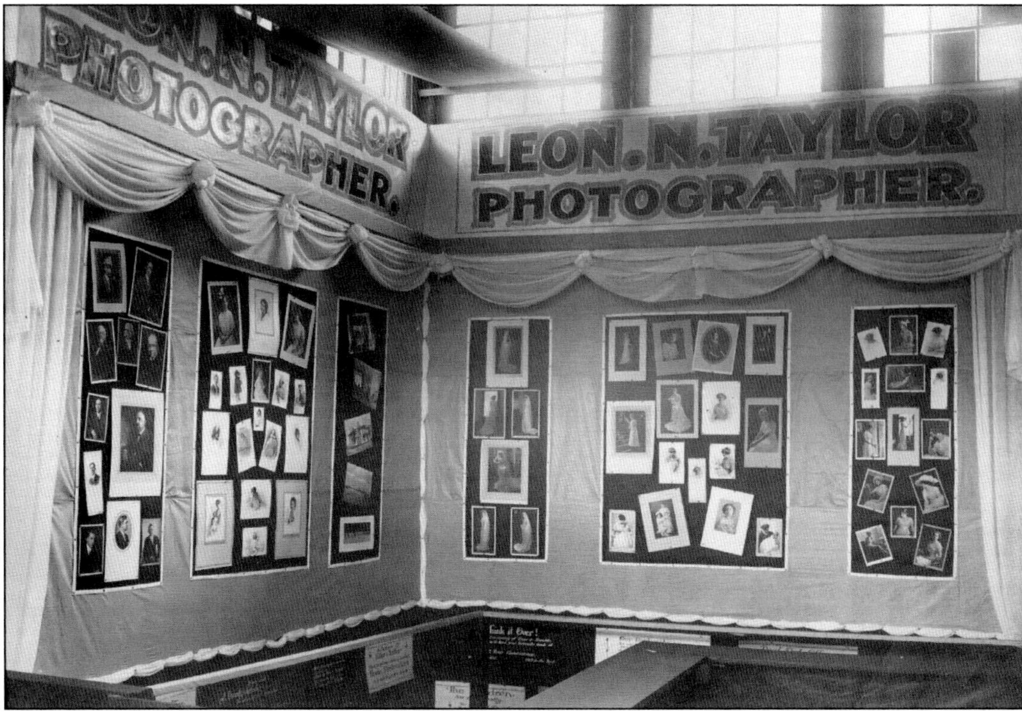

Most professional photographers stayed in business by taking portraits of local citizens, as reflected in this display of Leon Taylor's handiwork. He proved to be a man of many talents who was well prepared by his mentors. Before he established his own studio, Taylor served as an apprentice with the Eutsler Brothers Studio at 317 Main Street. (Photograph by Leon Taylor.)

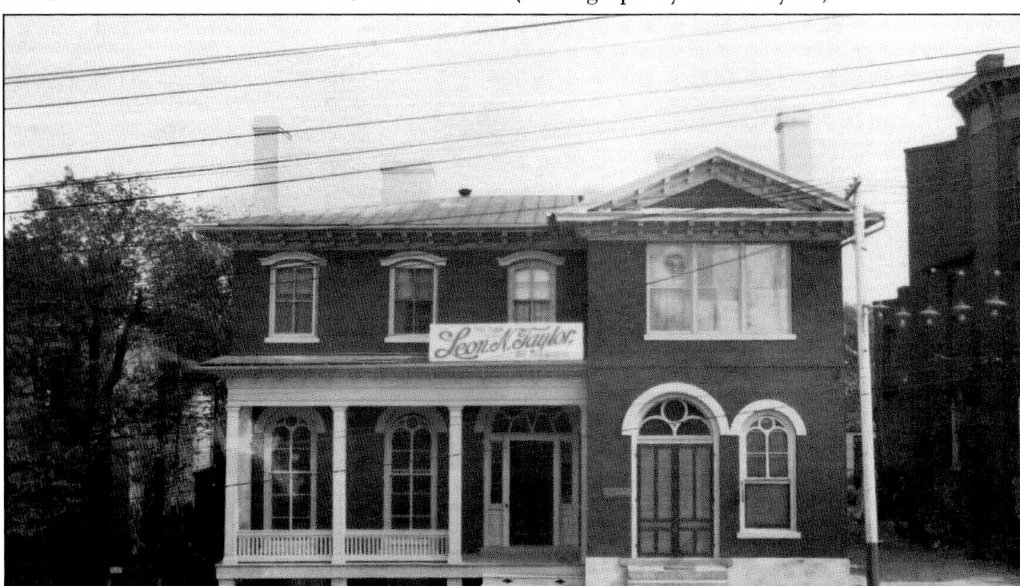

In 1914, Taylor opened his own photography studio in a house built in 1860 for John M. Johnston at 563 Main Street (the present-day site of Rippe's Shoes). Taylor captured the flavor of early Danville with a variety of surviving images of people, events, street scenes, and buildings. (Photograph by Leon Taylor.)

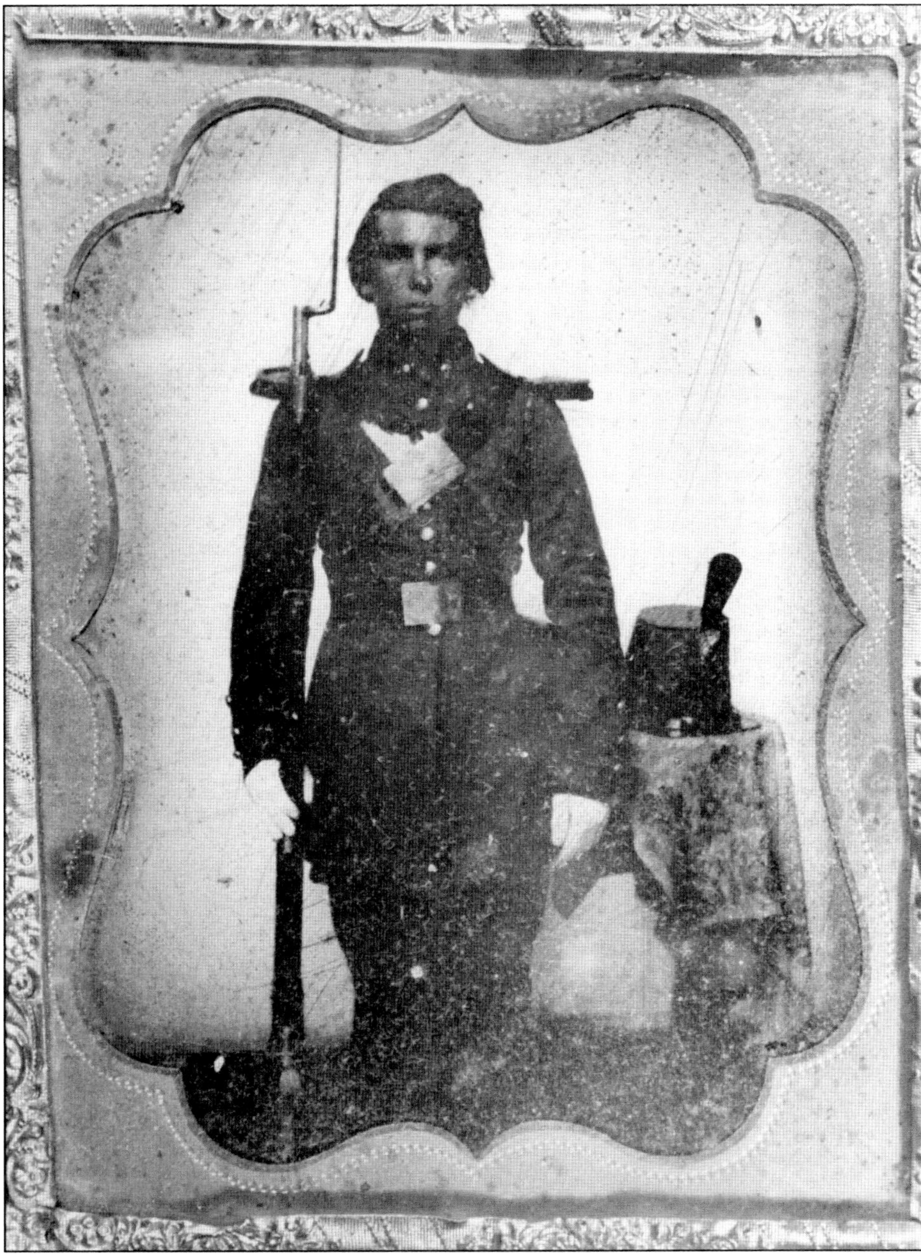

Born in Danville in 1844, Harry Wooding attended school at the Danville Male Academy on Academy Street (now Chambers Street), near Grove Street Cemetery. Like many young men who opt into military combat today, Wooding faced the grim realities of war early—by his mid-teens. In this daguerreotype from the mid-1860s, Wooding stands in his Confederate uniform with his bayonet and hat. When war broke out between the states, Wooding enlisted in the Danville Grays at age 16, serving under J.E.B. Stuart in the "Bloody Fifth" Virginia Cavalry. Wooding fought in several skirmishes, including the Battle of Bull Run and the Battle of Gettysburg. He spent four years with the Confederate forces—the only years he lived away from the Danville area. In early July 1938, Wooding attended the Battle of Gettysburg's 75th reunion, the last such veterans' convention. He died the following November at age 93. (Courtesy of Geraldine Wilson.)

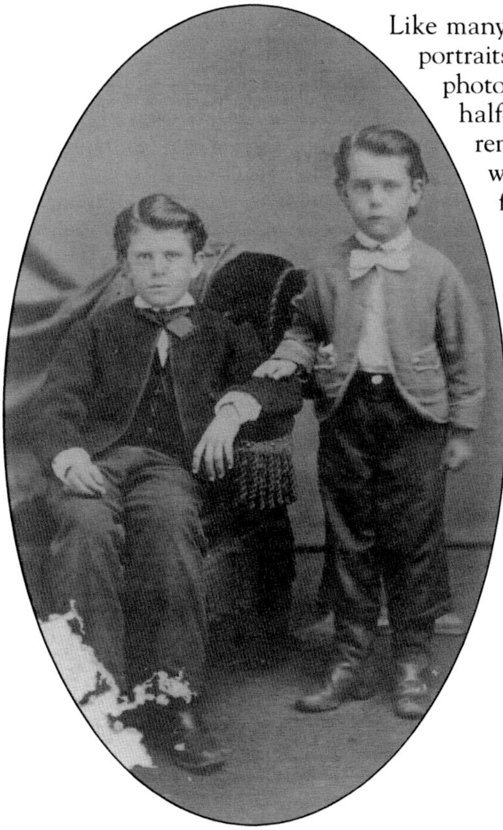

Like many Victorian families, the Woodings stored their portraits in a velvet-covered photograph album. This 1872 photograph shows Garland and George Wooding, the half-brothers of Harry Wooding, whose father had remarried after the tragic death of Harry's mother, whose dress was ignited when she passed too near the fireplace. (Photograph by J.M. South; courtesy of the Danville Museum of Fine Arts and History.)

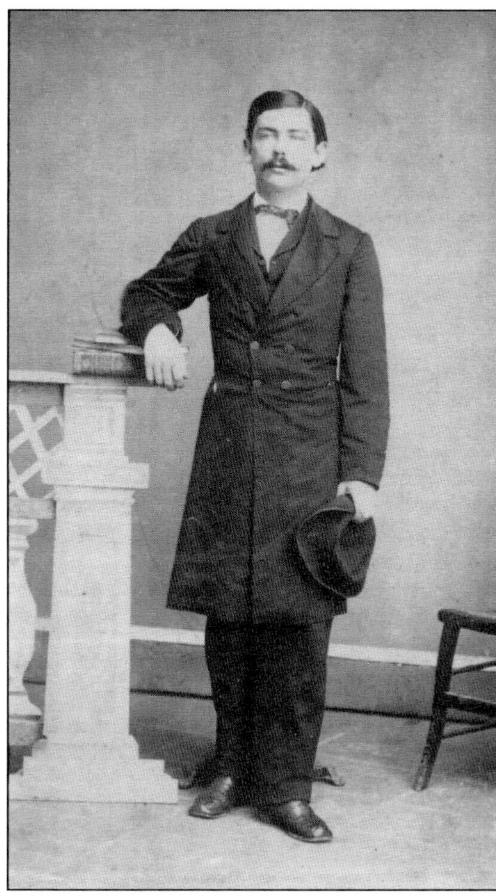

A partner in the dry-goods firm of Estes & Wooding, Harry Wooding continued in that business until 1892, when he won his first election and became mayor of Danville. He remained in office for 46 consecutive years. At the time of his death, in 1938, he held the record for the longest term in office of any mayor in the United States. (Photograph by Sanner & Medernach; courtesy of the Danville Museum of Fine Arts and History.)

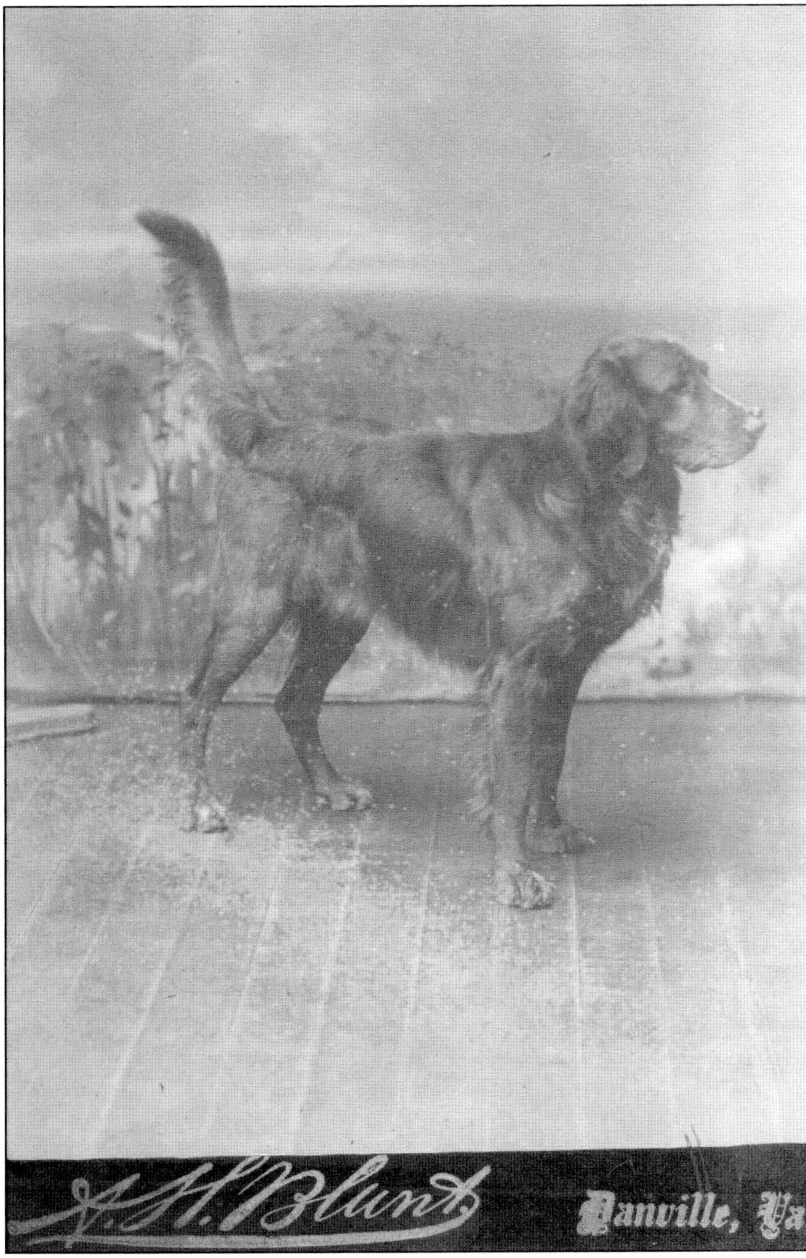

Harry Wooding's family commissioned this unusual portrait of Old Miller, the family dog. With the advent of cabinet cards, which were somewhat larger than earlier portraits, photographers now had room to stamp their names on the front of each image they produced. Harry Wooding was the sixth of ten children born to William Henry Wooding and Jane White Grasty, the daughter of Col. William C. Grasty. In 1873, William Henry "Harry" Wooding Jr. married Mary Ella Coleman, one of the twin daughters of Col. Daniel Coleman and Margaret Elizabeth Ayers. The Woodings had two daughters and one son. Before 1900, they lived in her parents' home at 722 Wilson Street. They then lived at 841 Main Street for many years before moving to their new residence, built in 1911 at 120 Holbrook Avenue. (Photograph by A.H. Blunt; courtesy of the Danville Museum of Fine Arts and History.)

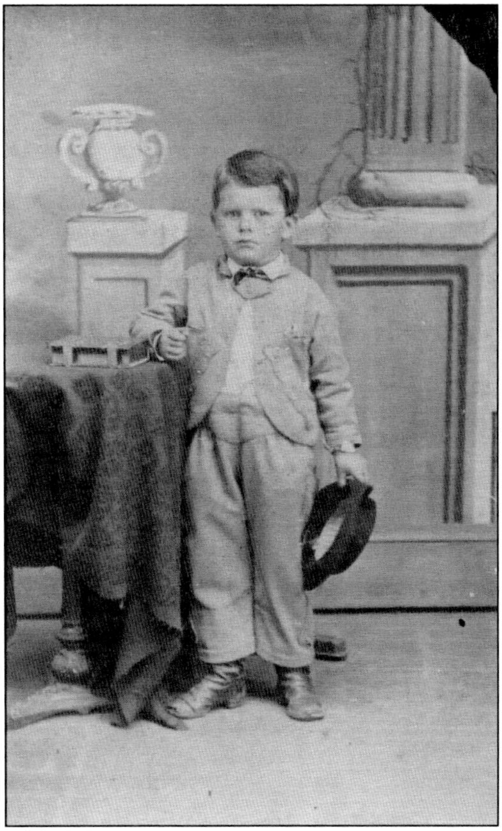

As is too often the case with family photographs, most images from the Wooding album were not labeled by name or date. This adorable four-year-old, who is unidentified, seemed to be holding his breath as well as his hat while waiting for the photographer to take his picture in 1868. (Photograph by Eugene N. Medernach; courtesy of the Danville Museum of Fine Arts and History.)

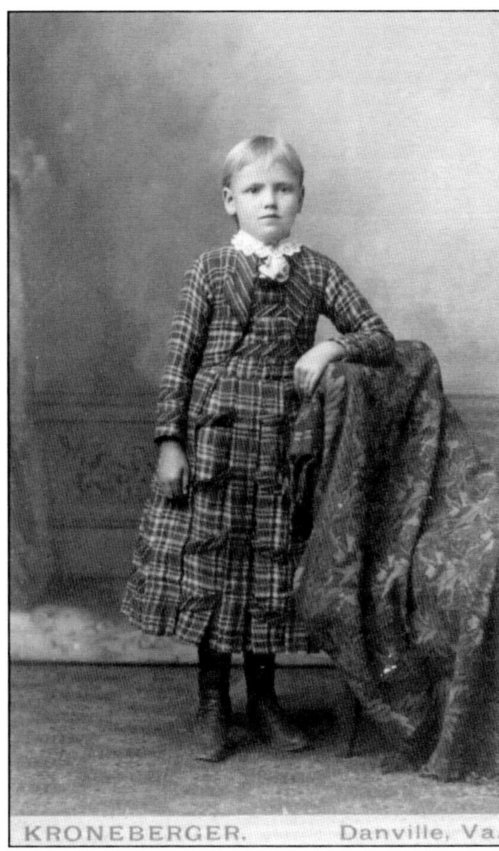

An 1850s innovation for coating glass plates with a wet solution made it possible to make multiple paper prints from one negative. Images attached to a small piece of cardboard, like this 1892 photograph of an unidentified girl, are known as *cartes de visite* (CDV). Itinerant photographers like Frank Kroneberger traveled widely and used this process in their work. (Photograph by F.A. Kroneberger; courtesy of Joan Daniel.)

Andrew Morton, a successful entrepreneur in Danville, was a barber who managed his own barbershop on Hotel Burton's ground level off North Union Street. His former shop had been located in the Hotel Arlington, which stood on the same site as the Hotel Burton. After moving to Danville in 1874, Morton also ran a dray line using two of his own fine horses for his delivery service. (Courtesy of Thelma B. Motley.)

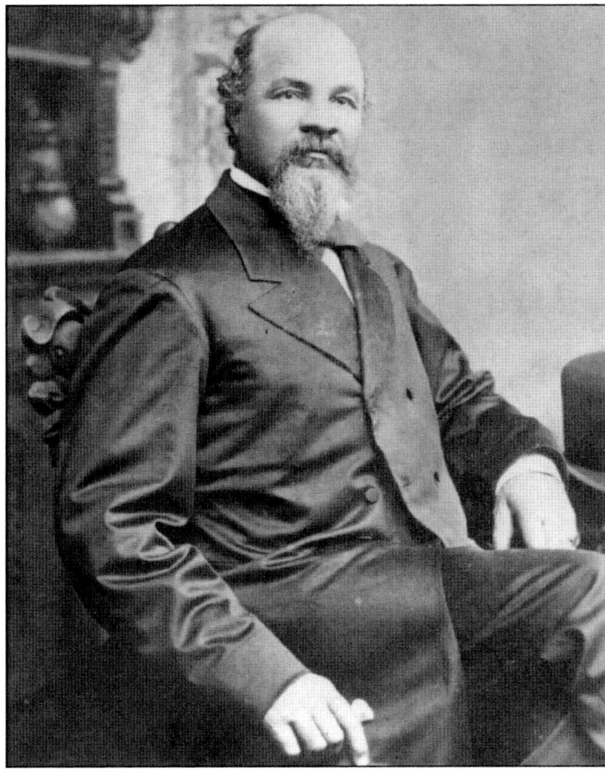

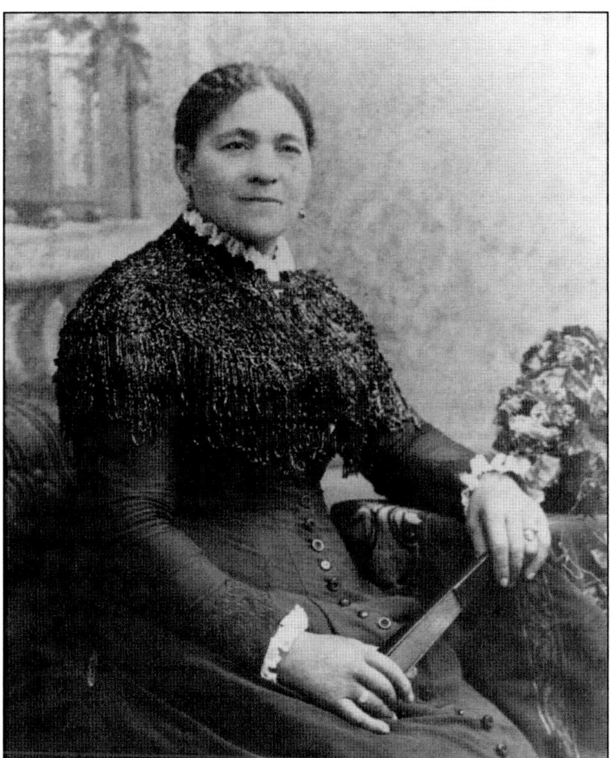

Mary Morton, Andrew's wife, held title to a large corner lot west of downtown, in Mechanicsville, where the couple built a fashionable mid-Victorian house at 543 Monroe Street. The Mortons were instrumental in organizing Calvary Baptist Church, located on the corner of Holbrook and Calvary Streets. (Courtesy of Thelma B. Motley.)

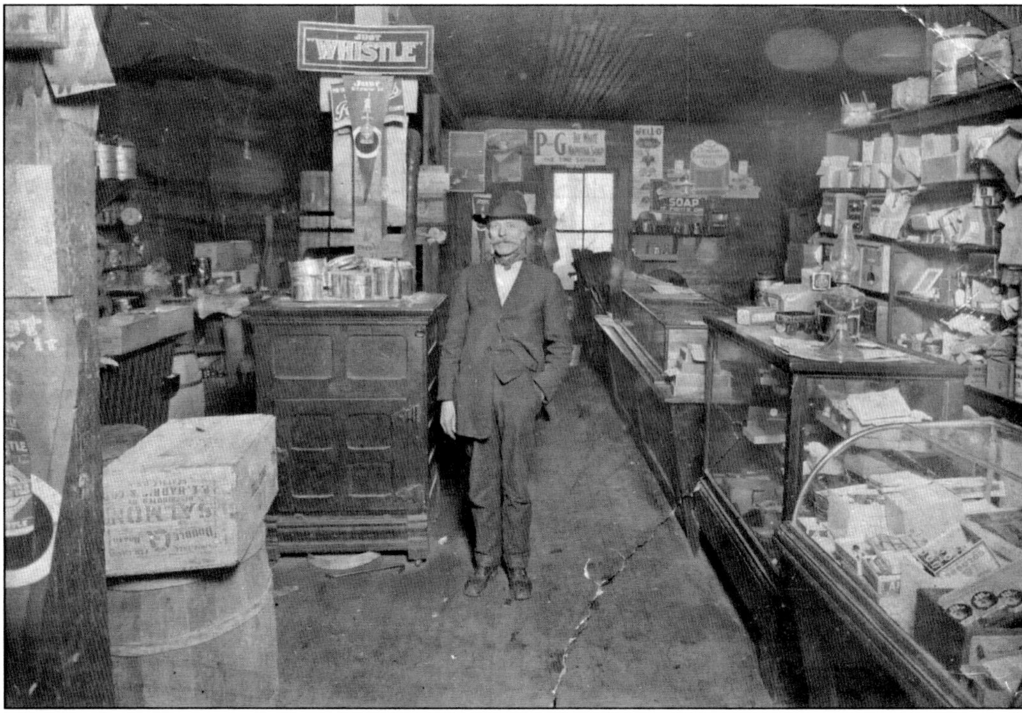

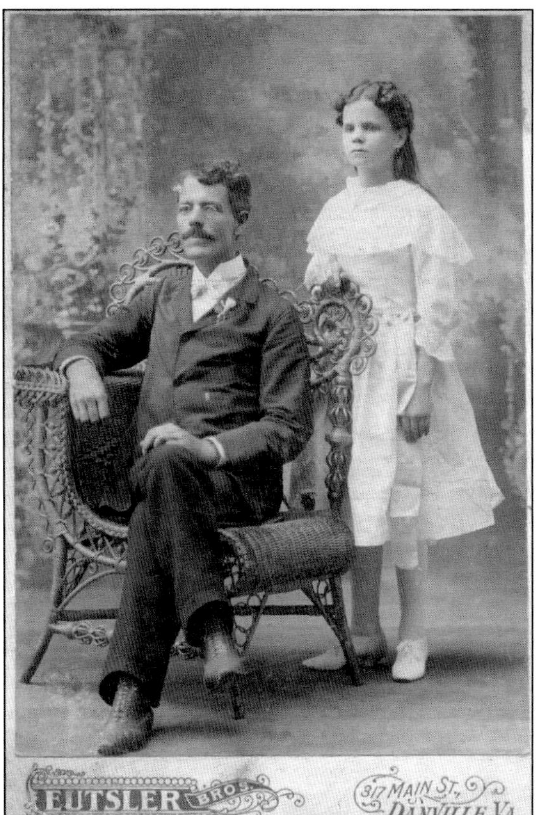

John W. Forbes owned a general store (pictured above in the 1920s) at 404 North Main Street. He married Lula Hamlett, one of the five daughters of James and Permelia Oliver Hamlett of North Danville. His father, Rev. John H. Forbes, was a Methodist minister who was hired by William T. Sutherlin to comfort soldiers during the Civil War. (Courtesy of Dee Smith.)

In 1898, John Forbes married Lula Hamlett when she was only 15 years old. He lied to her about his age, telling her he was 25 when he actually was 40. Interestingly, the couple stayed happily married for 57 years. (Photograph by Eutsler Brothers; courtesy of Dee Smith.)

Kate Hamlett, of North Danville, married George Forbes, the brother of John Forbes, who married Kate's sister Lula. Kate and George had three children who died before age five. In 1908, George fell on ice and died. The widowed Kate next married Joseph C. Bratcher, who died of a heart attack. She later married William A. Howard. (Photograph by Samuel Scott; courtesy of Dee Smith.)

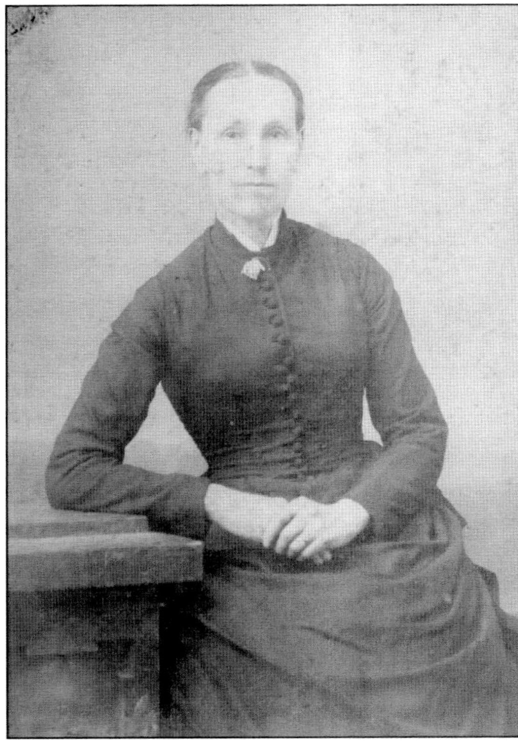

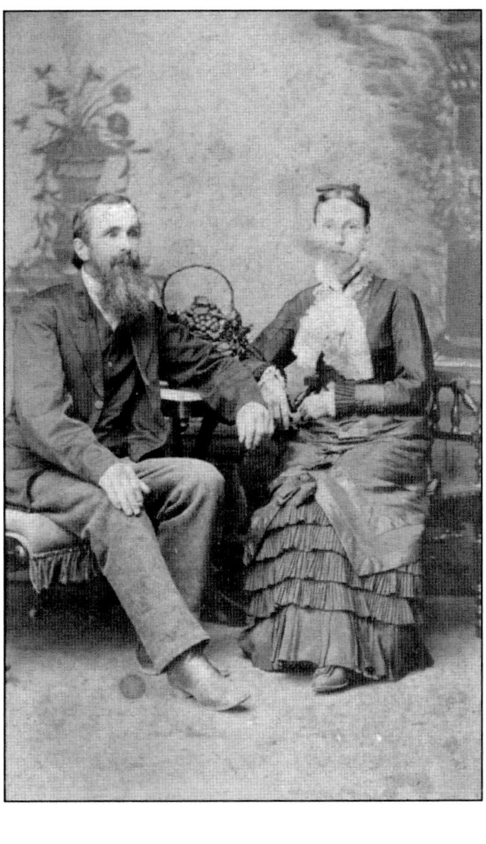

Married in 1900, Kate and George Forbes sat for their portrait in the studio of C.M.C. Woolwine. City directories listed Woolwine only in the years 1880 and 1881; he later worked in the studio of Eugene N. Medernach. Woolwine's wife, Emma, worked in the millinery store of Kate Medernach. (Photograph by C.M.C. Woolwine; courtesy of Dee Smith.)

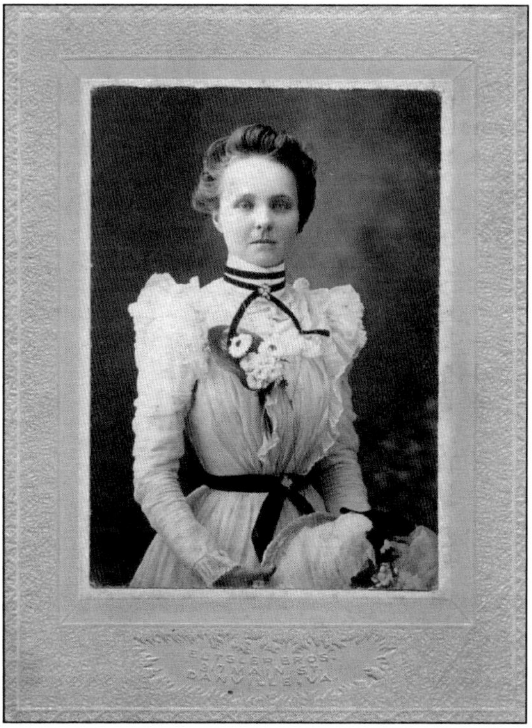

Mattie Hamlett, one of five sisters, married Thomas Tanner of North Danville. Based on its small size—only three inches by four inches—this photograph may have been one of Eutsler Brothers' earlier portraits. The Tanners had two sons, Roy and George, and a daughter, Ruth, who married Clyde Parsons and lived on Paxton Street. (Photograph by Eutsler Brothers; courtesy of Dee Smith.)

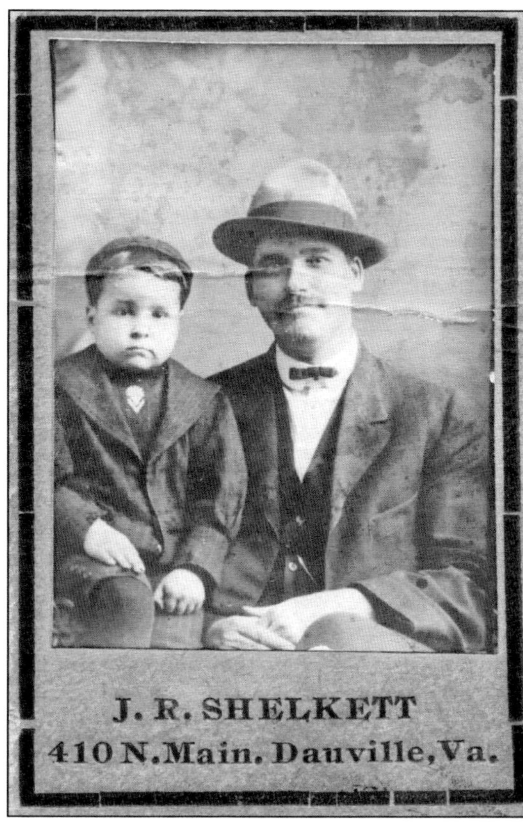

Thomas Tanner and his son Roy sat for their portrait in the North Main Street studio of John R. Shelkett. This tiny portrait, glued onto a piece of orange card stock, measured just 1.75 inches by 2.125 inches. On its reverse, Shelkett advertised the cheapest photographs in town: one dozen for 25¢. (Photograph by J.R. Shelkett; courtesy of Dee Smith.)

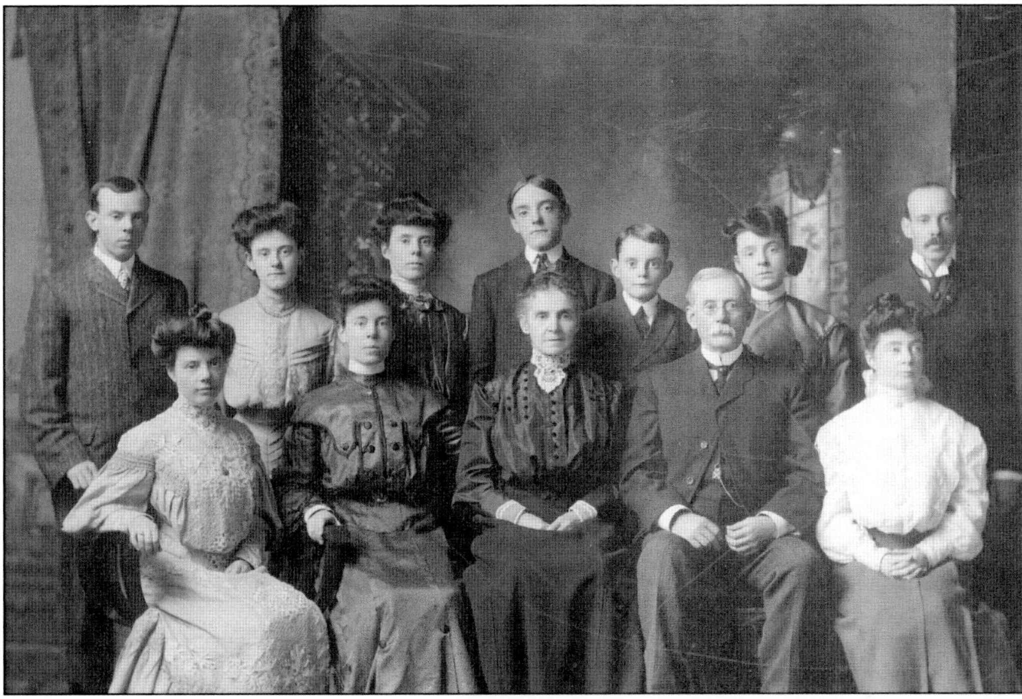

Dr. Lewis Edwin Harvie and Martha Rutherfoord Harvie moved to Danville in 1871. In 1903, on their 35th wedding anniversary, they posed for this group portrait with their 10 children. Pictured are, from left to right, (first row) Martha, Mary, Martha R., Lewis, and Fannie; (second row) Lewis Jr., Jane, Sadie, Rutherfoord, Edwin, Ellen, and John. (Photograph by Oliver W. Cole; courtesy of Dr. Edwin Harvie Jr.)

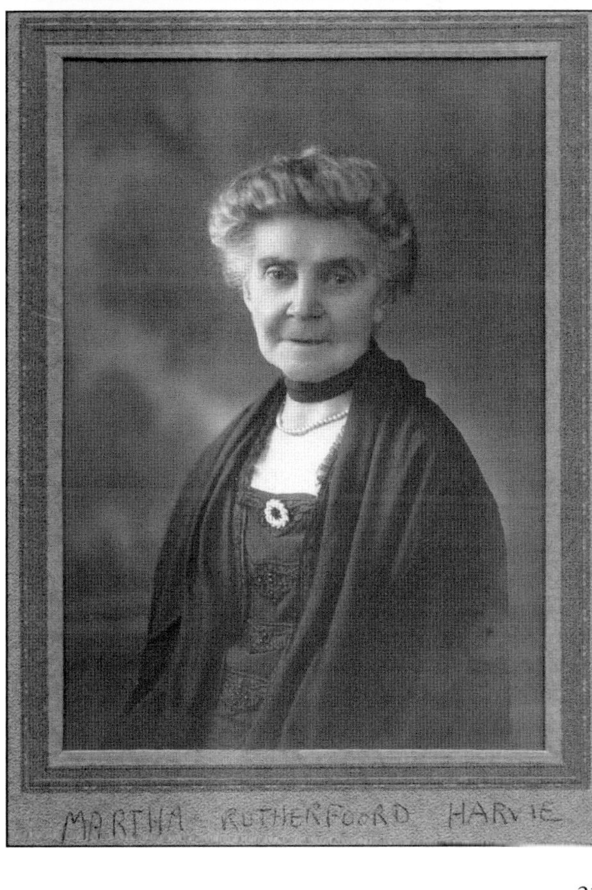

In 1868, Martha Rutherfoord married Dr. Lewis Edwin Harvie, who had served the Confederacy as a surgeon. The couple lived in Richmond for three years before moving to Danville. In 1874, they built the house that still stands at 954 Main Street. Born in 1845, Martha lived to be 92 years old. (Photograph by Leon Taylor; courtesy of Dr. Edwin Harvie Jr.)

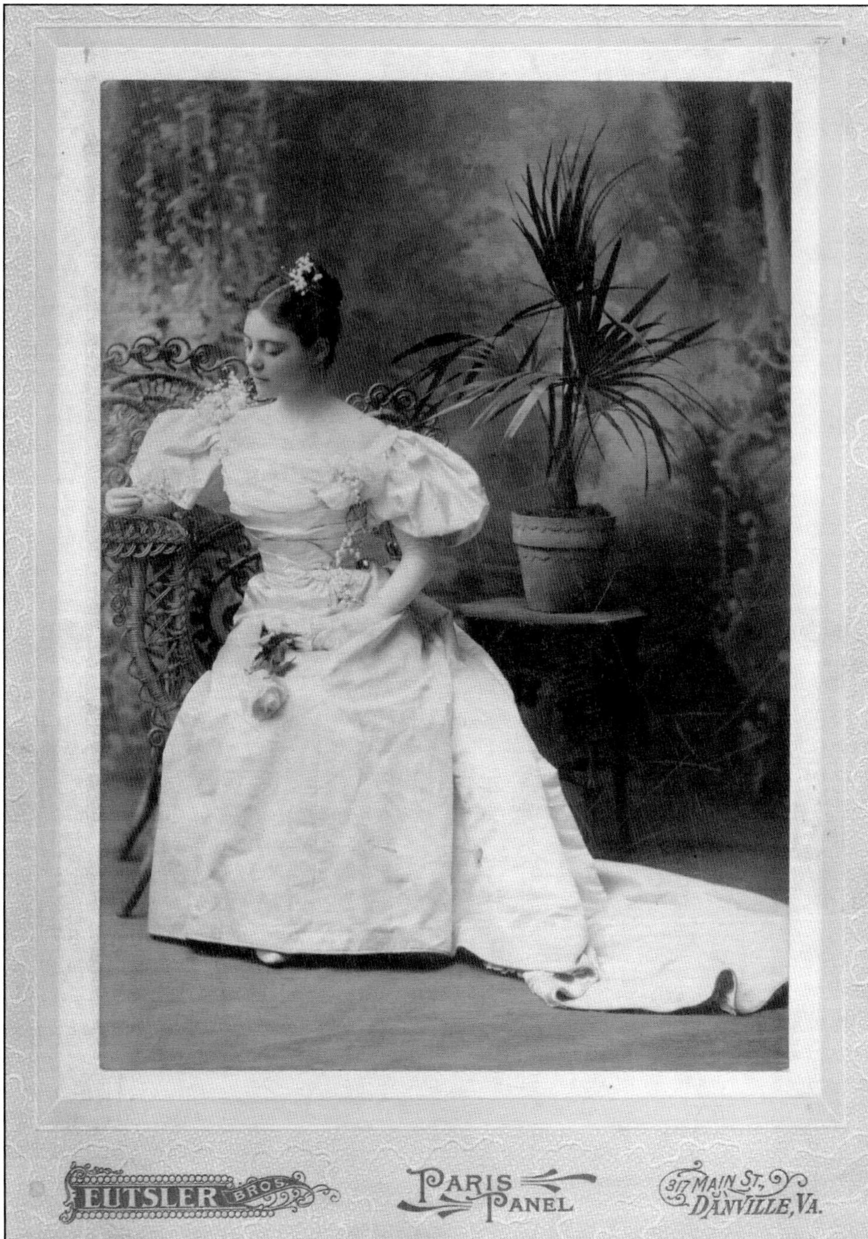

Frances "Fannie" Harvie, daughter of Dr. Lewis Edwin Harvie, posed for this portrait in 1896, three years after her marriage to J. Pinckney Williamson of Danville. Pinckney married the charming Fannie in his parents' brick mansion at 137 Holbrook Avenue, which had recently been built on one of the first lots subdivided from the rear yard of the William T. Sutherlin estate. The couple lived there for one or two years before moving into their own home at 819 Main Street. Later, they lived for some years at 119 South Main Street. Following several years' absence from Danville, the couple returned in 1909. Fannie died unexpectedly in 1920. Eutsler Brothers portraits were considered top of the line; they took all the photographs for the 1896 issue of *Headlight*, a magazine showcasing Danville's growth and progress. (Photograph by Eutsler Brothers; courtesy of Dr. Edwin Harvie Jr.)

Samuel Rutherfoord Harvie worked for 30 years as a clerk for the Danville school board. A lifelong bachelor, he became known for his recollections of Danville's life and times in the early 1900s, when he was a young man. Later, he chronicled events around town in numerous letters mailed to friends outside the city. (Photograph by Oliver W. Cole; courtesy of Dr. Edwin Harvie Jr.)

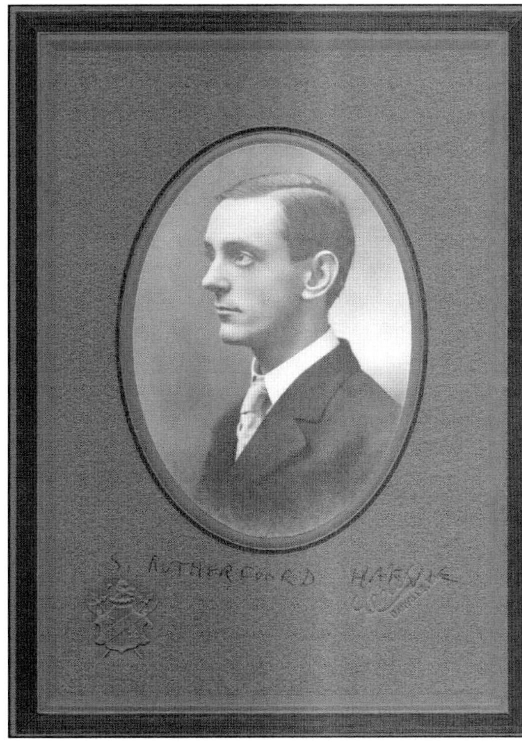

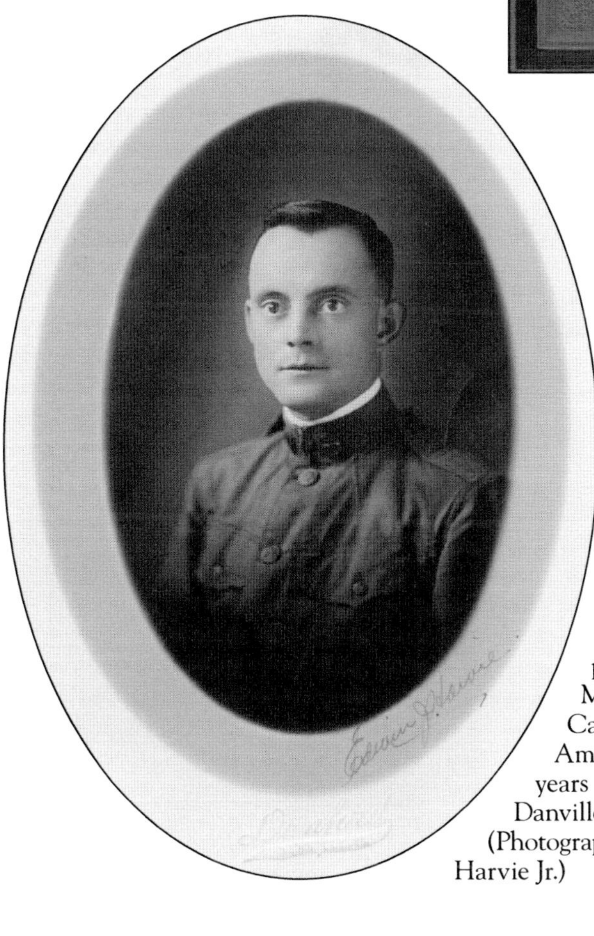

Edwin James Harvie, father of Danville physician Dr. Edwin Harvie Jr., married Mary Roane of Winston-Salem, North Carolina, in 1928. An agent with British American Tobacco Company, he spent seven years in Shanghai, China, before returning to Danville as an office manager for Dan River Mills. (Photograph by P.W. Dunford; courtesy of Dr. Edwin Harvie Jr.)

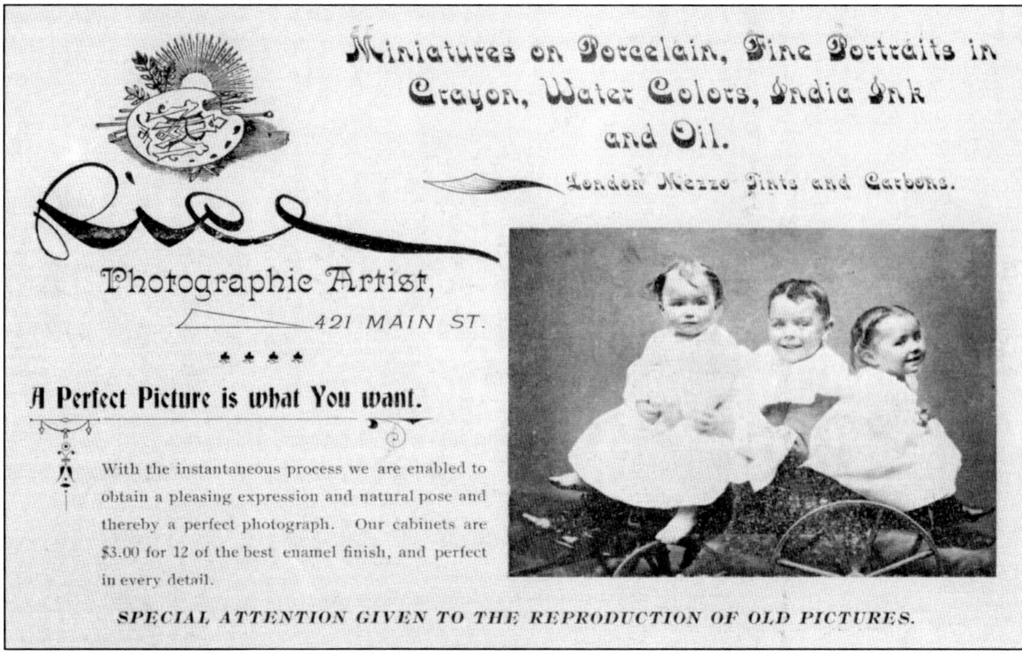

Alfonso D. Rice worked in Danville for only one year, but he left quite a photographic legacy. Many local citizens sought him out for studio portraits, as well as some commercial clients, including Waddill Printing Company, which published the city's *1898 Sketch Book*. (Courtesy of the Danville Historical Society.)

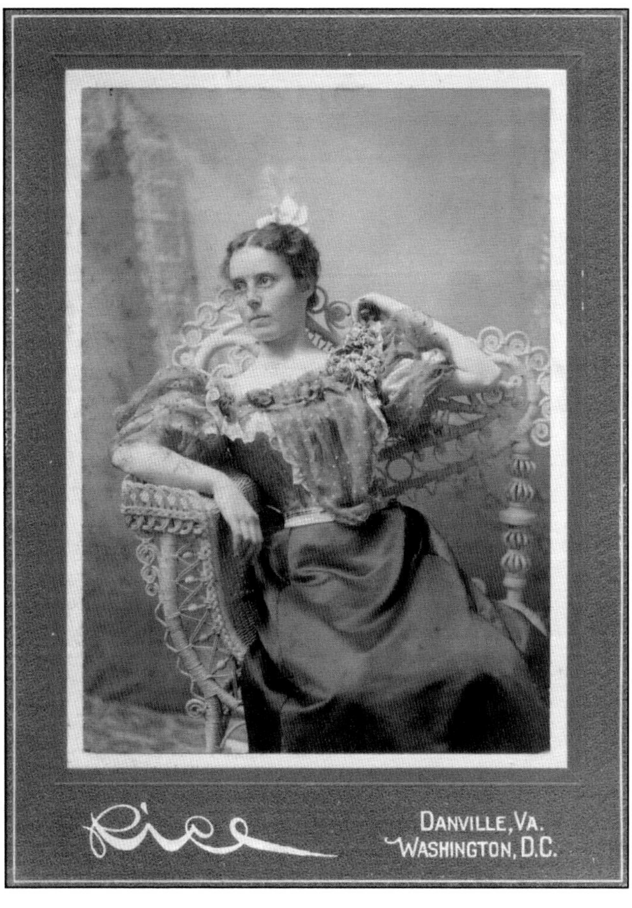

Named for her mother, Martha Old Harvie taught for many years in Danville schools. She married William Ayres Johnson, also of Danville. Around 1898, Alfonso D. Rice captured her likeness in this elegant studio portrait. Rice worked from his Danville studio at 421 Main Street for just one year before moving to Washington, DC. (Photograph by A.D. Rice; courtesy of Dr. Edwin Harvie Jr.)

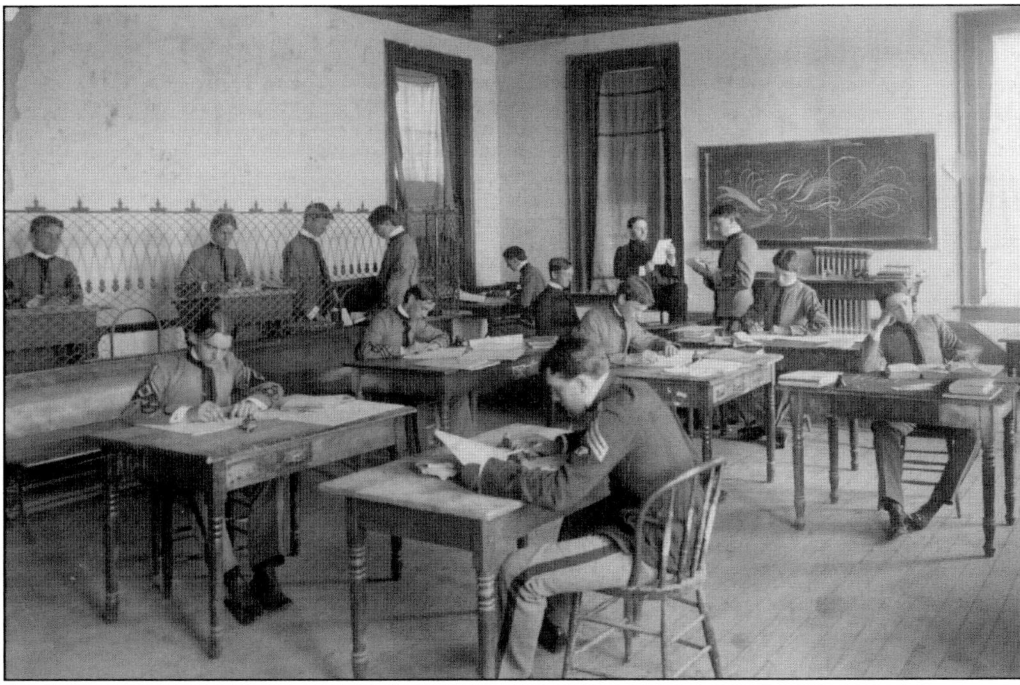

Danville Military Institute (pictured above) was chartered in May 1890 by professor Isaac H. Saunders. Most likely a continuation of the old Danville Male Academy, DMI sat atop a hill overlooking south Danville. The school survived many changes in name and purpose—since 1968, it has been Danville Community College—but its main hall, fondly known as the Castle on the Hill, was razed in 1974. (Courtesy of Carol and Charlton Strange.)

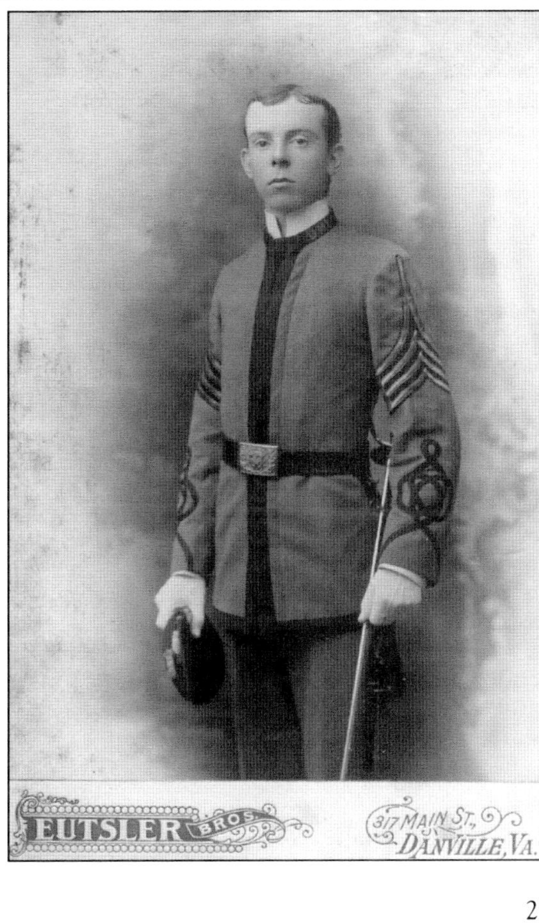

Lewis Edwin Harvie Jr. attended Danville Military Institute before beginning his career as a lawyer and judge in Kentucky. He remained a bachelor throughout his life, returning to Danville in 1948 after his health failed. He was one of the first patients at Hilltop Nursing Home. (Photograph by Eutsler Brothers; courtesy of Dr. Edwin Harvie Jr.)

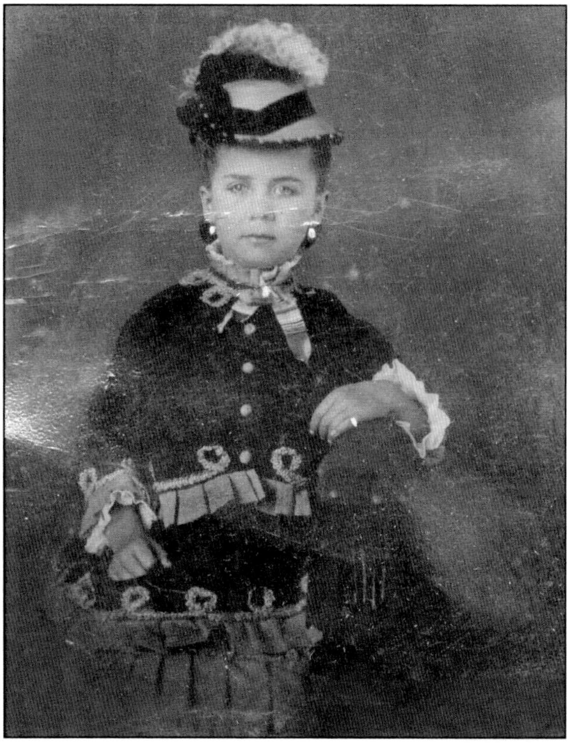

Attired like a fashion plate from *Godey's Lady's Book*, this unidentified woman looks self-assured in an outfit embellished with box pleats and fancy trims and topped by a pert hat. This 1870s tintype (an image on a thin sheet of iron) was one of many nameless portraits placed lovingly into a Victorian photograph album belonging to the Harry Wooding family. (Courtesy of the Danville Museum of Fine Arts and History.)

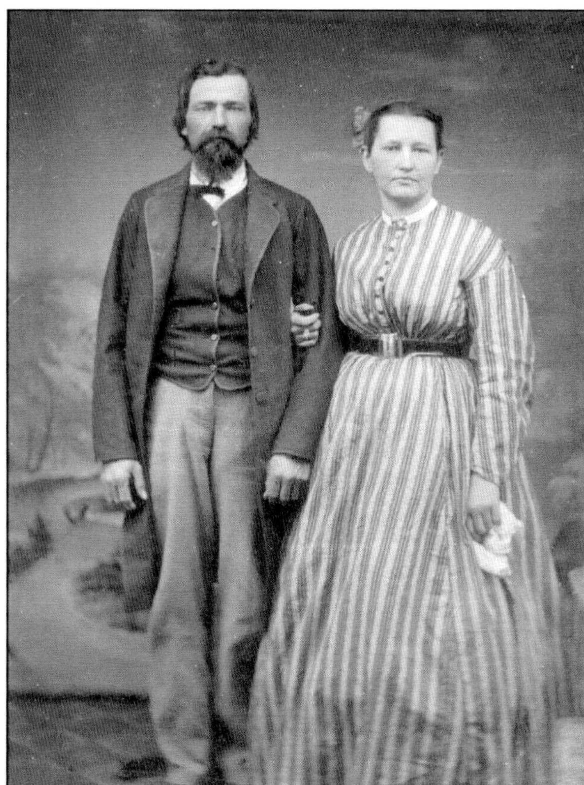

Locating tintypes of local citizens proved almost as challenging as finding local daguerreotypes; there were not many to be found. But an unknown photographer took this tintype portrait of full-length figures in the 1880s. Identified as "Uncle Pomp and Aunt Lizzie Dyer," they are ancestors of local dentist Charlton B. Strange Jr. (Courtesy of Carol and Charlton Strange.)

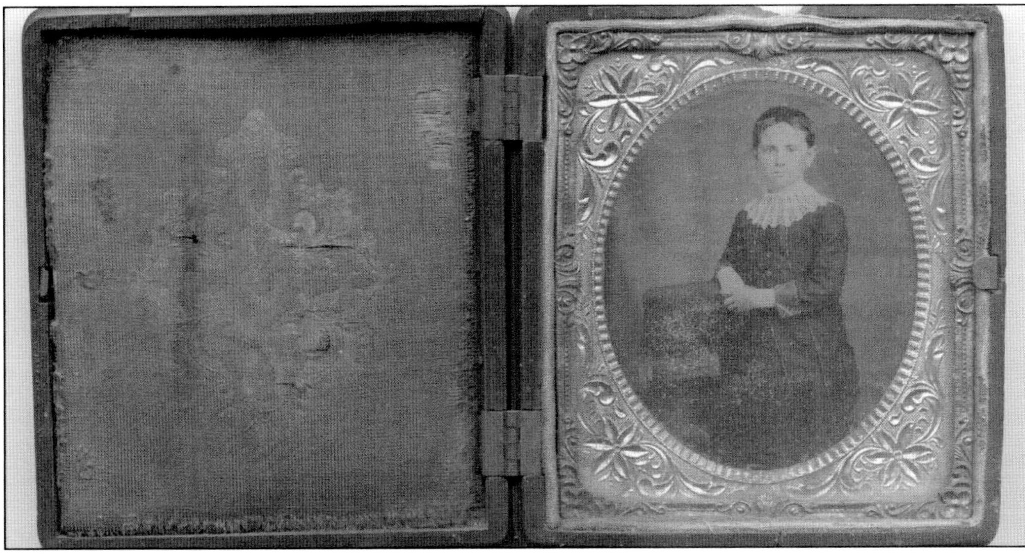

Daguerreotypes, the first type of photographic image accessible to the American public beginning in the early 1850s, were always placed under glass inside a protective case. This unidentified young girl was a member of Danville's Gwynn or Noell families, forebears of Charlton Strange. (Courtesy of Carol and Charlton Strange.)

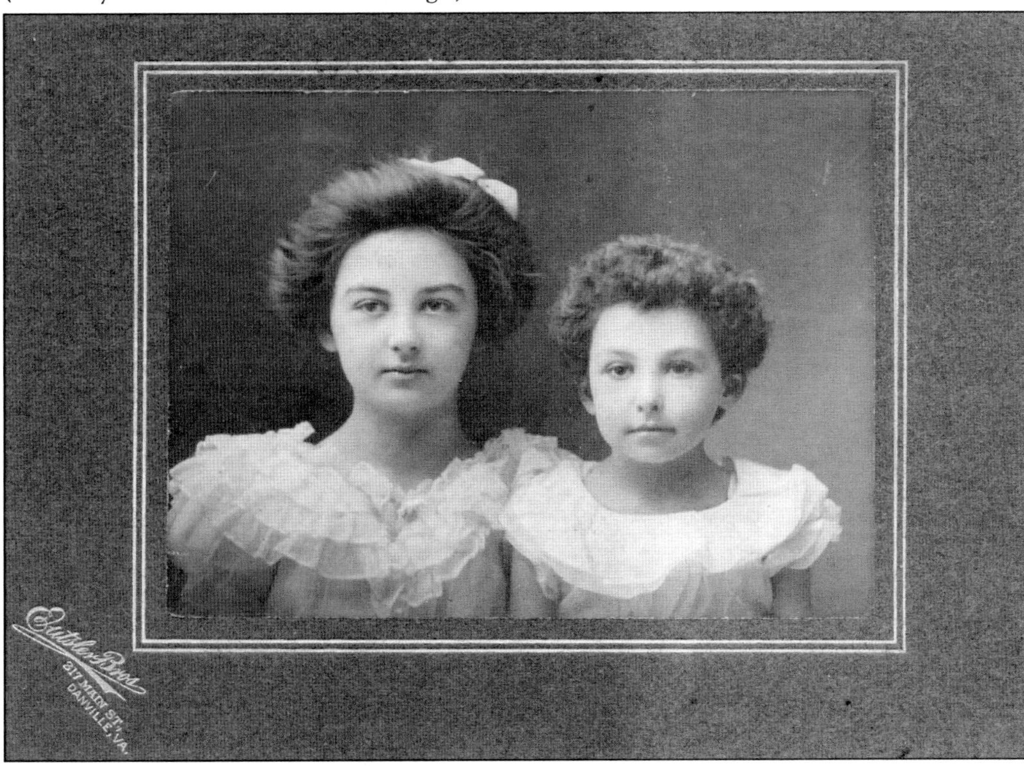

Willa and Frances Strange, sisters of Charlton B. Strange Sr., posed for this portrait around 1892 in the Eutsler Brothers photography studio at 317 Main Street. Children's portraits were the bread and butter of most professional photographers, and the Eutsler Brothers offered portraits in crayon, sepia, and watercolors. (Photograph by Eutsler Brothers; courtesy of Carol and Charlton Strange.)

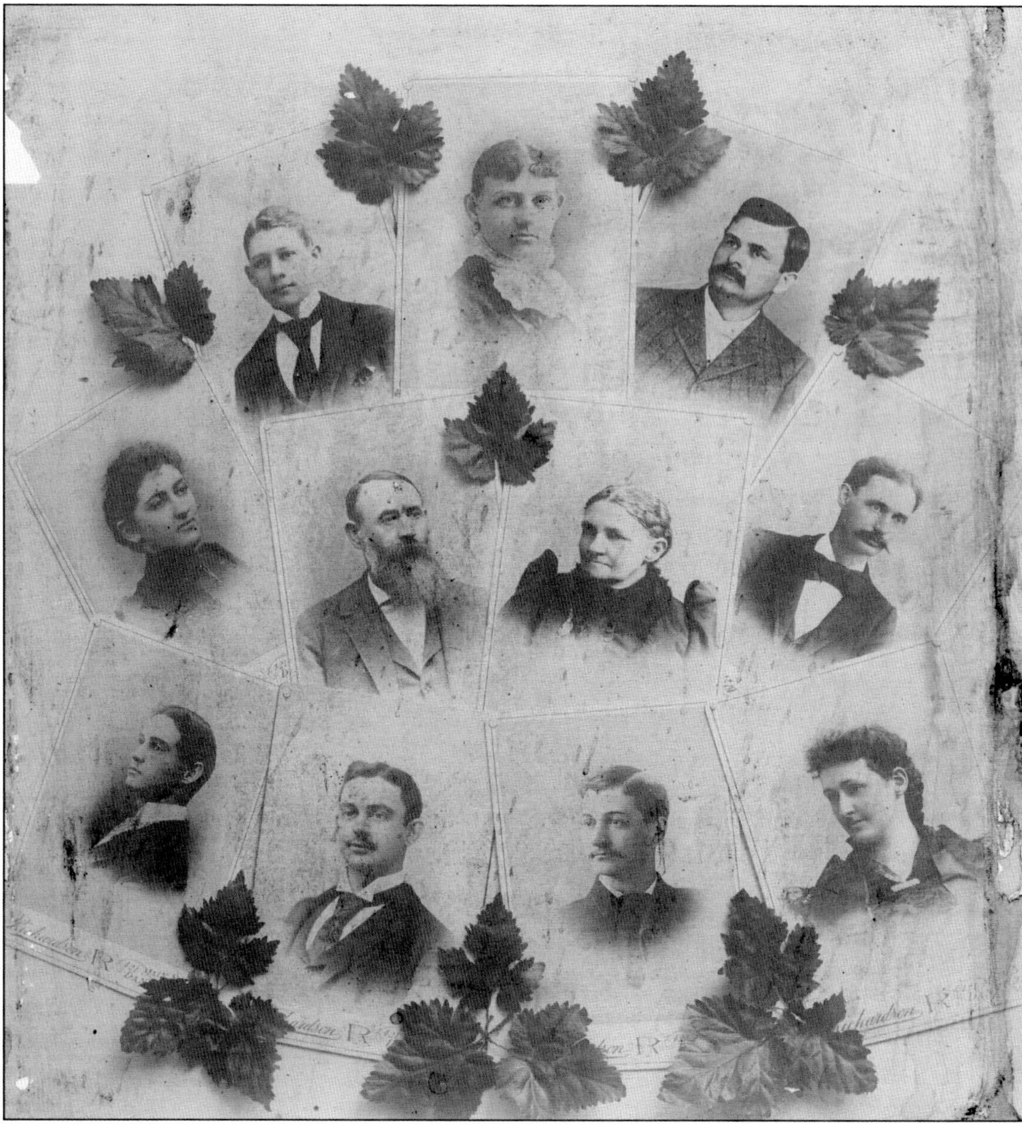

One interesting form of collage appeared in Victorian England in the 1860s and 1870s. With the 1854 standardization of *carte de visite* photographs, a precursor of the small pictures that emerge from modern photograph booths, women with time on their hands experimented with photographic collages more than 100 years before the creation of Photoshop. They arranged small photographs into a single piece of art, moving them around like pawns on a chessboard. Some women even combined family portraits with items from nature to create the illusion of a family tree. This delightful collage was made in 1894 from individual portraits of the Noell family members. In the center are Jesse Roland Noell and his wife, Ann Elizabeth Dabbs. Starting at the top center and continuing clockwise are their nine children: Louisa Elizabeth, George Livingston, Charles Daniel, Annie Susan, Jesse Roland Jr., Joseph Dabbs, Green, Frances, and Walter Carlton Noell. (Photograph by F.H. Richardson; courtesy of Carol and Charlton Strange.)

Two

Main Street

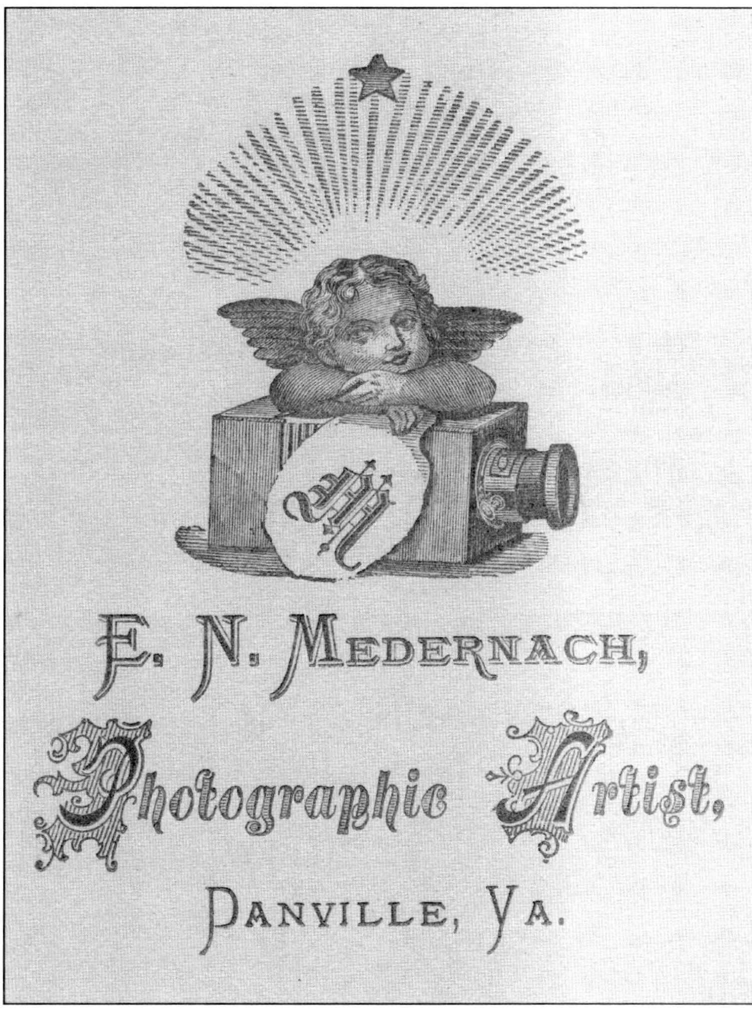

Eugene N. Medernach was born in France, came to the United States, married Sarah Catherine Bagby, and then moved to Danville in the 1860s. Medernach was the first known photographer to set up a professional studio in town; it was located on lower Main Street near the bridge. He died in 1891 in Salisbury, North Carolina. (Courtesy of the Danville Historical Society.)

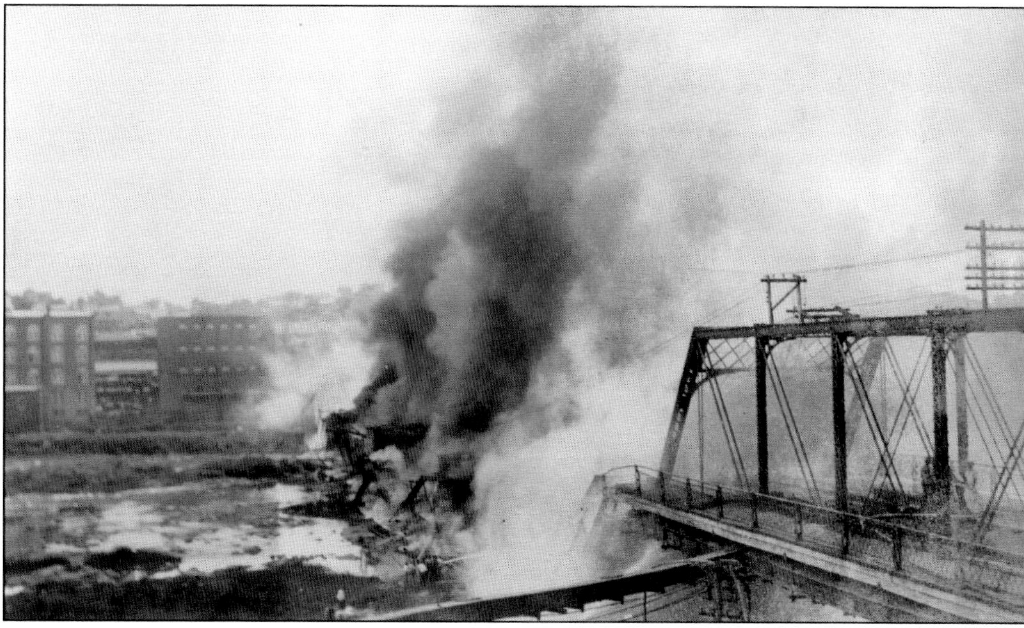

On June 30, 1927, Danville's "fireproof" Main Street bridge burned. Constructed in 1887, the iron-truss structure was touted as being immune to fire or flood, despite the fact that its flooring was wooden and coated with tar. A tar kettle reportedly ignited the floor while repairs were being done on the bridge. (Photograph by George C. Stone; courtesy of David Eagle.)

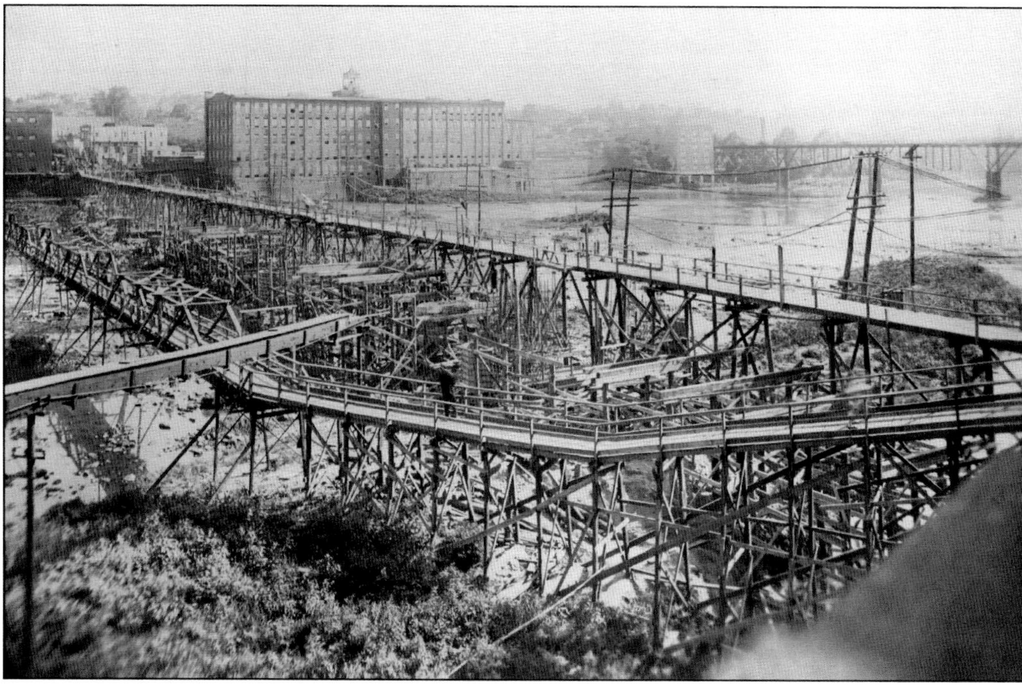

Immediately after workmen removed the mangled iron remains of the bridge, they constructed this wooden footbridge so pedestrians, at least, could cross the river. After months of inconvenience, a large group of spectators watched as the new concrete bridge, designed by Indiana engineer Daniel P. Luten, finally opened to traffic on January 12, 1928. (Photograph by William E. Land.)

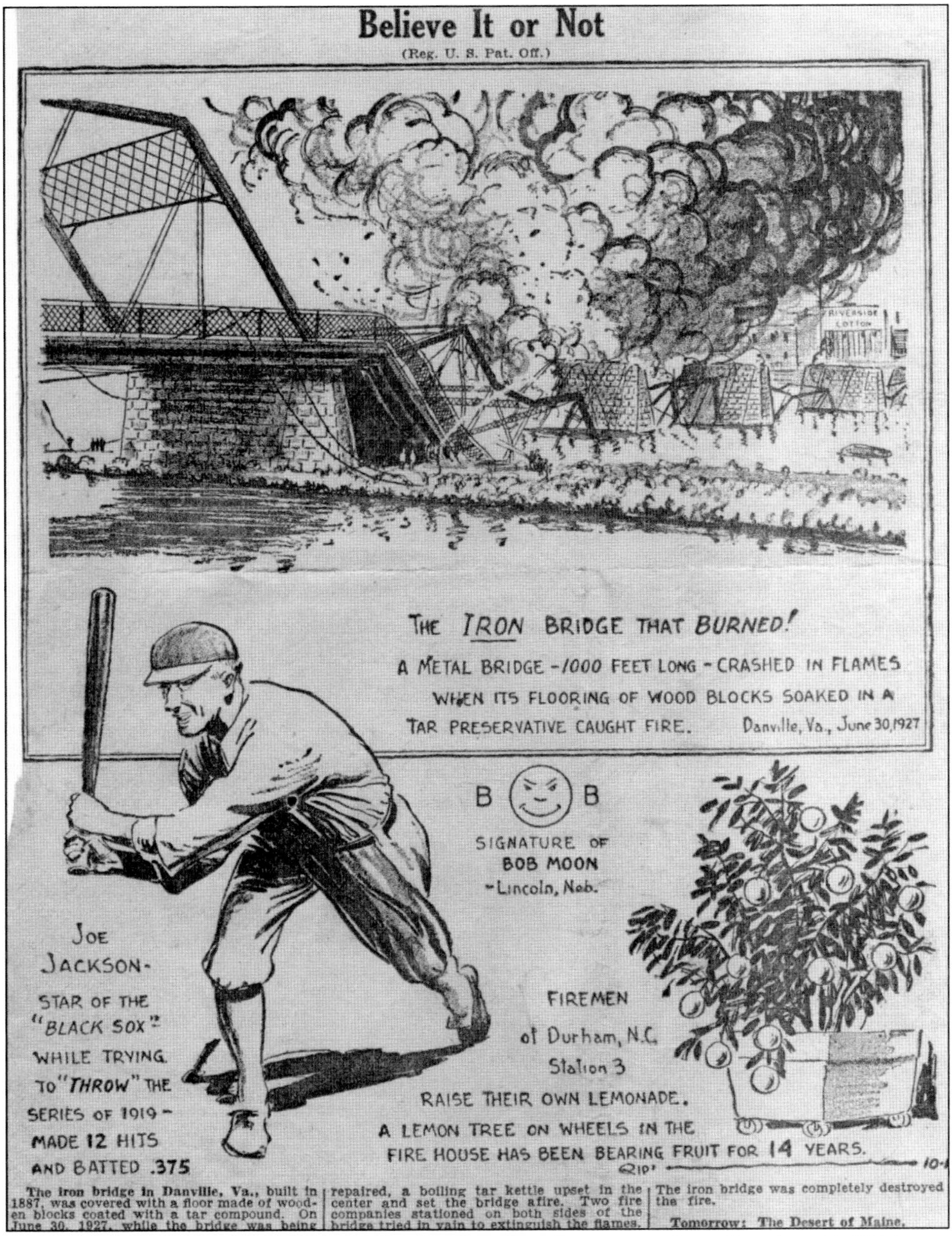

Once just a rumor, this recently unearthed newspaper illustration from October 11, 1933, proved that the burning of Danville's fireproof bridge in 1927 actually made it into the *Ripley's Believe It or Not*! collection of odd facts. Robert Ripley placed his syndicated comic drawings into newspapers all over the country. This article from an unknown newspaper had been carefully squirreled away in the genealogical materials of Earle Garrett Jr., the father of coauthor Clara Fountain. In the early 1930s, Danville mayor Harry Wooding wrote that, after the fire, the city salvaged parts of the burnt iron span to fill in ravines that separated some streets. New roads over these gorges enabled easier travel on foot and by automobile, and several shorter and more convenient connections linked the Jefferson Avenue extension to Grove Street, Washington Street to Claiborne Street, and Worsham Street to Scales Street. (Courtesy of Clara Fountain.)

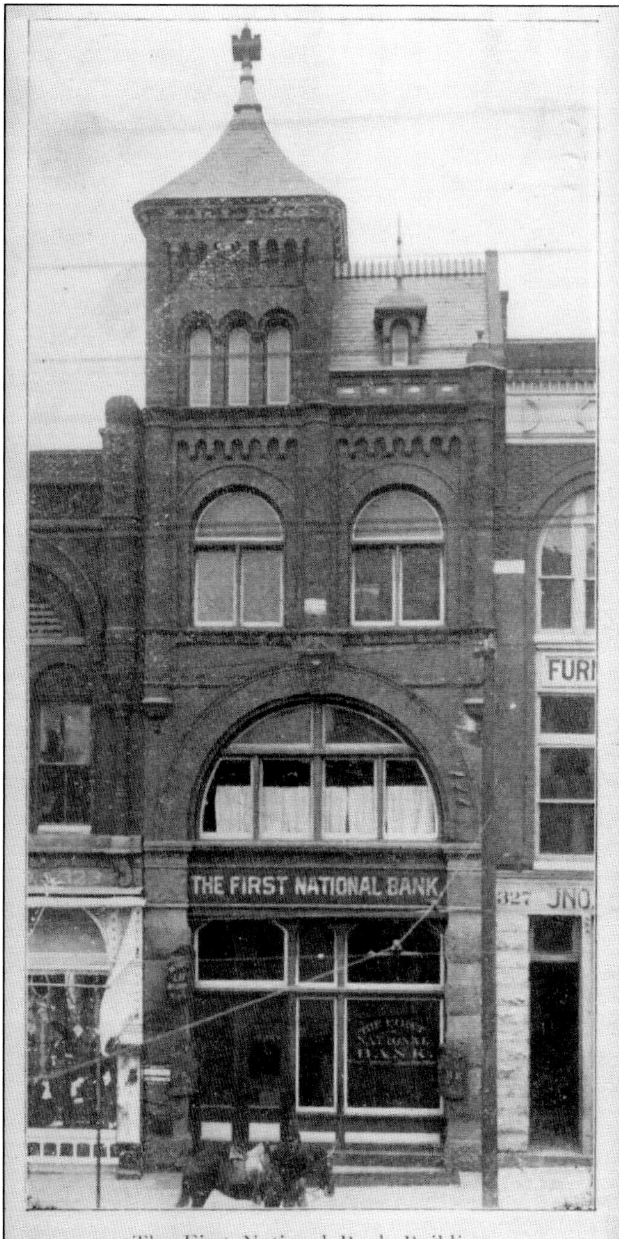

Planters' National Bank opened on May 18, 1872, at 325 Main Street, just below the Bijou Theatre (later the Rialto). In 1899, the bank became First National (above). In 1910, First National moved to the corner of Main and South Market Streets, where it remained for more than 60 years. In 1978, as a holding company, it evolved into First & Merchants National; it became Sovran National in 1983, NationsBank in 1990, and Bank of America in 1998. In 1948, First National Bank opened the city's first branch bank on West Main Street at Ballou Park, signaling a trend followed by most of the banks in Danville. In 1973, First National Bank and Trust Company razed its classically inspired second home at 341 Main Street to construct a block-wide contemporary building. The changing world of finance led Bank of America to vacate this building in 1999, and the Ballou Park branch closed in late 2012. (Courtesy of Sue B. Glidewell.)

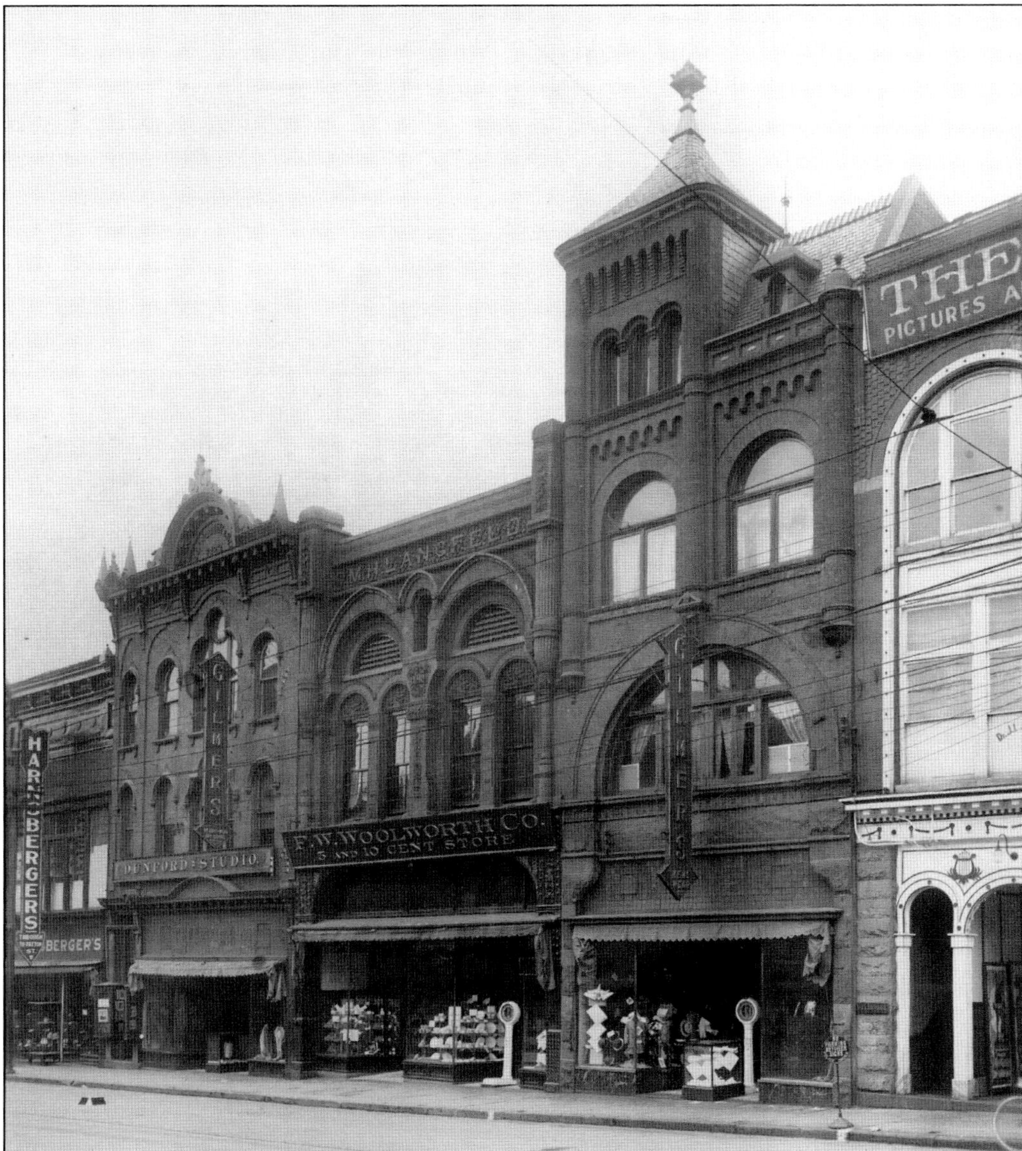

Around World War I, some of Danville's leading stores lined Main Street's 300 block, just downhill from the Bijou Theatre. Harnsberger's department store, Gilmers bakery (which housed Phillip W. Dunford's photography studio), F.W. Woolworth's, and Gilmers ready-to-wear and dry goods store all operated behind substantial late-Victorian facades. These buildings survived until 1973, when the First National Bank cleared the block for its new headquarters. Gilmers Department Store, one of the city's leading retailers, had an extensive inventory that filled two expansive brick storefronts that dominated the block from Main Street to Patton Street. Gilmers men's, women's, and children's ready-to-wear filled all three floors at 325 Main Street, and their bakery occupied the basement of the building two doors down at 317 Main Street, where Dunford maintained his photography studio on the second floor. Long before the F.W. Woolworth's chain expanded its operation on the site of the old Holland Building on Main Street at South Union Street, the company's earlier store was in the Langfeld Building in the center of Main Street's 300 block. (Photograph by Leon Taylor.)

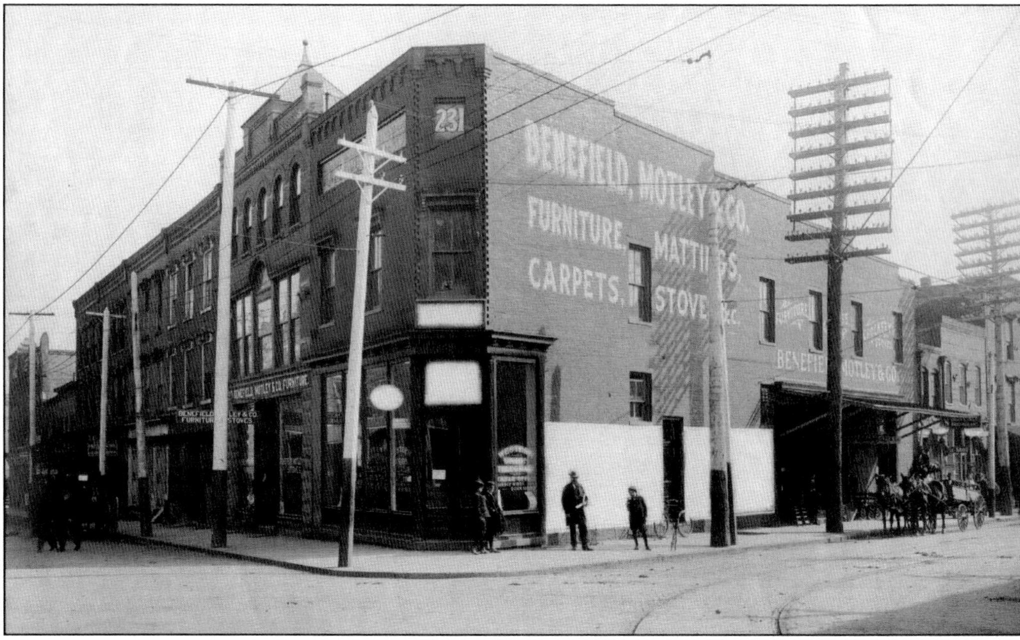

In 1895, W.G. Benefield founded Benefield, Motley & Company, a home furnishings store at 229 Main Street, on the corner of Craghead Street. Its officers included R.C. Thompson, J.A. Motley, and E.P. Motley. Later, Schewels Furniture Company used this building until a fire destroyed it in 1958. Soon thereafter, Schewels constructed a new, block-long building, which is currently the home of Lou's Antique Mall. (Photograph by Leon Taylor.)

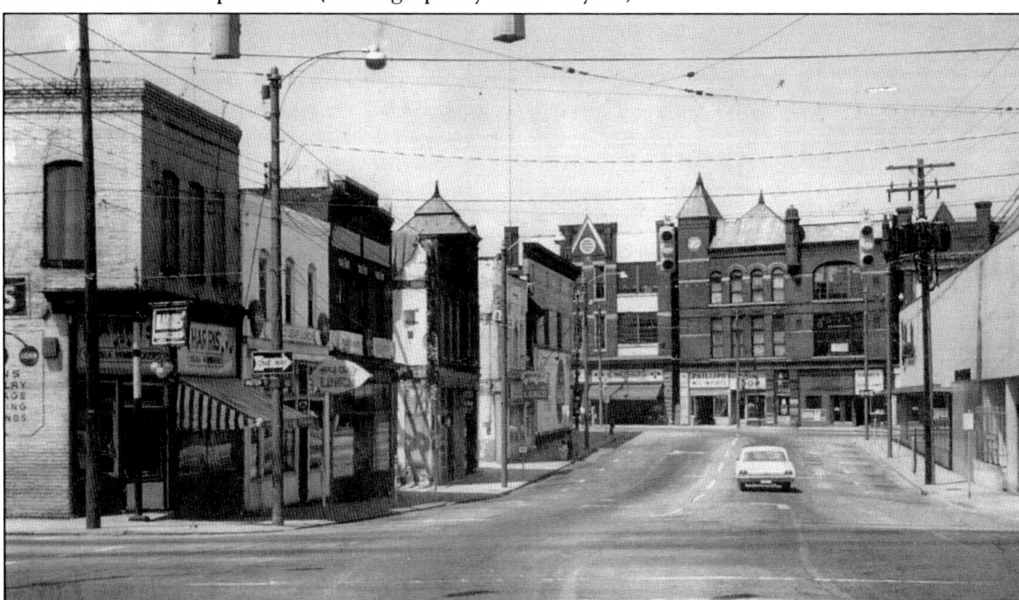

The area of Craghead Street near Main Street once bustled with eateries and small stores like Harris' Pawn Shop (far left), where a saloon with a second-floor dance hall once flourished. Next door, John P. Maurakis owned and managed the Gold Leaf Lunch from 1935 to 1972. By 1973, gaps in Craghead Street's once-solid 100 block foreshadowed its demolition, and most of lower Main Street was razed at that time as well. (Photograph by John P. Maurakis.)

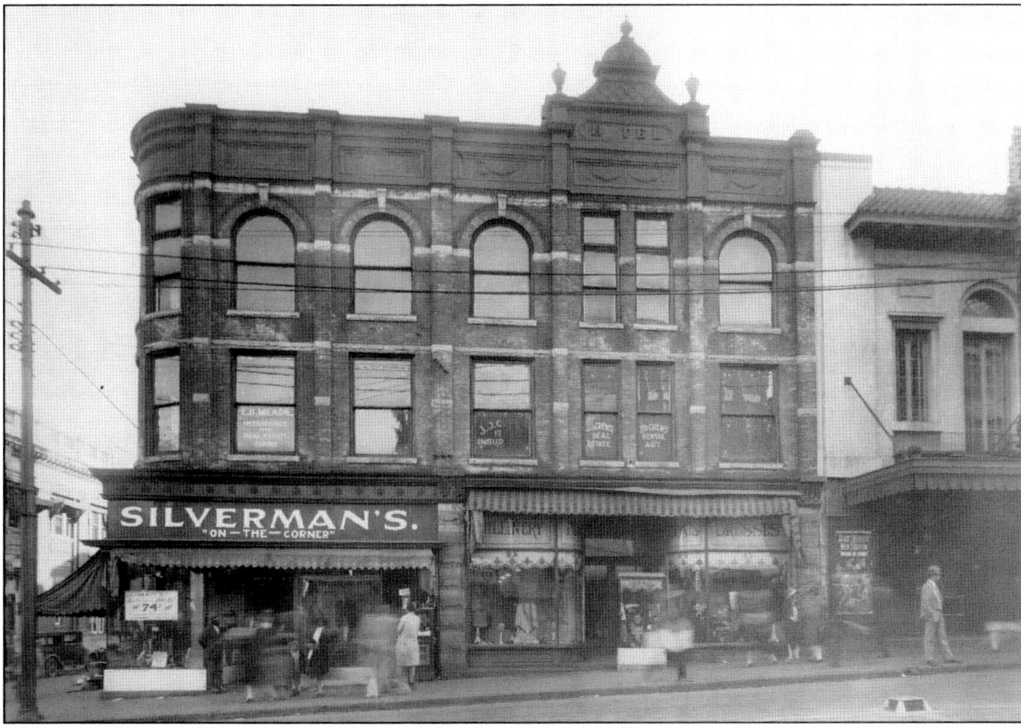

Kolman Silverman immigrated to the United States in 1887 and moved to Danville soon afterward to run a men's clothing store. By 1917, the business relocated from South Market Street to 401 Main Street, as seen here next to the Broadway Theater (later the Lea). By 1943, W.T. Grant's five-and-dime store occupied a newer, Georgian-inspired building on this site. (Photograph by Leon Taylor.)

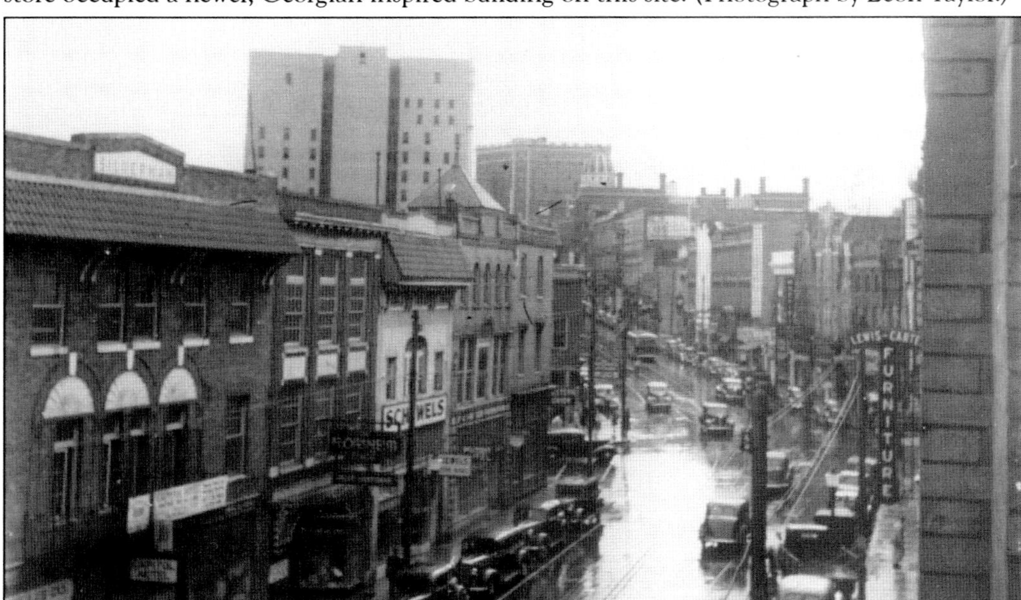

Jacob "Jake" Silverman, cut from the same cloth as his father, Kolman Silverman, began his own men's store just after World War I. Located at 223 Main Street (far left), it was a couple of doors down from Schewels' first 1920s-era storefront. (Courtesy of Clara Fountain.)

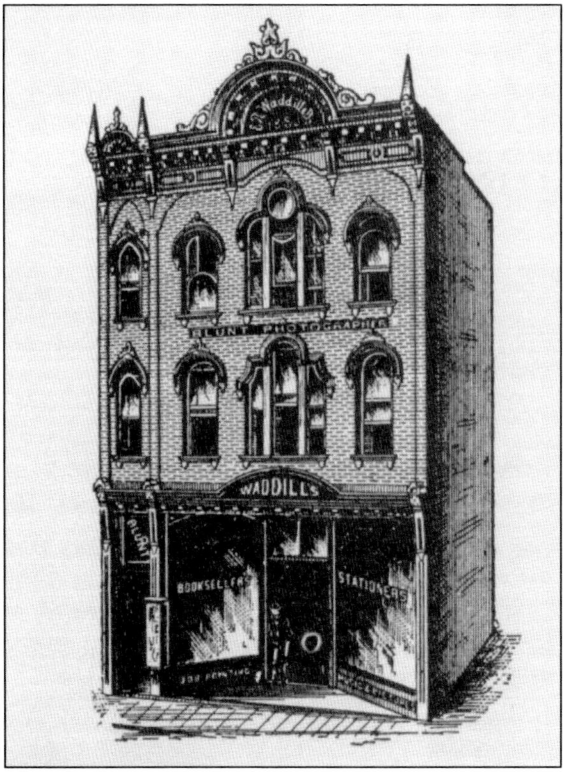

In 1886, brothers Edward R. and Walter W. Waddill, the co-owners of Waddill Printing Company since 1869, moved into new facilities at 317 Main Street, a lavish three-story brick building between Market and Craghead Streets. Their new building also housed the photography studio of Anthony H. Blunt. Waddill Printing Company published local works such as the *1898 Sketch Book*, a promotional review of Danville's business prospects. (Courtesy of the Danville Historical Society.)

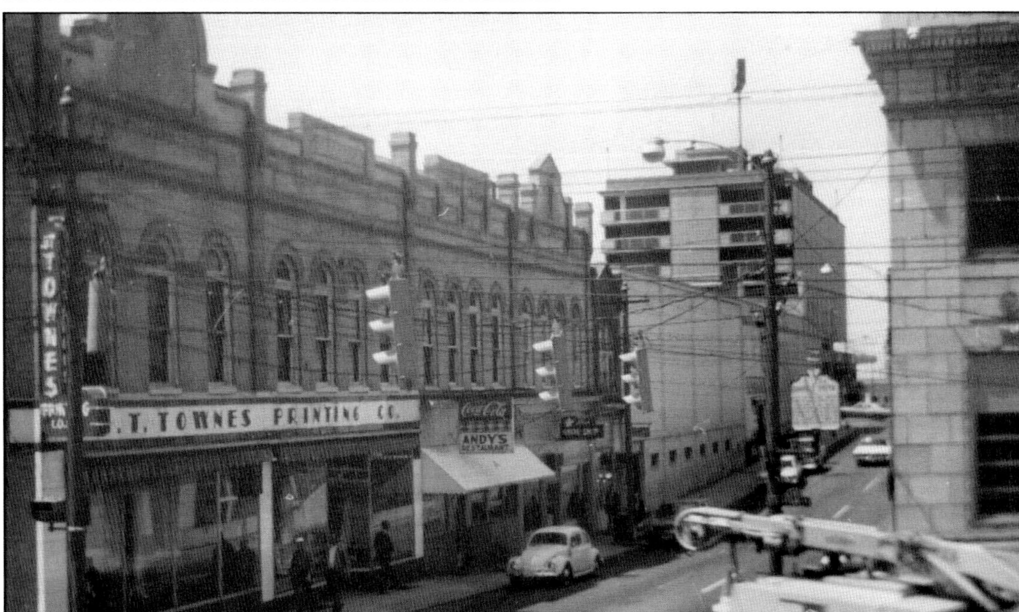

In 1897, J.T. Townes established a printing business in the Holland Building on Main Street. In the mid-1930s, the firm moved to this location, pictured here in the 1960s, at the corner of South Union and Patton Streets, where they remained for decades. J.T. Townes specialized in commercial printing, bookbinding, and the sale of office supplies and equipment. (Photograph by Wayne Brumfield.)

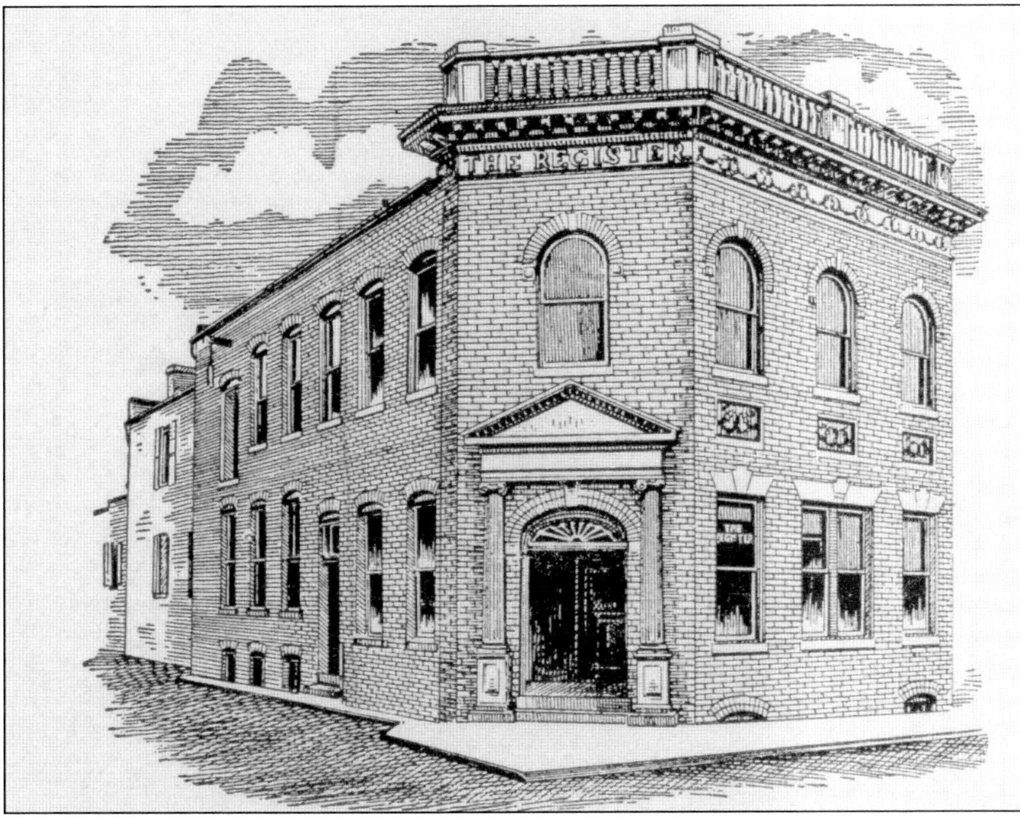

Early in the 1900s, printers and publishers dominated much of South Union Street. In 1901, the *Register* newspaper occupied its new headquarters, which are depicted in this line cut. Next door, at 117 South Union Street, the Boatwright Brothers Company, who bought out Thomas H. Averett, offered retail and commercial printing and bookbinding in a former tobacco prizery running back to Patton Street. It was destroyed in a 1911 fire. (Courtesy of the Danville Public Library.)

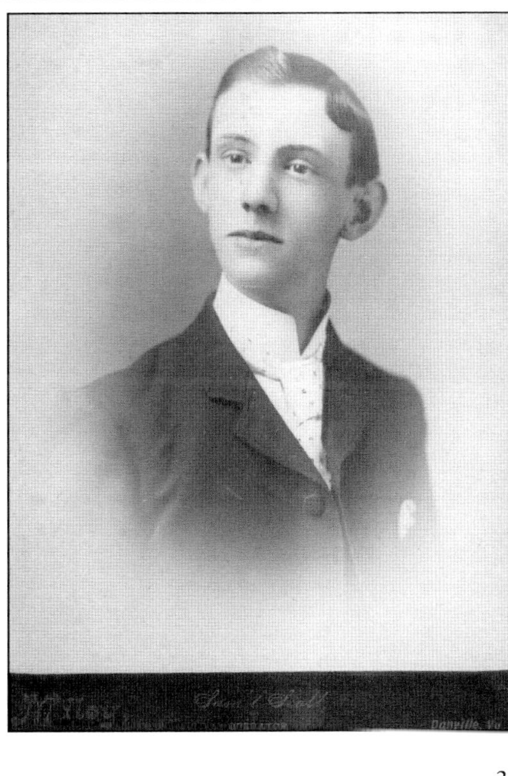

Joseph Overton Boatwright married Ellen Coleman Wooding, the daughter of Harry Wooding. Joseph served as the secretary of the Boatwright Brothers Company, a family business of printers and stationers. Here, a youthful Joseph strikes a serious pose for Michael Miley, a photographer most famous for his portrait of Robert E. Lee on his horse Traveller. (Photograph by Michael Miley; courtesy of the Danville Museum of Fine Arts and History.)

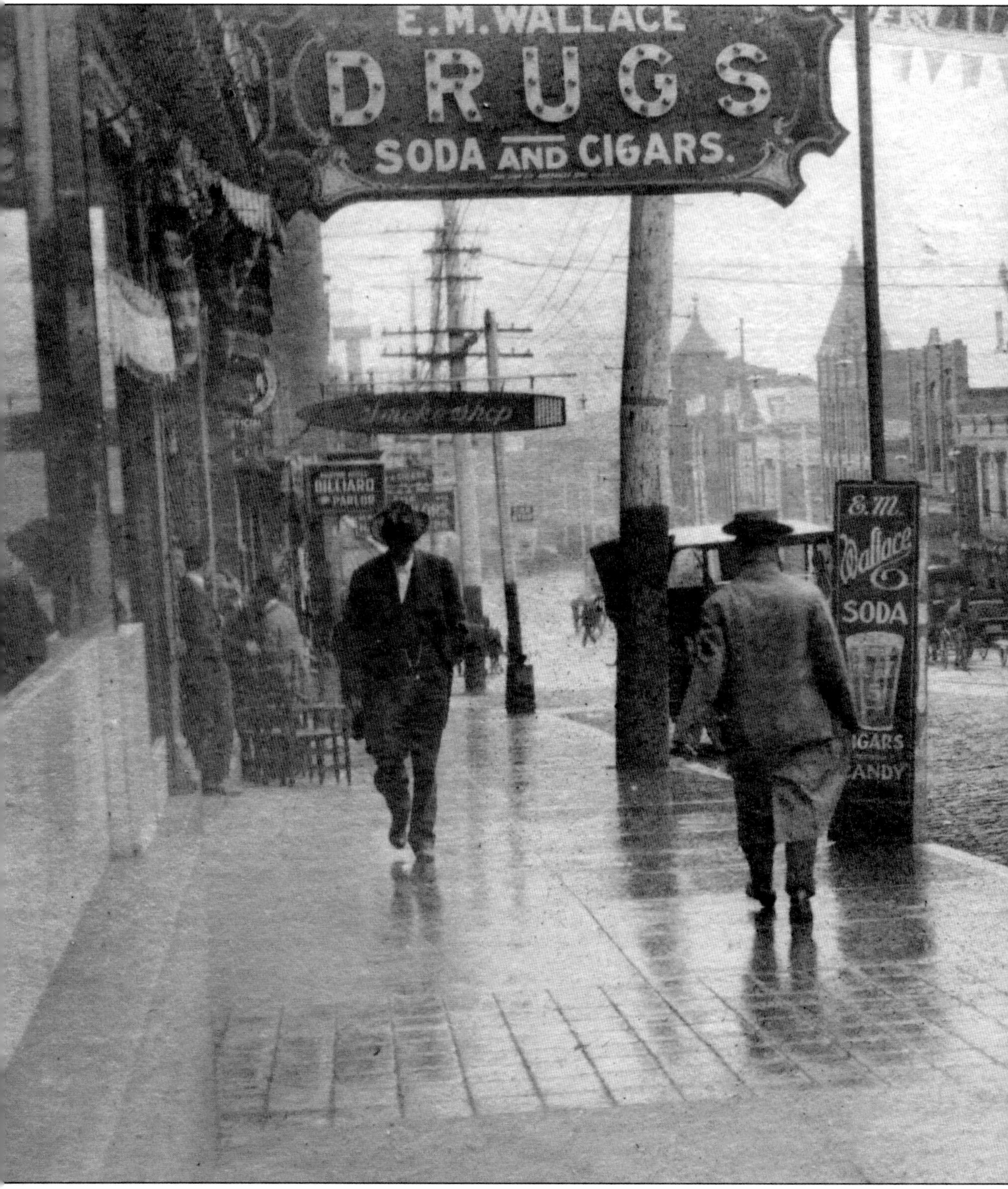

Standing just up Main Street from the Burton Hotel at North Union Street, photographer Leon Taylor captured the rhythm of a rainy day around 1905. At 512 Main Street (on the left), Emmet M. Wallace offered pharmaceuticals, cigars, and a soda fountain at his drugstore. A tobacco shop, not far from a billiard parlor, shared retail space at the Burton and lured smokers by way of a huge cigar hanging above the sidewalk. Regarded as the city's crossroads, the intersection of Main

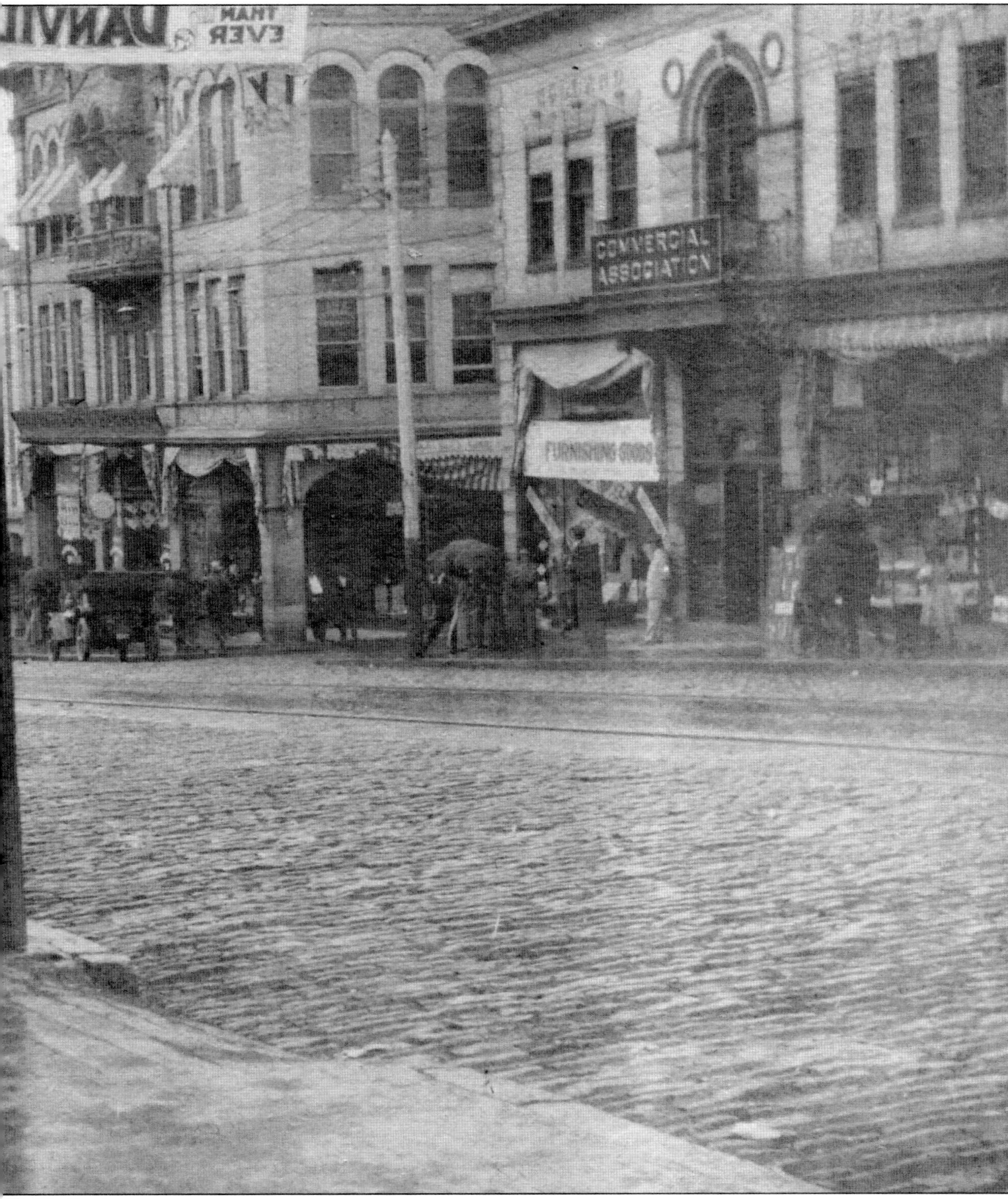

and Union Streets attracted some of Danville's most elite offices and professional development. Continuing the mid-19th-century pattern, important landmarks anchored each corner of South Union Street: Danville's second Masonic temple (since 1851), built in 1901, and the antebellum Holland Building, home to the Danville Commercial Association, which was refurbished around 1900. (Photograph by Leon Taylor.)

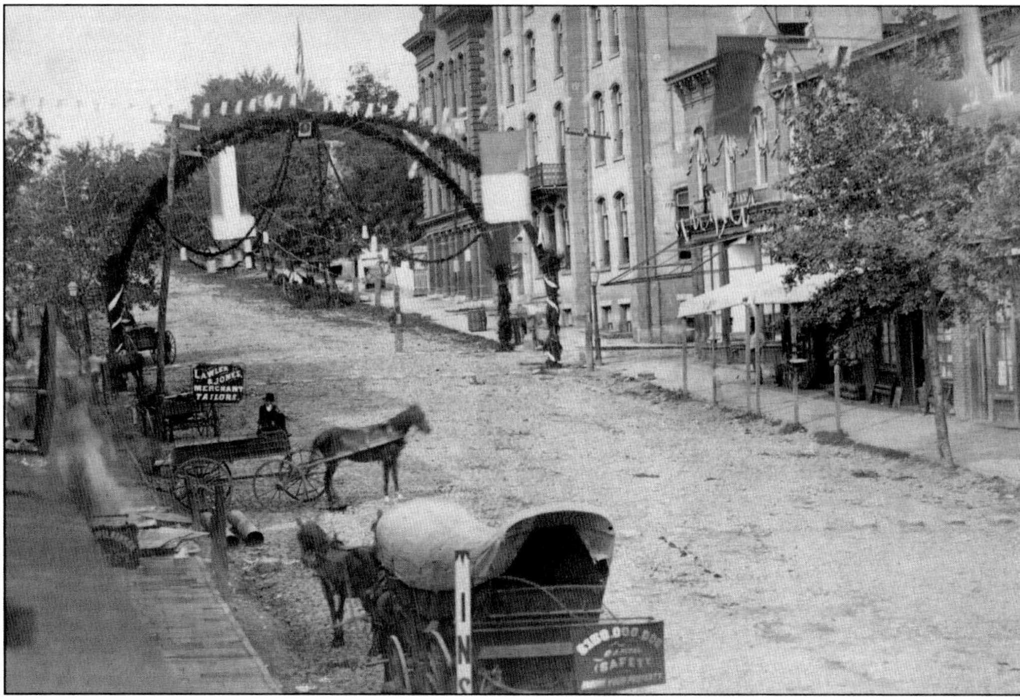

Eyewitnesses to the 1878 dedication of Danville's Confederate Monument reported that the whole town shut down for the celebration. Some of the trappings of that fete are visible in this photograph by Eugene Medernach, whose studio was downhill near the bridge. The Arlington Hotel is just to the right of the festooned arch over Main and Union Streets. (Photograph by E.N. Medernach; courtesy of the Danville Historical Society.)

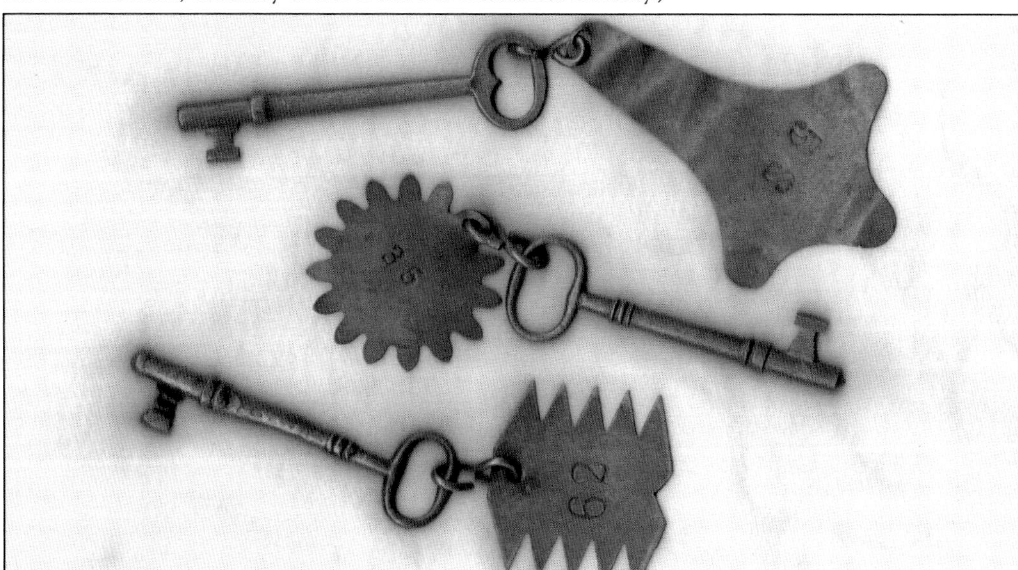

Heavy skeleton keys, each with a fancy die-cut brass key tag, identified rooms at the Arlington Hotel, where tobacconists and other businessmen traveling to Danville came to expect only the best accommodations. The key and tag together, some six inches long on average, must have weighed heavily in a guest's pocket compared to today's plastic key cards. (Courtesy of Gary Grant.)

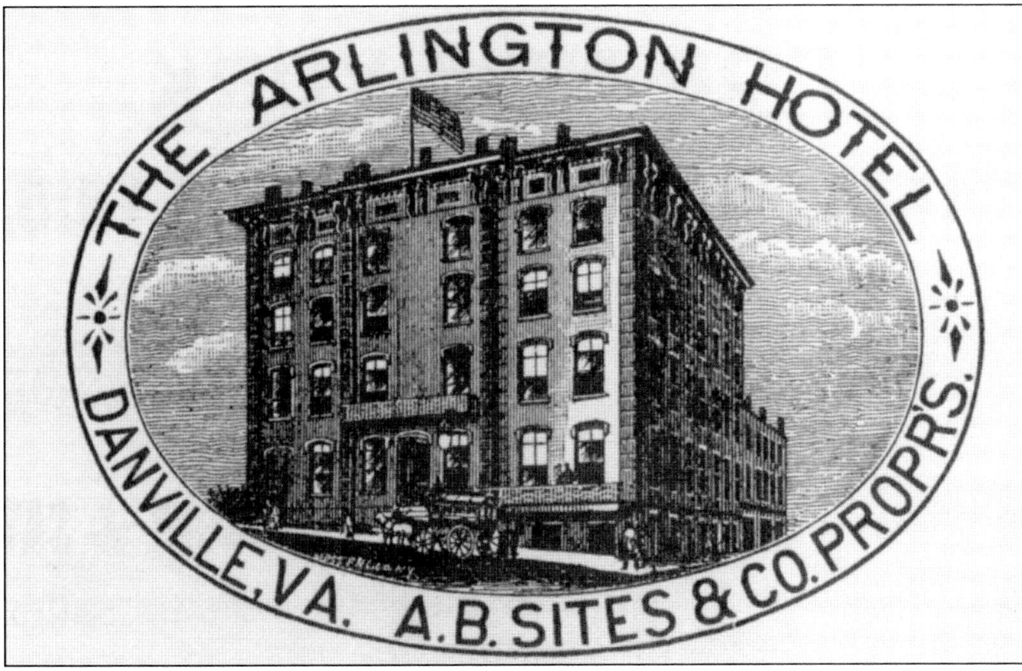

Danville's Civil War–era mayor, Robert Walker Williams, built the Arlington Hotel in 1869 on the former site of John W. Paxton's hostelry, the Red Castle Inn, which was described in its day as a "house of entertainment." Thomas Jefferson Lee, North Danville's fourth mayor, purchased the Arlington in 1883. Its first-class bar and billiards room flourished until Prohibition. (Courtesy of the Danville Historical Society.)

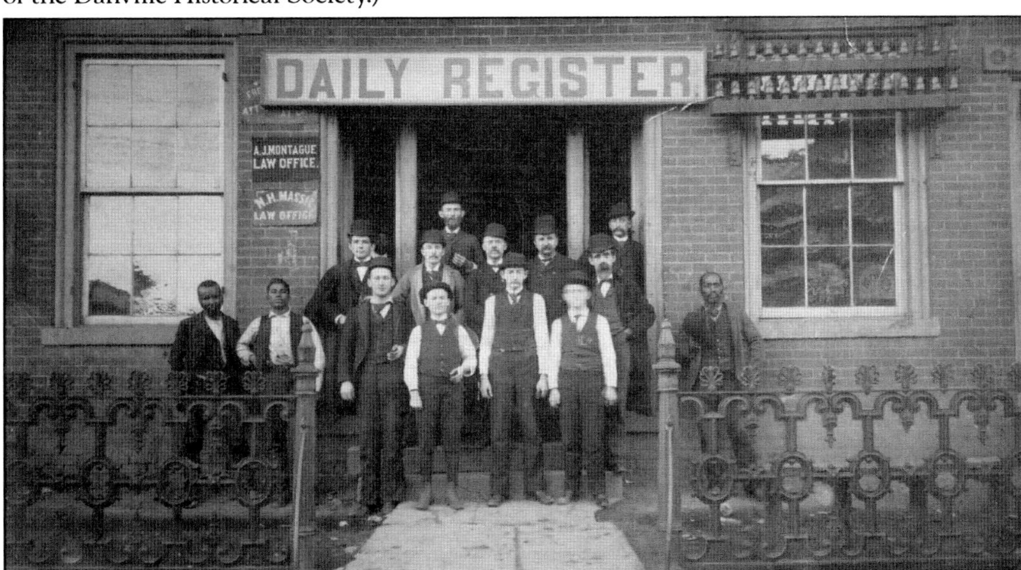

The *Daily Register*, one of Danville's early newspapers, began in 1832 as a weekly. After several name changes, it continues today as the *Register & Bee*. In 1880, the newsroom and circulation staff posed here in front of the paper's office at 503 Main Street in the Holland Building, opposite the Arlington Hotel. Woolworth's operated from a new building on this site for much of the 20th century. (Courtesy of Richard T. Davis.)

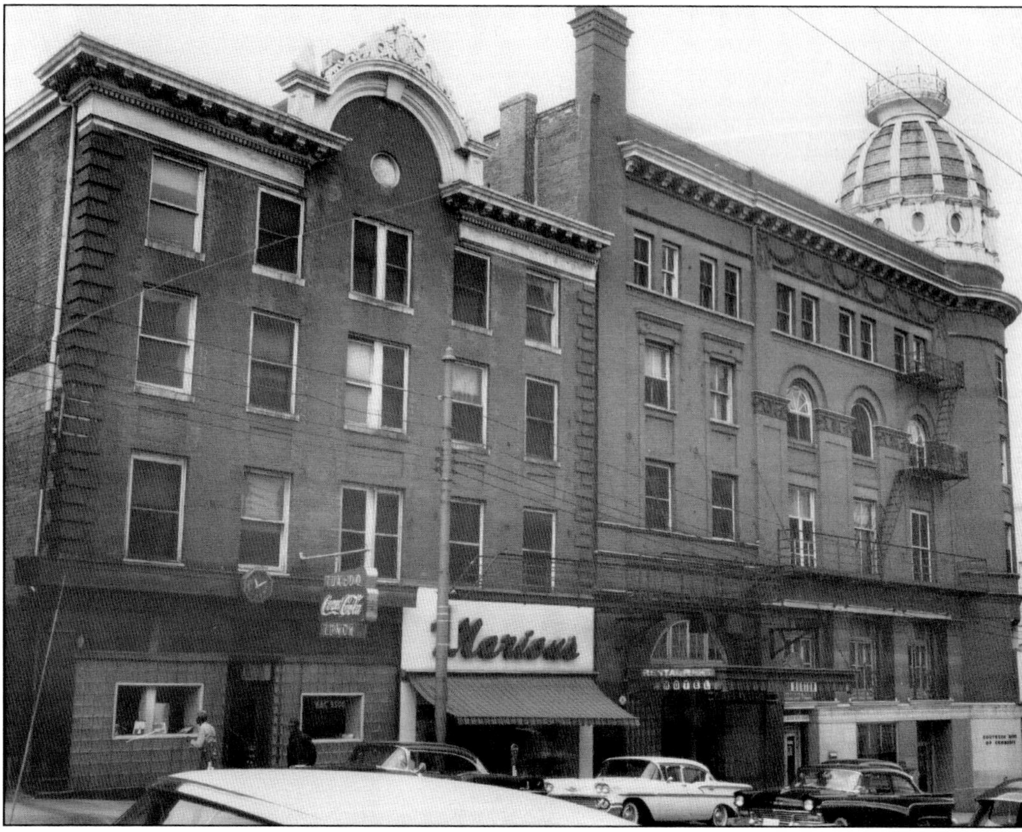

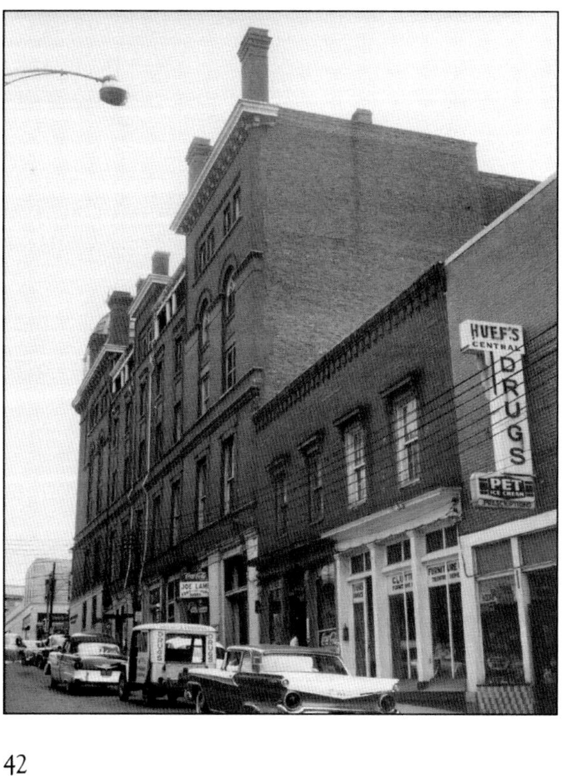

Four successive hotels, spanning 180 years, made the corner of Main and North Union Streets (above) preeminent in Danville hostelry. John W. Paxton built the Red Castle Inn in the early 1830s, Robert Walker Williams replaced it with the Arlington Hotel in 1869, and F.X. Burton built his Hotel Burton there in 1891. Investors built the Midtowner (Downtowner) there in 1962. (Photograph by John Tate; courtesy of the Danville Historical Society.)

This late-1950s oblique view of the Hotel Burton shows the businesses behind the Burton on North Union Street. Each of the hotels that occupied the busy Main Street corner—diagonally across from three successive Masonic temples over 150 years—also housed a prominent bank on the first floor. (Photograph by John Tate; courtesy of the Danville Historical Society.)

A grand hotel like the Burton sealed its reputation with luxurious amenities for its guests. This well-staffed and equipped barbershop, owned and managed by Andrew Morton, was on the ground floor of the hotel, with its entrance on Union Street. With six barber chairs, Morton provided quick and quality work. His clientele included many prominent men of Danville. (Photograph by Leon Taylor.)

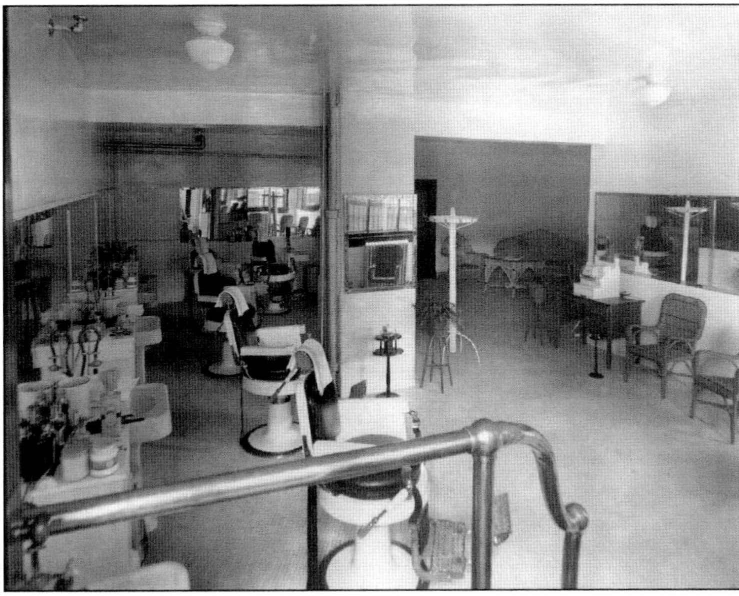

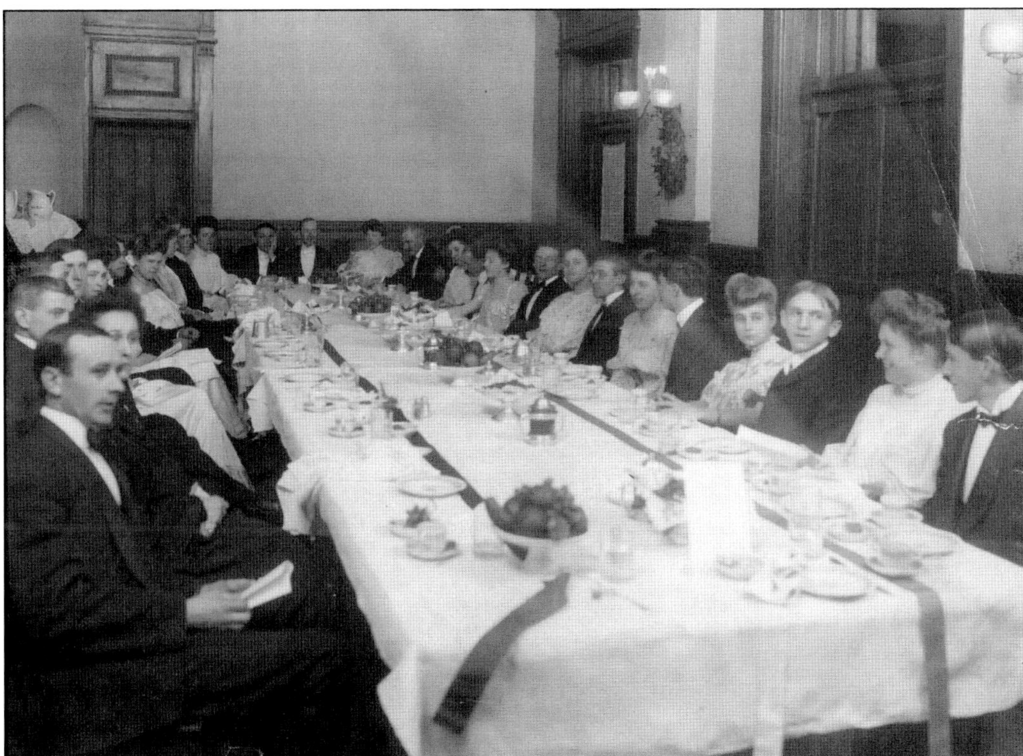

In this rare c. 1900 interior view of the Hotel Burton, an elegantly dressed group sits at a banquet table in the dining room. The Burton offered fine food and a popular catering service. Even in its later days, the Burton ranked among the city's top three hotels, along with the Stonewall and the Danville. (Photograph by Leon Taylor.)

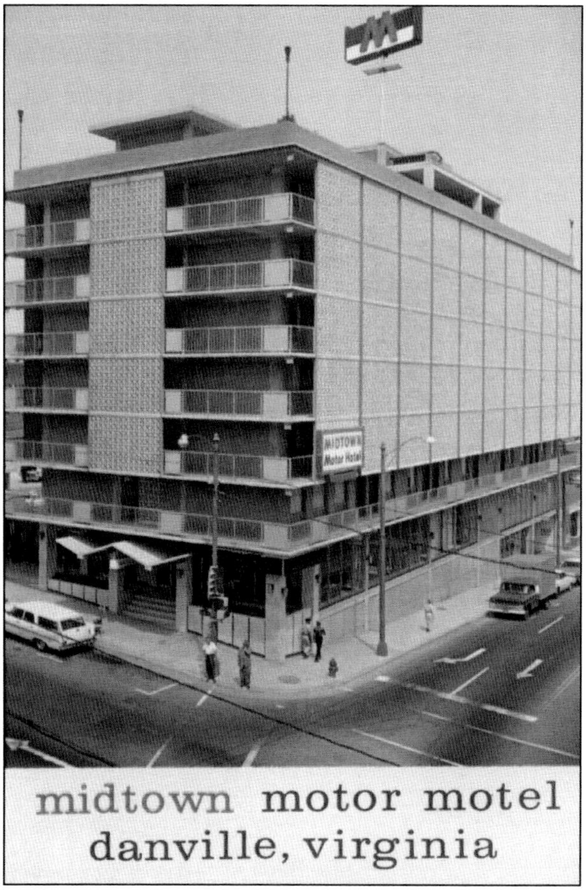

In 1962, investors razed the 60-year-old Hotel Burton in order to redevelop the site. It was replaced with a modern motel, the Midtowner (a local nickname), which had 118 rooms, a restaurant, a cafeteria, and a lounge. Later called the Downtowner, it met the same fate as many center-city hotels, closing in the mid-1980s. Stavros Calos of Danville took this photograph for his postcard business, the Piedmont Greeting Card Company. (Photograph by Stavros Calos.)

Over time, several attempts to refurbish the Downtowner stalled, including a late-1980s effort to reopen it as a hotel and subsequent efforts to reuse the building adaptively, first as housing for the elderly and then for college students. The city's River District Initiative included razing the 50-year-old hotel in the second half of 2012 (as shown below). Plans for the reuse of the site remain unresolved. (Photograph by Stuart Craig.)

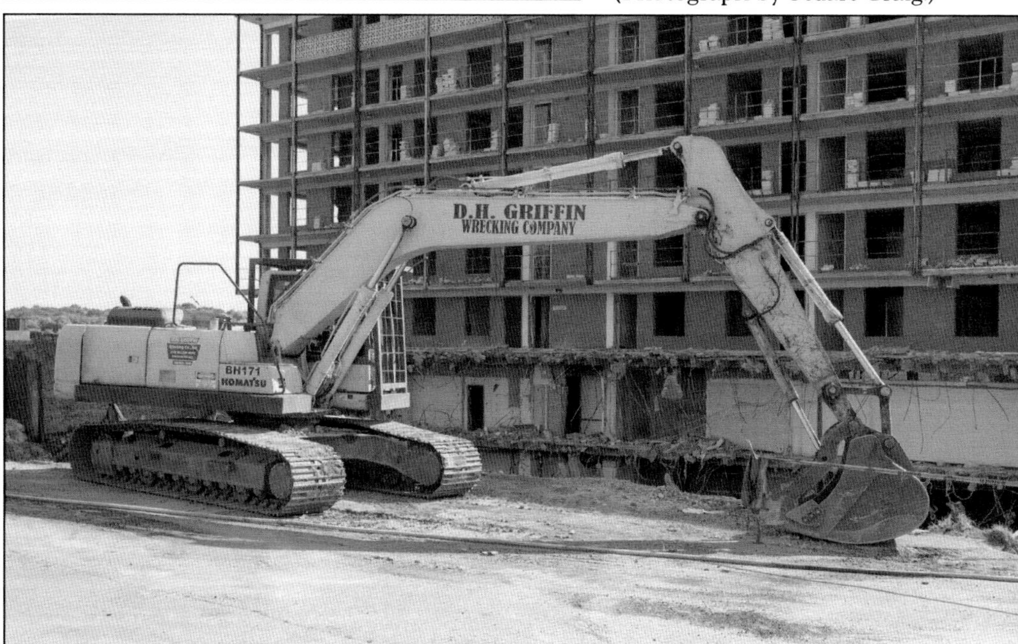

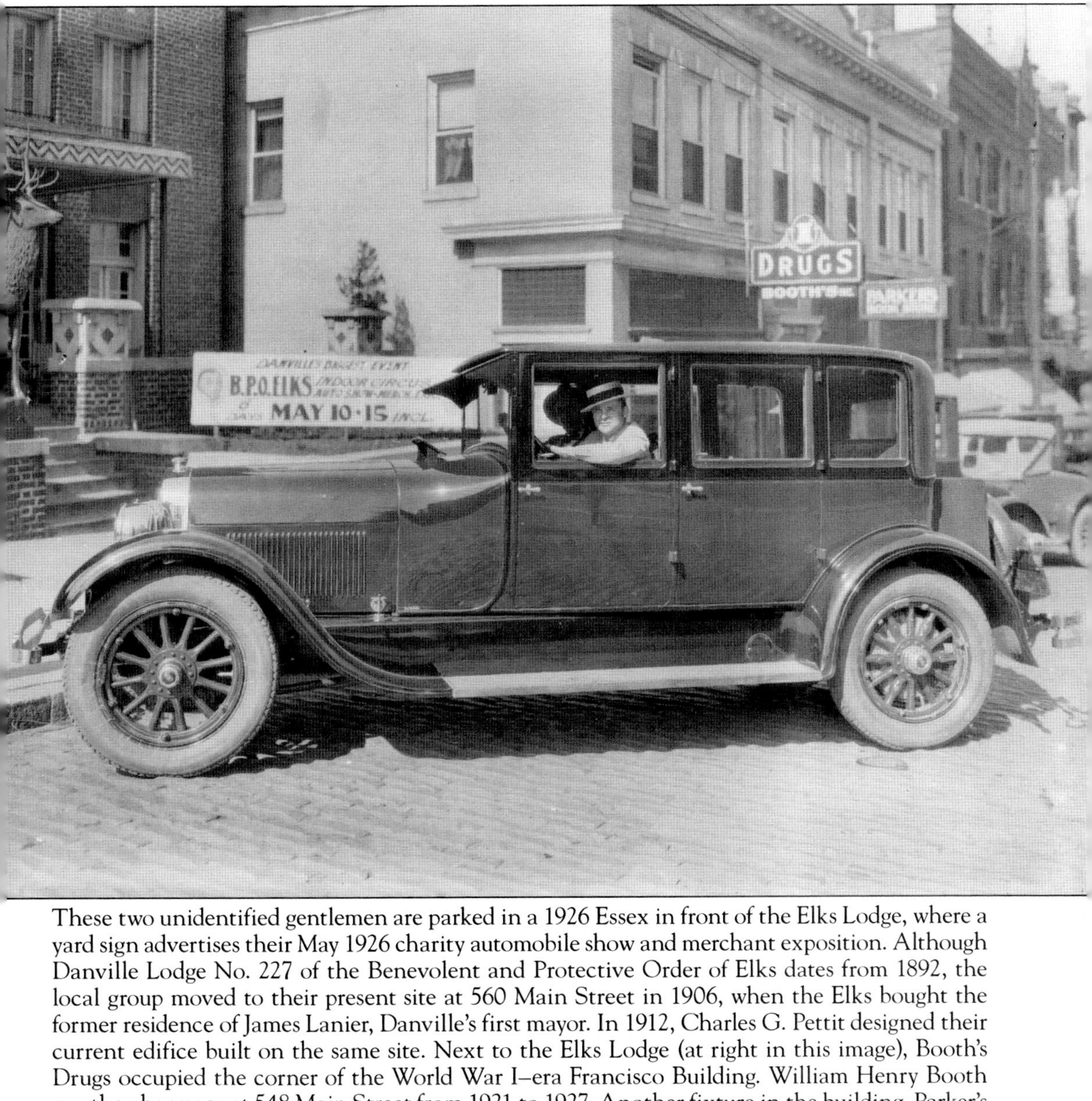

These two unidentified gentlemen are parked in a 1926 Essex in front of the Elks Lodge, where a yard sign advertises their May 1926 charity automobile show and merchant exposition. Although Danville Lodge No. 227 of the Benevolent and Protective Order of Elks dates from 1892, the local group moved to their present site at 560 Main Street in 1906, when the Elks bought the former residence of James Lanier, Danville's first mayor. In 1912, Charles G. Pettit designed their current edifice built on the same site. Next to the Elks Lodge (at right in this image), Booth's Drugs occupied the corner of the World War I–era Francisco Building. William Henry Booth ran the pharmacy at 548 Main Street from 1921 to 1927. Another fixture in the building, Parker's Book & Stationery Company at 544 Main Street, remained there for about 30 years, closing in 1955. Parker's had opened down the hill in 1902, when William Henry Parker came to Danville from Tennessee to join his father J.F. Parker in the landmark business, which sold books, musical instruments, sporting goods, art prints, and frames. (Photograph by Leon Taylor.)

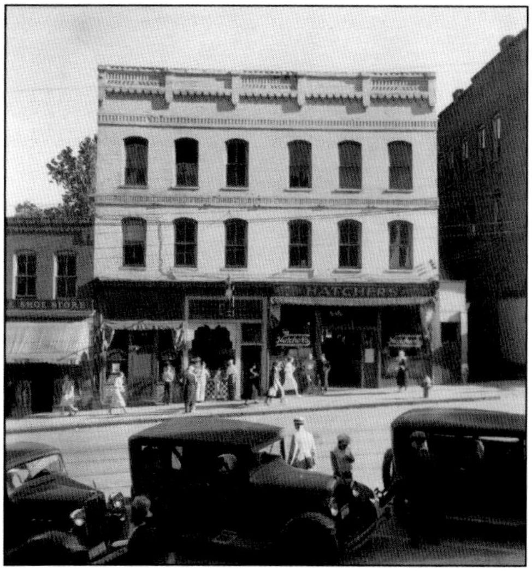

Leon Taylor took this photograph of the Gravely-Holland Insurance & Real Estate Company (at left) at 535 Main Street in the early 1930s. Hatcher's cigar and billiards store (at right), owned by Peyton R. Hatcher, proclaimed itself "Danville's oldest sports center." The Gravely-Holland company, under the watch of W. Tredway Gravely and Archer R. Gravely, managed and owned the building, which was constructed in the 1880s for S.H. Holland. (Photograph by Leon Taylor.)

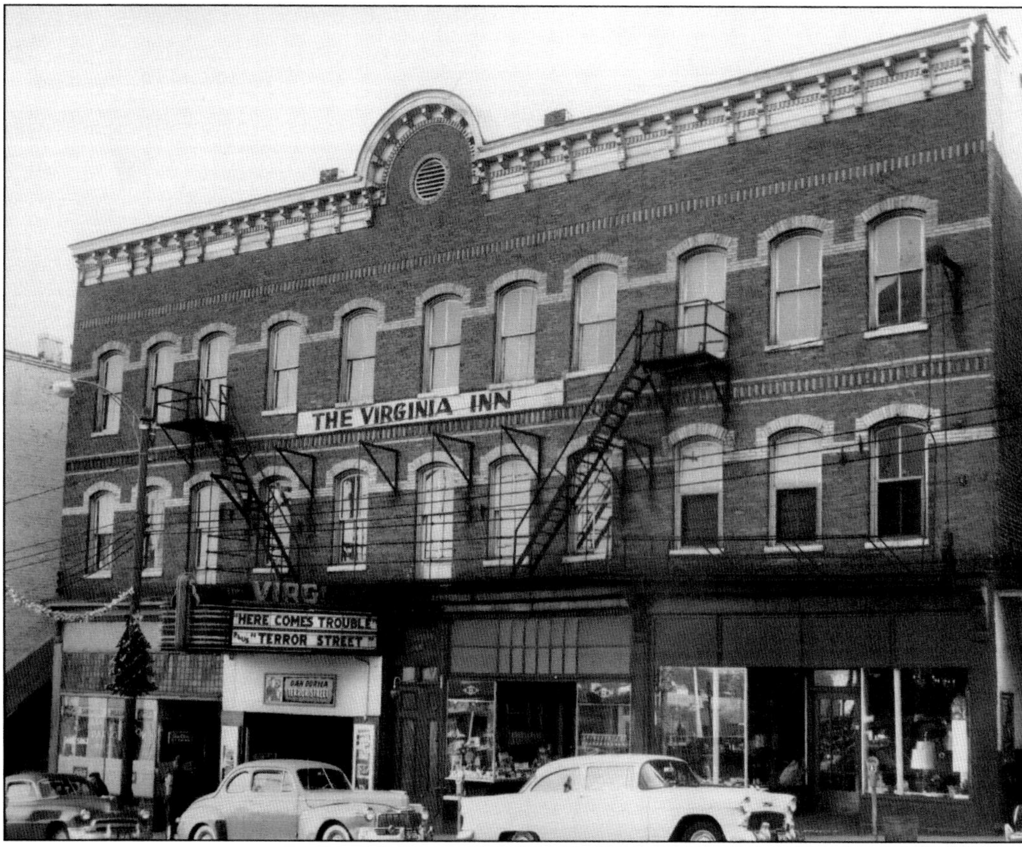

The Virginia Theater, one of Danville's premier movie houses between World War I and World War II, evolved out of Danville's Academy of Music, which was attached to the Hotel Carolina (later the Virginia Inn) at 543 Main Street. This early-1890s vaudeville hall succeeded Danville's first opera house, located down the street in the iron-front Pace Building. After the Virginia closed, the building's top two stories were removed in 1962. (Photograph by John Tate; courtesy of the Danville Historical Society.)

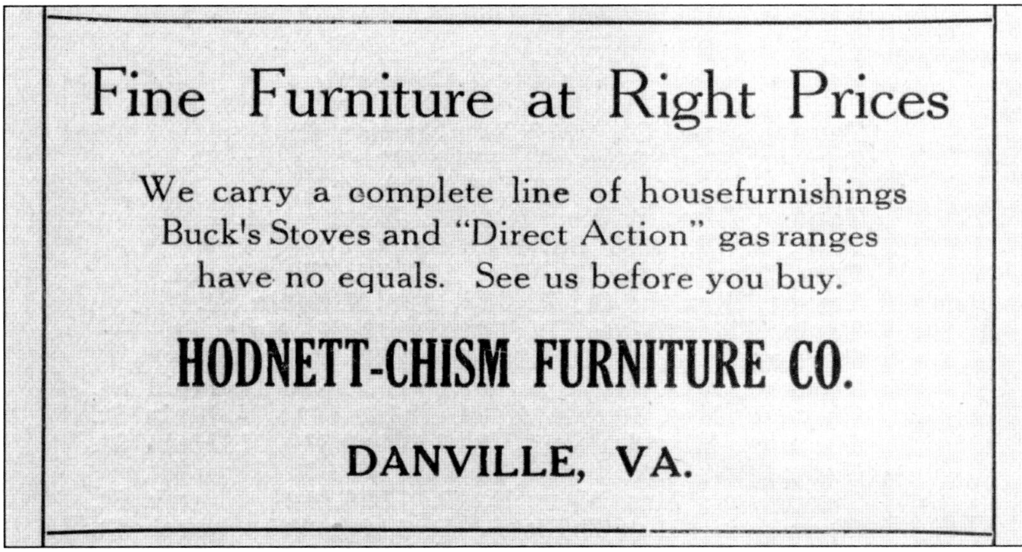

The Hodnett-Chism Furniture Company at 416 Main Street succeeded the former Crumpecker, Chism & Company, founded in 1880 and located down the hill at 220 Main Street. Years later, it became Clements, Chism & Parker; and, finally, Clements & Parker. Advertised as "Danville's Greatest Store," it offered a generous supply of household furnishings. (Courtesy of Clara Fountain.)

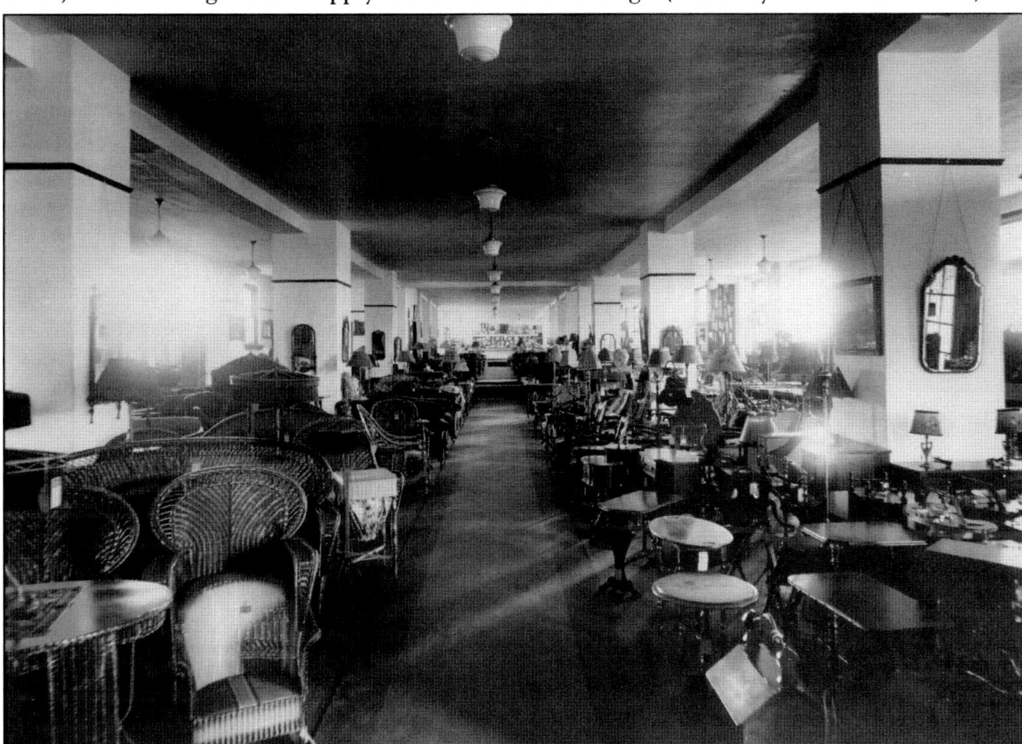

When Hotel Danville opened its doors in 1927, Clements, Chism & Parker Furniture Company occupied most of the street-level commercial space. This interior view of the store from the late 1920s shows the scope of furnishings available. Regarded for many years as Danville's largest retail furniture enterprise, the store closed its doors in the early 1980s. (Photograph by Leon Taylor.)

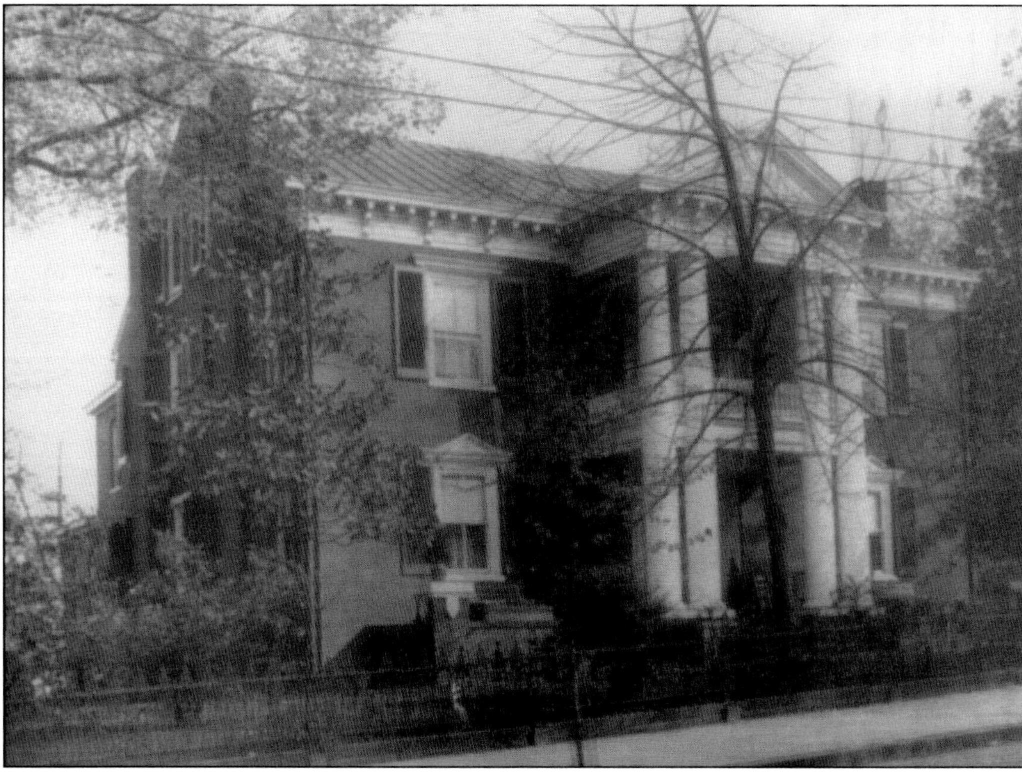

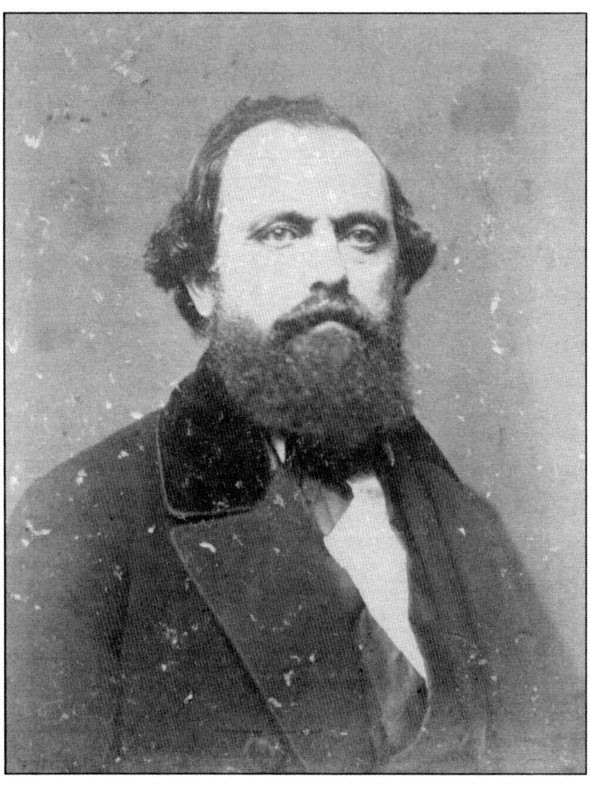

Double end chimneys distinguished this antebellum mansion built at 711 Main Street in 1840 for William W. Williamson and his wife, Mattie, the daughter of William T. Clark and the second cousin of Harry Wooding. For over 75 years, this classically inspired house stood juxtaposed to the Victorian home of F.X. Burton. Both houses were razed in the early 1960s to make way for a modern bank on the site. (Courtesy of the Danville Historical Society.)

Born in 1820, William Thomas Clark of Danville married Barbara Freeman of Culpeper County, Virginia. They made their home on Ridge Street, between Main and Patton Streets. A tobacco manufacturer and president of the Danville Female Academy, Clark also served two terms as the mayor of Danville (in 1860 and 1865). (Courtesy of the Danville Museum of Fine Arts and History.)

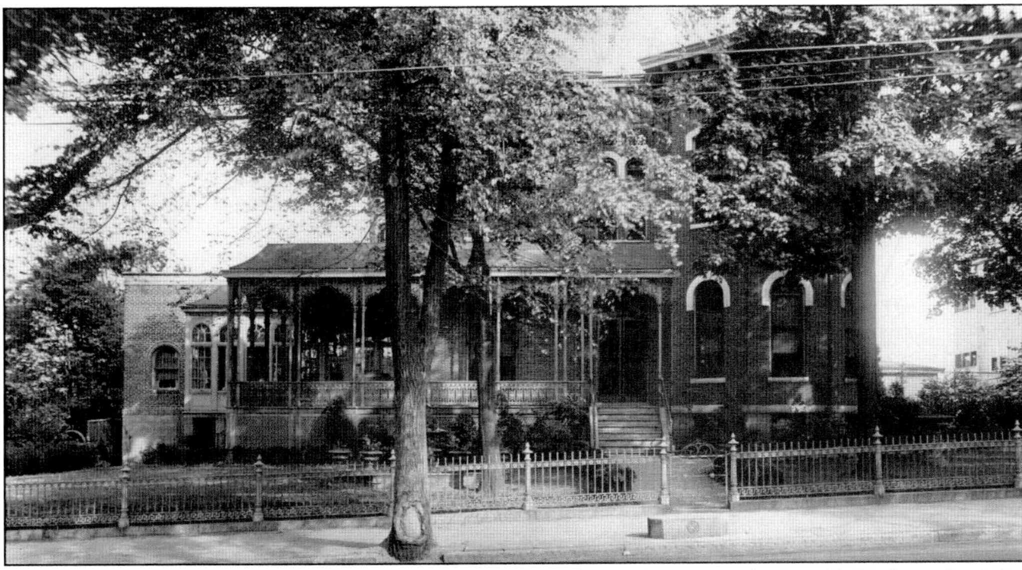

In 1873, F.X. Burton married Alice Shelton, the daughter of W.N. and Mary F. Shelton. In 1884, Burton built this mansion, designed by architect Albert West, on the site of the old Shelton home, at 723 Main Street. A prominent local tobacco manufacturer, Burton also built the Morotock Cotton Mill, near the river, which was absorbed in 1890 by the larger Riverside Mills, the predecessor of Dan River Inc. (Photograph by Leon Taylor.)

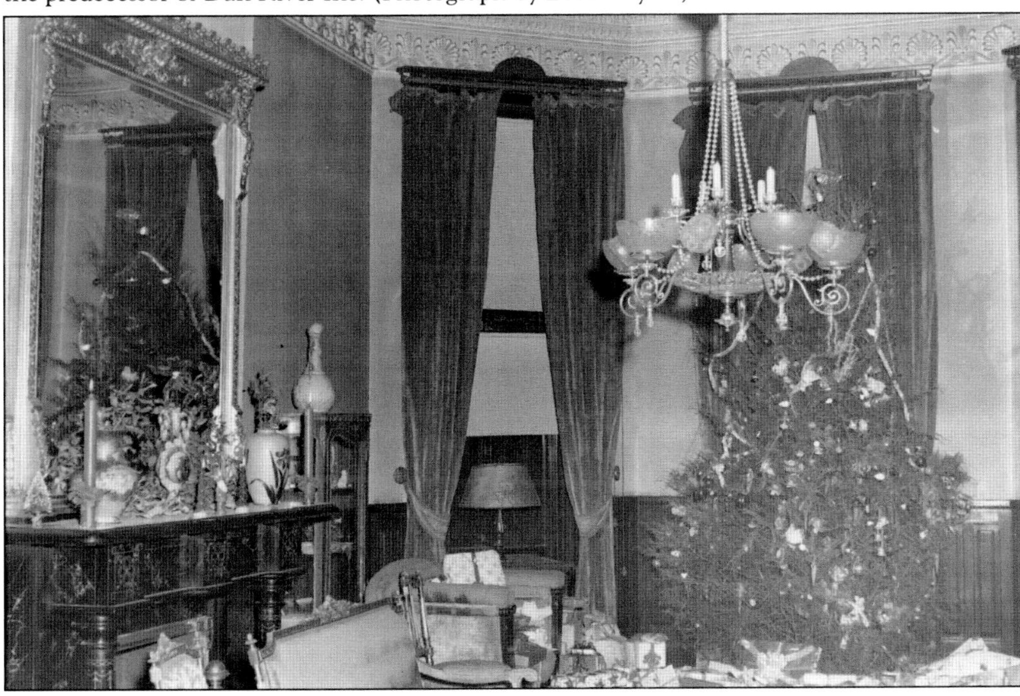

In this interior view of the Burton home, gifts rest under a World War I–era Christmas tree reflected in a gilt mirror over the black, faux-marble mantel. Crowned by ornate plaster, the lofty ceiling supported a gas-electric chandelier that illuminated the parlor's Victorian splendor. Alice Shelton Burton died in 1930, willing her house to the First Presbyterian Church to be used by elderly churchwomen as a residence called the Sunnyside Home. (Courtesy of Zoe Edmunds.)

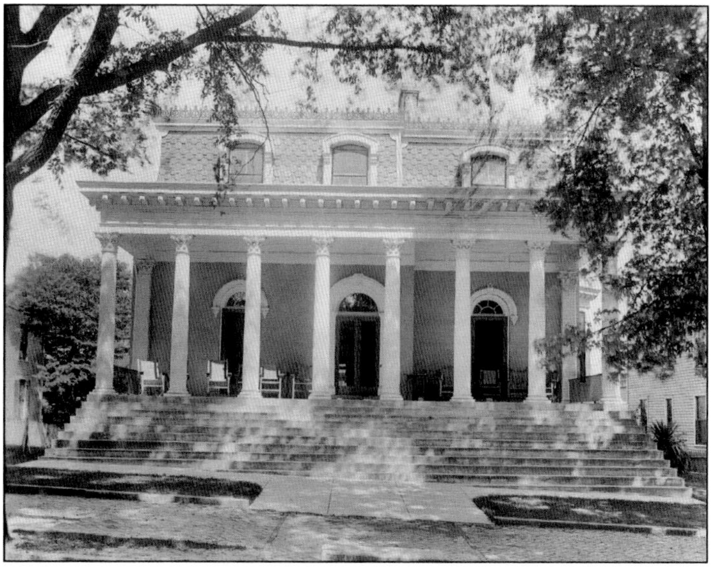

One of Danville's architectural masterworks was the Italianate dwelling of John M. Johnston, who served as the Confederate States depositary during the Civil War. His "cottage," built in 1872 at 712 Main Street, was one and a half stories and featured a decorative mansard roof. The Johnston house served as the Tuscarora Club from 1912 to 1932, after which it was replaced by the federal courthouse and post office. (Photograph by Leon Taylor.)

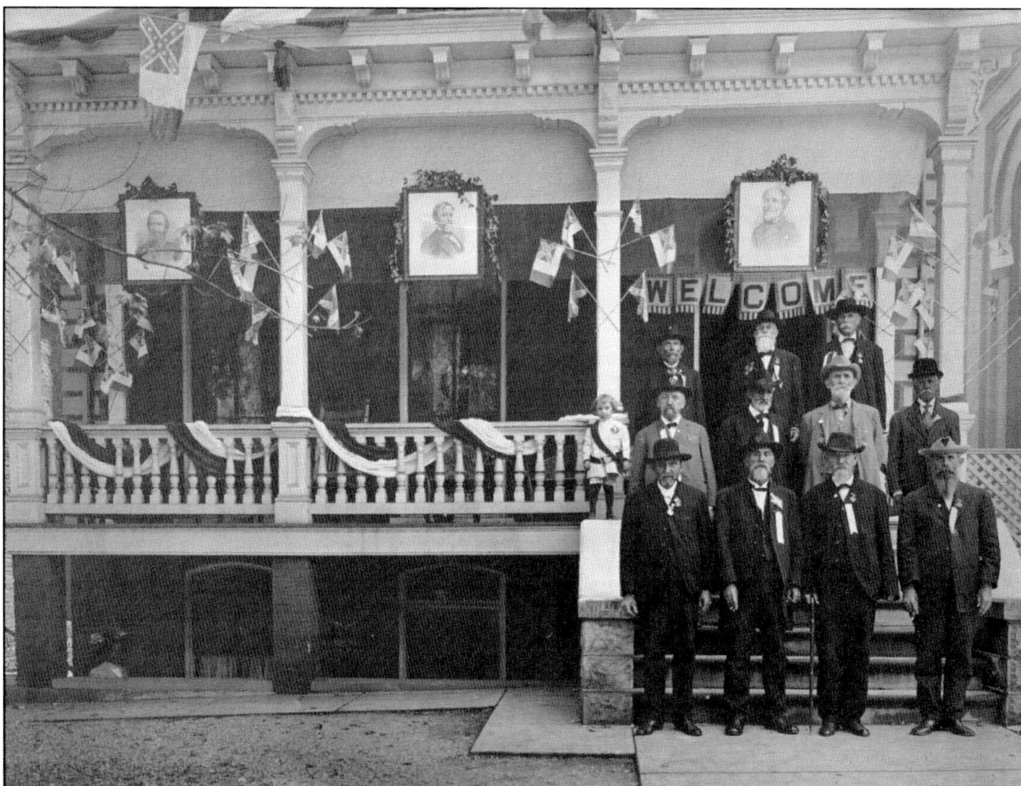

Harry Wooding (first row, second from left) attended many Confederate reunions. Here, unidentified fellow veterans pose proudly alongside Captain Wooding, who fought in the Battle of Bull Run and the Battle of Gettysburg, on the steps of the home of Dr. W.L. Robinson. Long known as the Professional Building, the 1877 house at 753 Main Street originally featured this ornamental wooden porch typical of brick Italianate dwellings. (Photograph by Leon Taylor.)

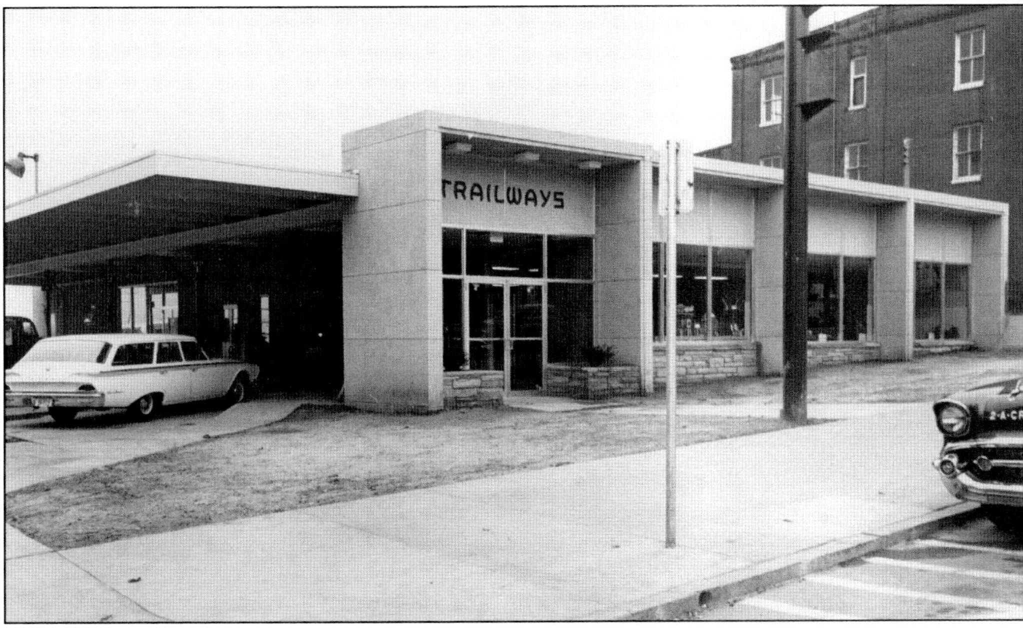

The Trailways Bus Company constructed a new station in 1959 on the 700 block of Main Street, just below Main Street Methodist Church. Two large apartment buildings were razed to accommodate the space required for buses to drive around the new hub. (Photograph by John Tate; courtesy of the Danville Historical Society.)

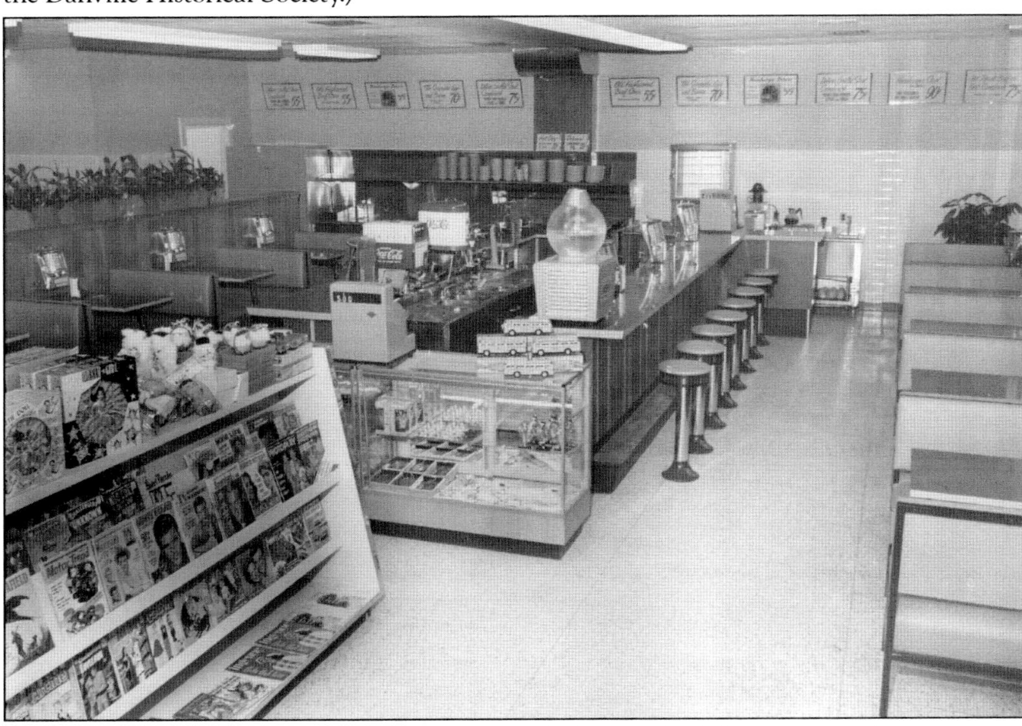

Trailways offered riders a convenient place to eat and relax inside while waiting for their connecting buses. In August 1960, this luncheonette opened its doors to become the first desegregated eating place in Danville. (Photograph by John Tate, courtesy of the Danville Historical Society.)

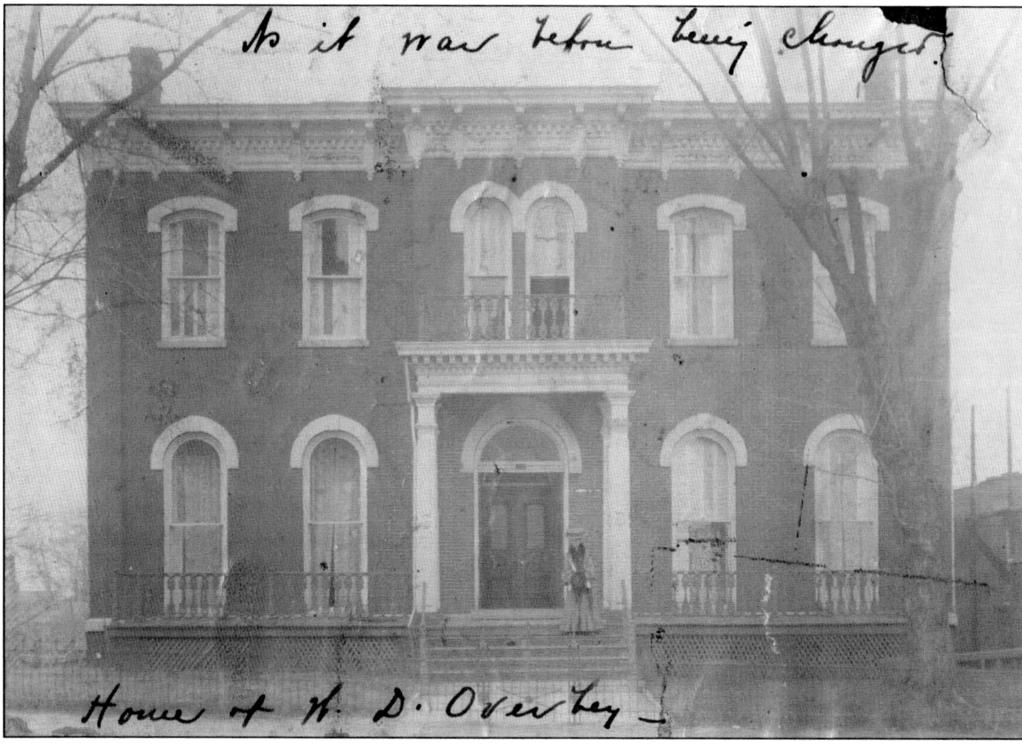

When Sgt. Robert W. Lawson built this dignified Italianate mansion at 782 Main Street in 1881, it represented the first wave of Danville's post–Civil War tobacco boom. It also reflected the talents of local architect/builder Thomas Benton Fitzgerald. After Lawson's death in 1884, his estate conveyed the property to Sallie Shepherd, the widowed daughter of one of Danville's founders, Capt. John Noble. (Courtesy of Cindy Castle.)

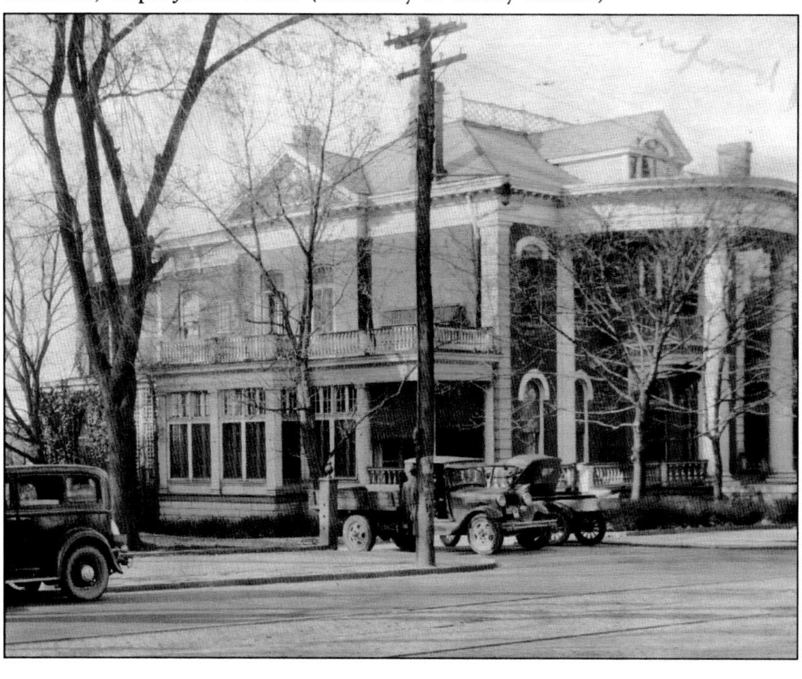

Sallie Shepherd's daughter, also named Sallie, married lumber dealer Daniel A. Overbey. In 1911, Daniel added a dramatic semicircular portico to the front of the house. The couple had two sons, William Daniel and John E. Overbey. (Photograph by P.W. Dunford; courtesy of Cindy Castle.)

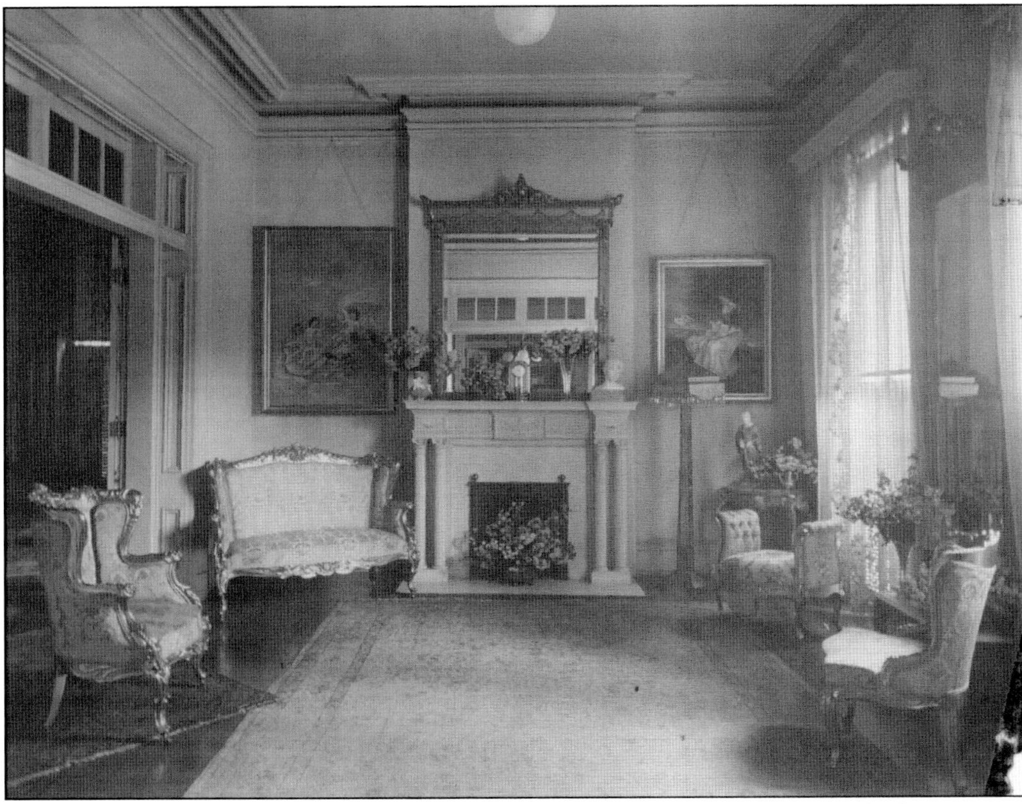

The Overbeys transformed not only the facade, but also the whole interior of the house at 782 Main Street. They redecorated all the rooms and added millwork, turning the staid house into a lavish showplace. William Daniel Overbey and his wife, May Hutchinson Overbey, the second generation to own the house, held extravagant parties in its opulent rooms for many decades. (Courtesy of Cindy Castle.)

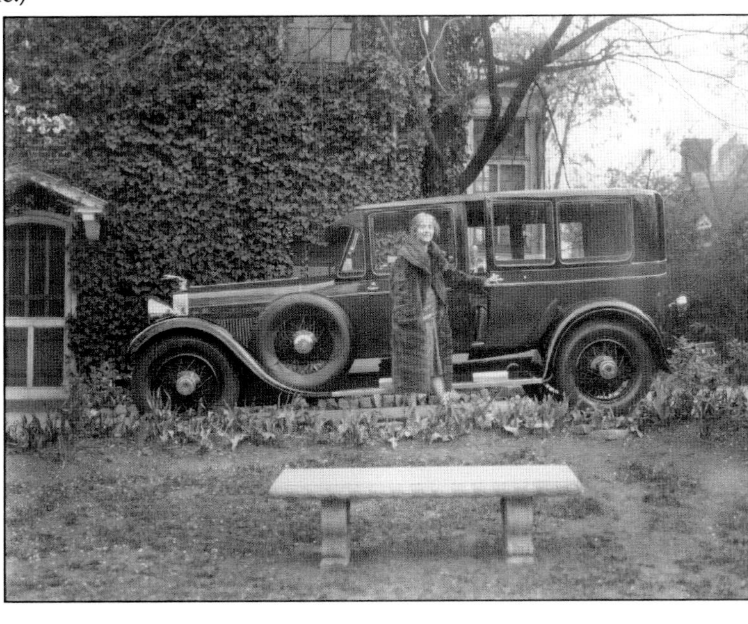

A Mississippi native and an honor graduate of Mary Baldwin College in Staunton, Virginia, May Hutchinson Overbey was also an avid gardener. Ornamental trees and perennials graced the grounds, descending from the garage off Jefferson Avenue Extension. This image also shows the family's handsome Pierce-Arrow and May's passion for fashion. (Photograph by Leon Taylor.)

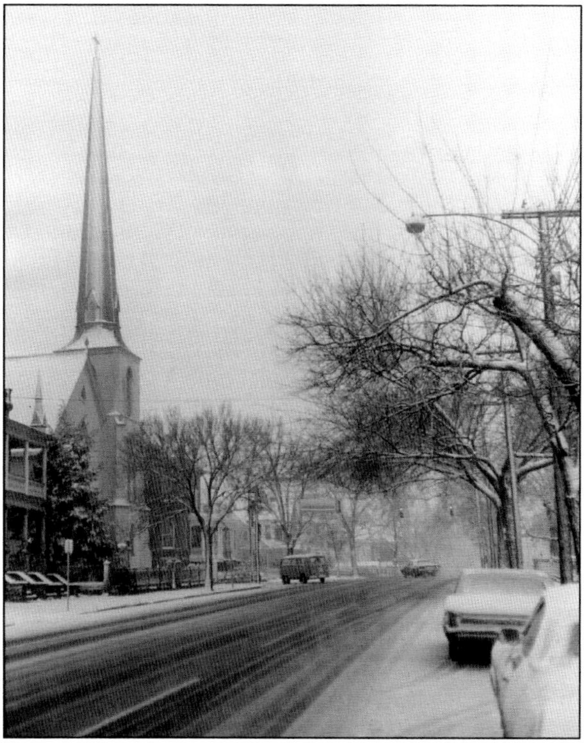

In this c. 1970 photograph, snow coats the slender steeple of the Episcopal Church of the Epiphany as traffic lumbers carefully onto Main Street from Jefferson Avenue. Led for over 50 years by founding rector Dr. George Washington Dame, Epiphany first occupied this site in 1844. Members began constructing the present Gothic Revival edifice in 1879. Sunday school students raised money for the cast-iron fence. (Courtesy of the Danville Historical Society.)

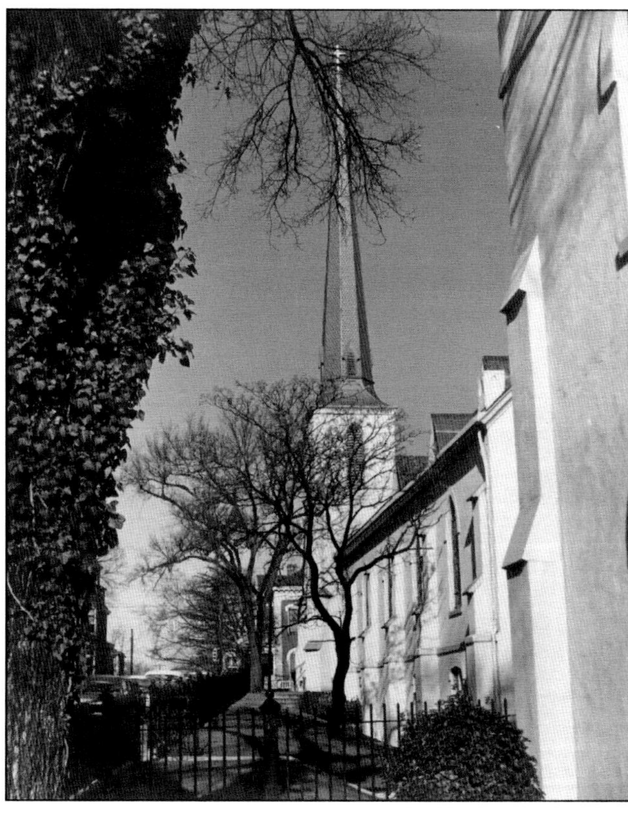

William E. Land served as a district court judge on the Danville bench for many years. Also an accomplished photographer, he captured the subtle shadows of picturesque elms on Epiphany's stuccoed walls along Jefferson Avenue, where the congregation built its 1950s parish house (now called Dame Hall). Church founder Dr. George Dame was the first superintendent of Pittsylvania County and Danville schools in 1870, when Virginia made public education compulsory. (Photograph by William E. Land.)

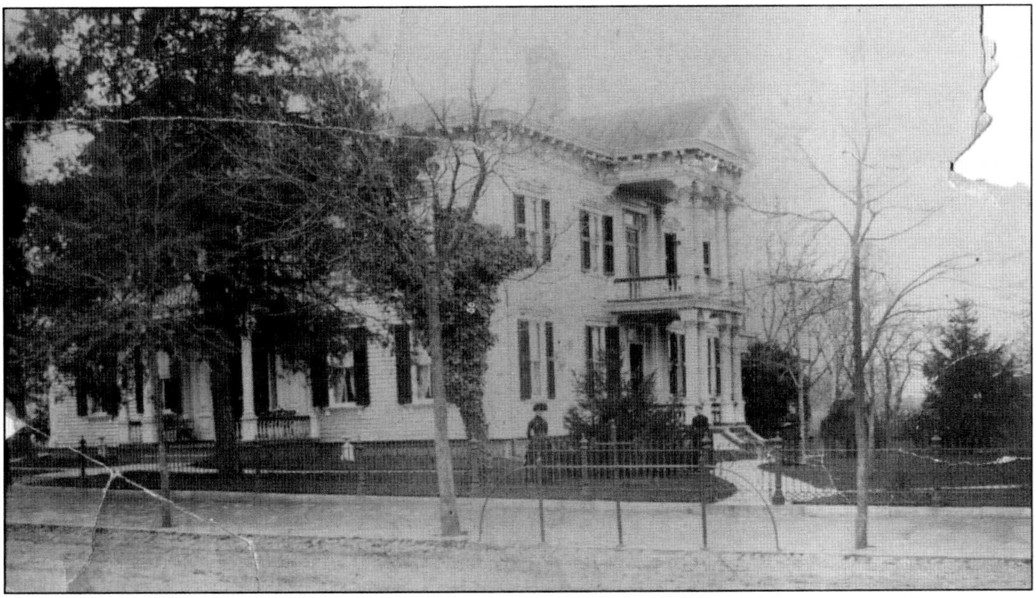

The mid-1800s mansion of C. Gilmore Holland, located at 818 Main Street, occupied expansive grounds on the current site of the Danville YMCA. The weatherboard house featured two-level porticos with elegant Corinthian columns. A brick summer kitchen stood at the rear of the house, set on landscaped grounds with winding paths. The Holland-Conrad square in Greenhill Cemetery, enclosed by limestone entry posts draped with carved "hands" of tobacco, eternally immortalizes the Hollands as among Danville's first families of tobacco. (Courtesy of Gary Grant.)

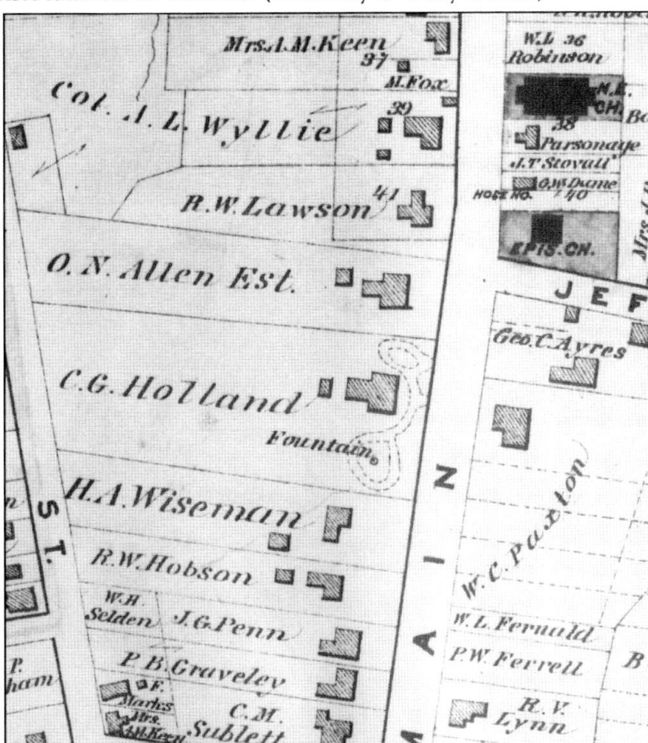

After the Civil War, Danville's nouveau riche crowded lavish new dwellings onto narrow Main Street lots, as seen on this 1877 Beers' Map. The footprints for these "townhouses" contrasted with that of the earlier C.G. Holland mansion, which was set on a two-acre lot. (Courtesy of the National Tobacco-Textile Museum.)

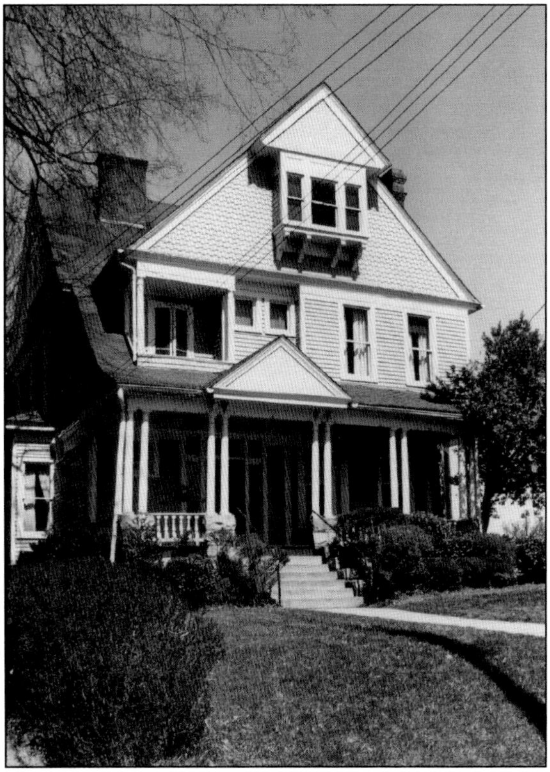

In the 1890s, James E. Perkinson and his family moved into this late-Victorian mansion built in the asymmetrical Queen Anne style at 828 Main Street, next door to the Holland mansion. Like most of the Hollands, Perkinson made his name as a leaf tobacco dealer. The house was razed in the 1970s to expand the parking lot for the Danville YMCA. (Photograph by Russell Wright.)

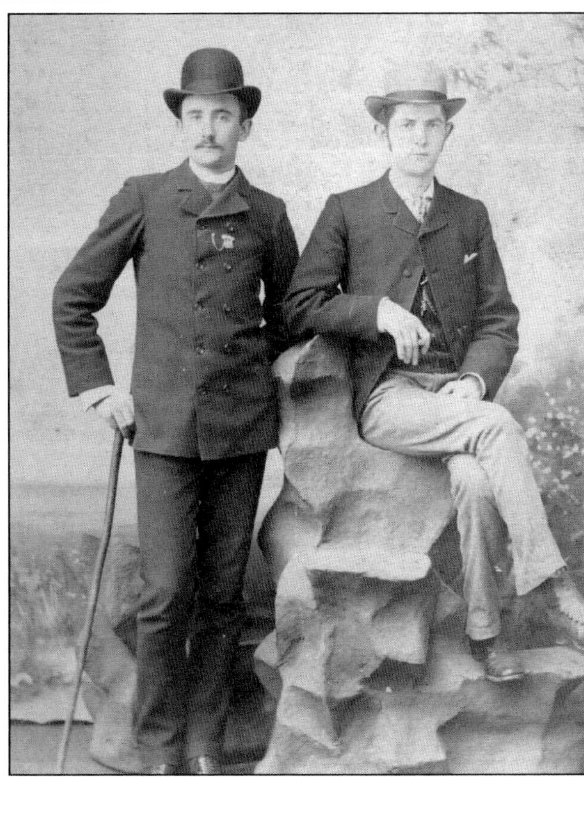

A youthful James E. Perkinson (right) and Alexander B. Carrington strike rakish poses around 1880 in the studio of the Blunt Art Palace. Carrington, known as "Colonel" for his Civil War service, was one of three principals—along with Richard L. Dibrell and H. Lee Boatwright—who helped make Dibrell Brothers a presence in international tobacco markets. (Photograph by A.H. Blunt; courtesy of the Danville Historical Society.)

On Monday, April 25, 1960, a fire broke out at 827 Main Street, the home of Ella C. Swanson, the wife of Henry C. Swanson. By the time firemen could get her out of the building, she had collapsed from smoke inhalation. Although she was not burned, she died the following Friday. The wind carried the fire to the roof next door, at 821 Main Street (below). That house, which was built in 1907 and owned by Kathryn B. Penn, the widow of James G. Penn Jr., burned extensively, with many valuable antiques inside. The two-house fire attracted many spectators, who gathered across the street. (Both photographs by John Tate; courtesy of the Danville Historical Society.)

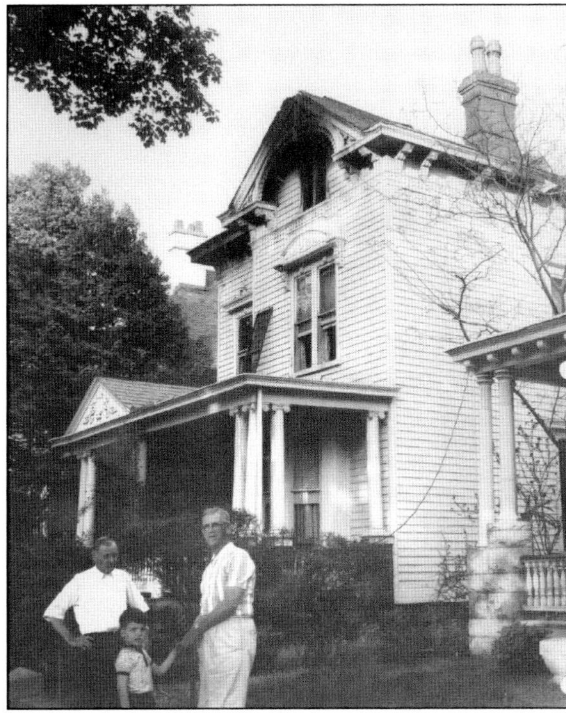

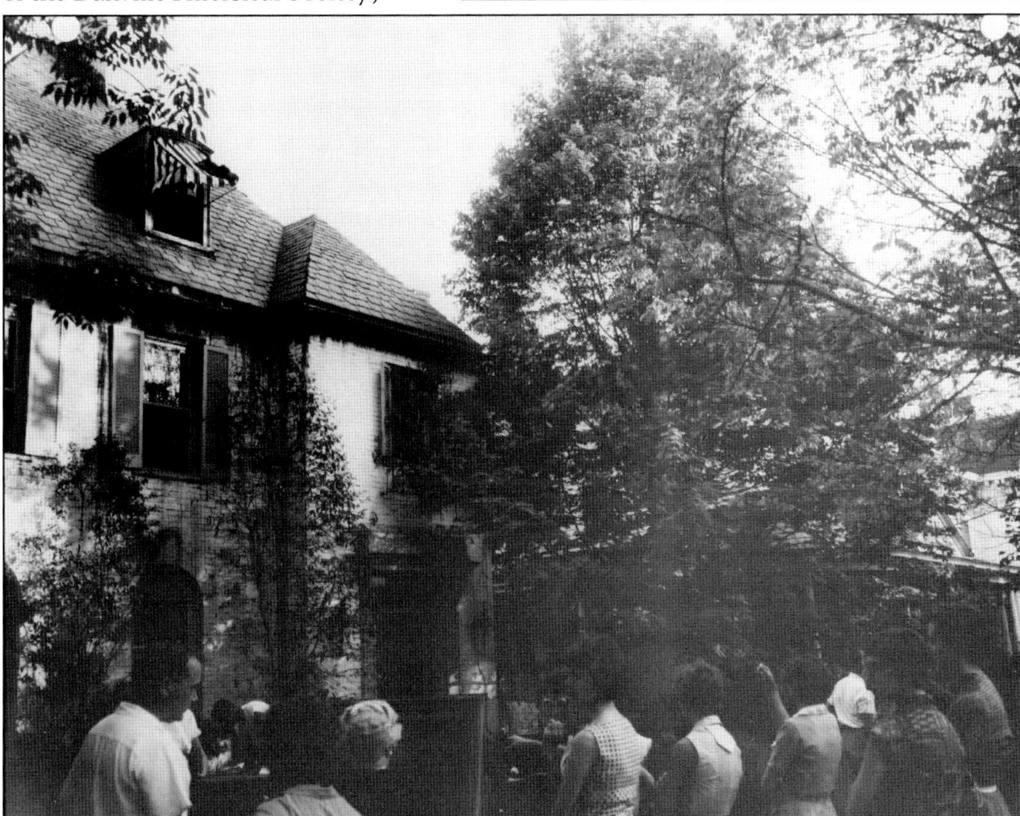

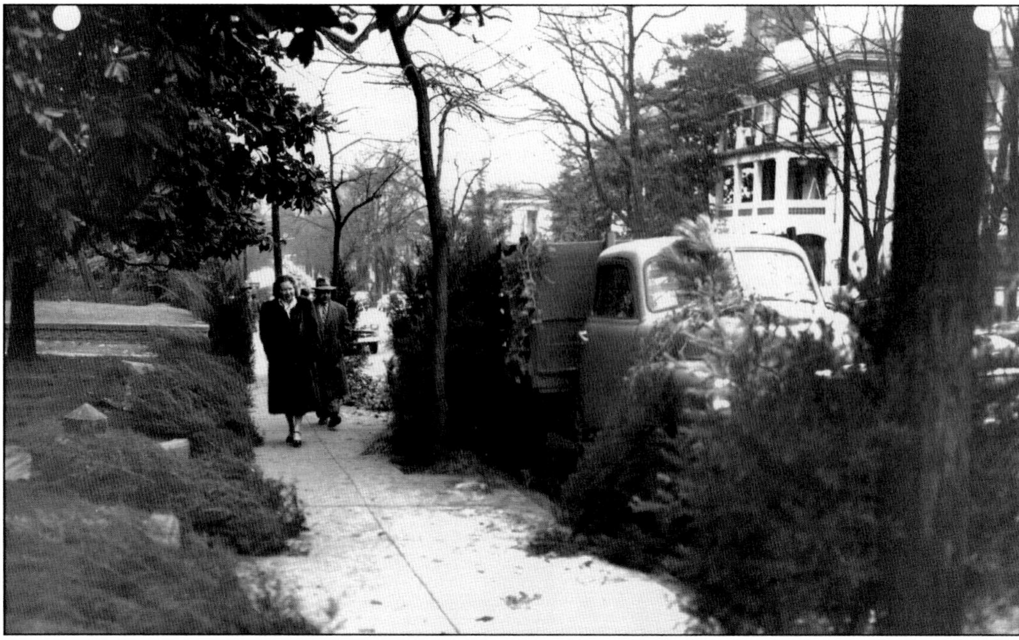

In this 1952 image, a vendor sells Christmas trees in the heart of downtown, laying out native cedars on the sidewalk in front of 918 Main Street. Danville's Christmas shopping season began the day after Thanksgiving, when throngs headed downtown after the Santa Claus parade. (Photograph by John Tate; courtesy of the Danville Historical Society.)

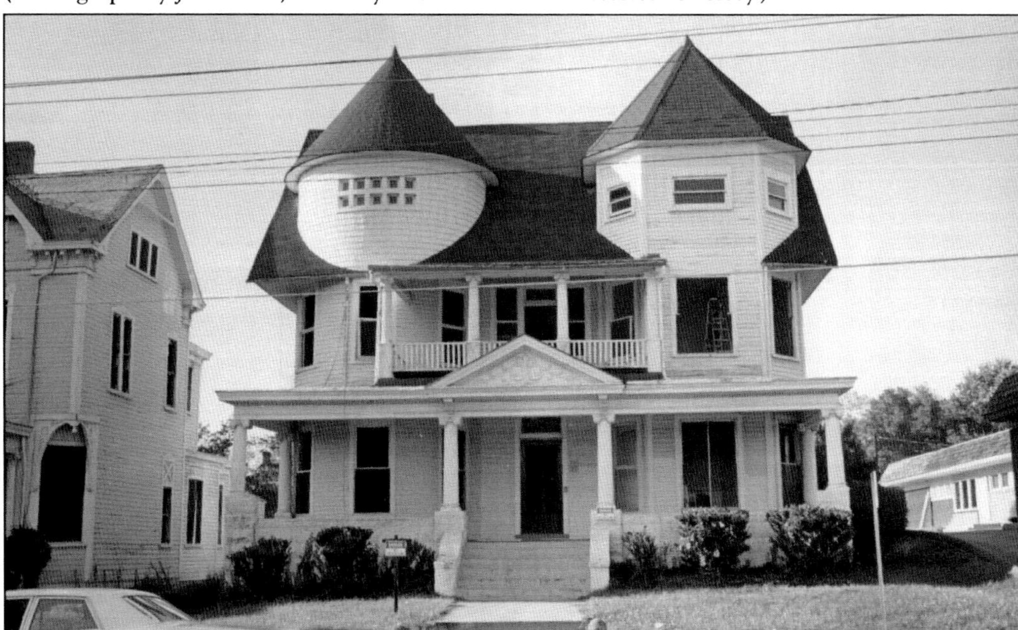

In 1895, grocer John R. Ferrell built this two-towered house at 1042 Main Street. Also known as the Isaac Rosenstock house (after an early department store owner who purchased the property in 1902), it later became four apartments. In the early 1970s, the nearby urologic clinic (right) expanded its parking, destroying the house, along with the neighboring Southall house (left). (Photograph by Steve Calos; courtesy of Sue B. Glidewell.)

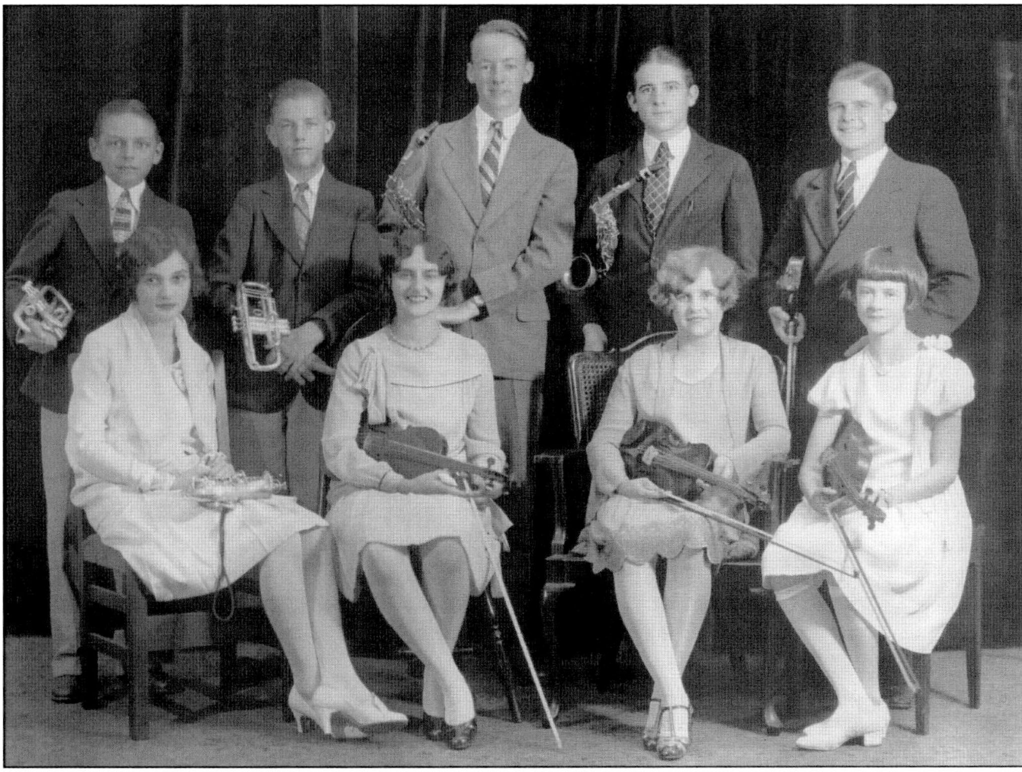

In the mid-1920s, Mount Vernon Methodist Church encouraged its teenaged members to play in the church's student orchestra. These young people are, from left to right, (first row) Virginia Payne, Ann Mary Sanford, Anne Elizabeth Garrett, and Elsie Hawkins; (second row) Bill Groff, Ira McMann, Billy Ragland, Thomas Blackwell Garrett, and Albert Earle Garrett Jr. (Photograph by P.W. Dunford.)

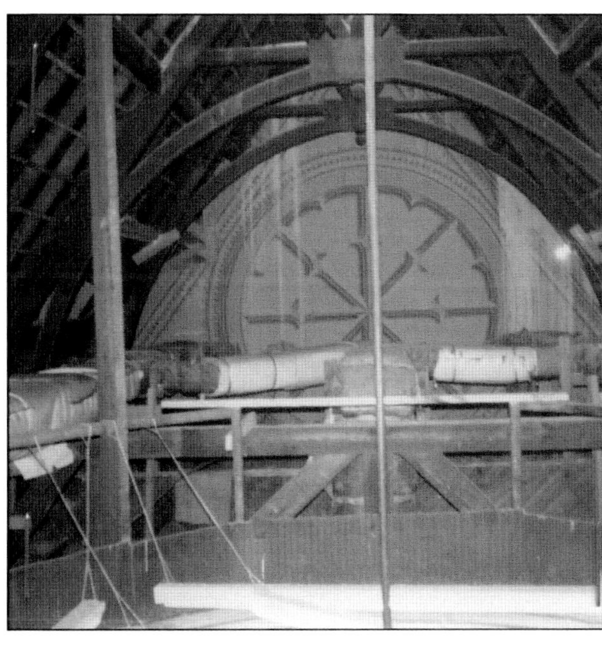

When Mount Vernon Methodist Church installed air-conditioning in its sanctuary in the late 1950s, church leaders considered removing the "false" coffered ceiling to restore the original interior cathedral's grandeur. When this course proved too expensive, workmen stretched the ducts above the lowered ceiling. In this space, vaulted wooden trusses framed the rose window on one wall, revealing some of its original drama. (Courtesy of Mount Vernon United Methodist Church.)

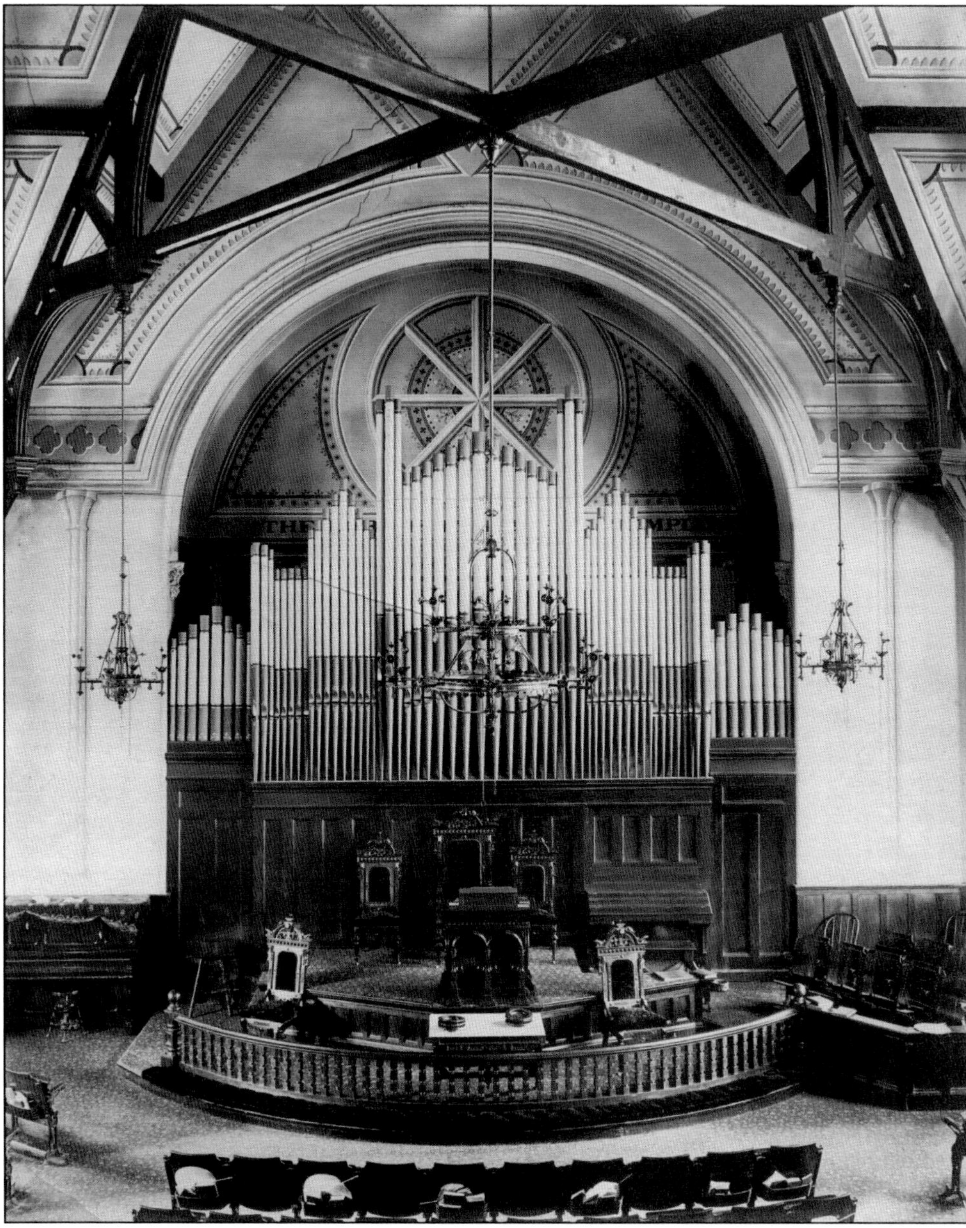

For years, members of Mount Vernon Methodist Church hoped to find a photograph of the sanctuary as it looked when the church was built in 1884. Repeatedly, but to no avail, they asked descendants of charter families to go through scrapbooks of their relatives, hoping to find views of ancestors' weddings or christenings taken inside the church. In the summer of 2012, the authors discovered this interior view photographed by Leon Taylor in 1910. The original design showed a semicircular chancel and altar rail in front of a five-sided raised platform for the pulpit. Geometric frescoes decorated the upper sections of several walls and the ceiling, which was tied together with massive wooden trusses. A dramatic eight-segment motif painted to mimic a rose window stretched above the choir loft and behind the new organ pipes. The pipes of the Hook & Hastings organ, which was added in 1905, covered a verse of scripture painted below the rose medallion: "The Lord is in His Holy Temple." (Photograph by Leon Taylor.)

The congregation of Mount Vernon Methodist Church celebrated Christmas 1916 in their recently refurbished sanctuary. New chandeliers suspended from a lower, coffered ceiling cast bright electric light on the congregation and the expanded choir loft. Small lights around the archway over the choir shed enough light for members to read their hymnals and anthems. (Courtesy of Mount Vernon United Methodist Church.)

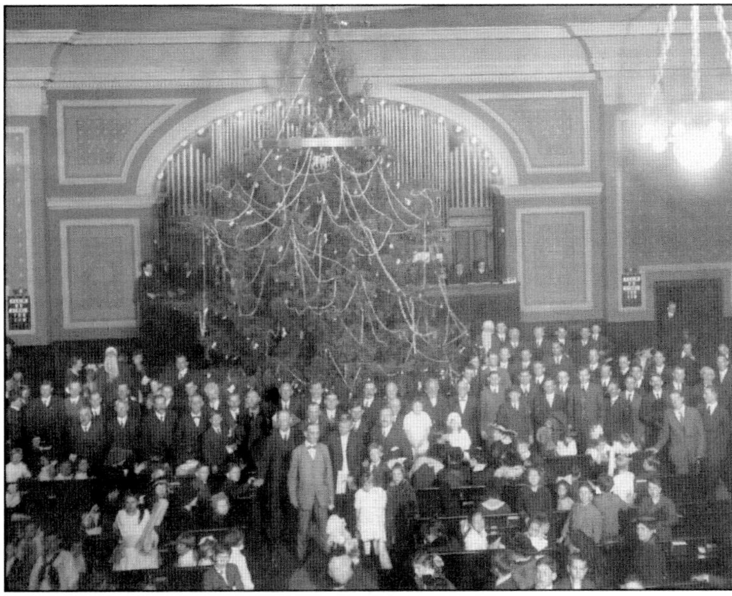

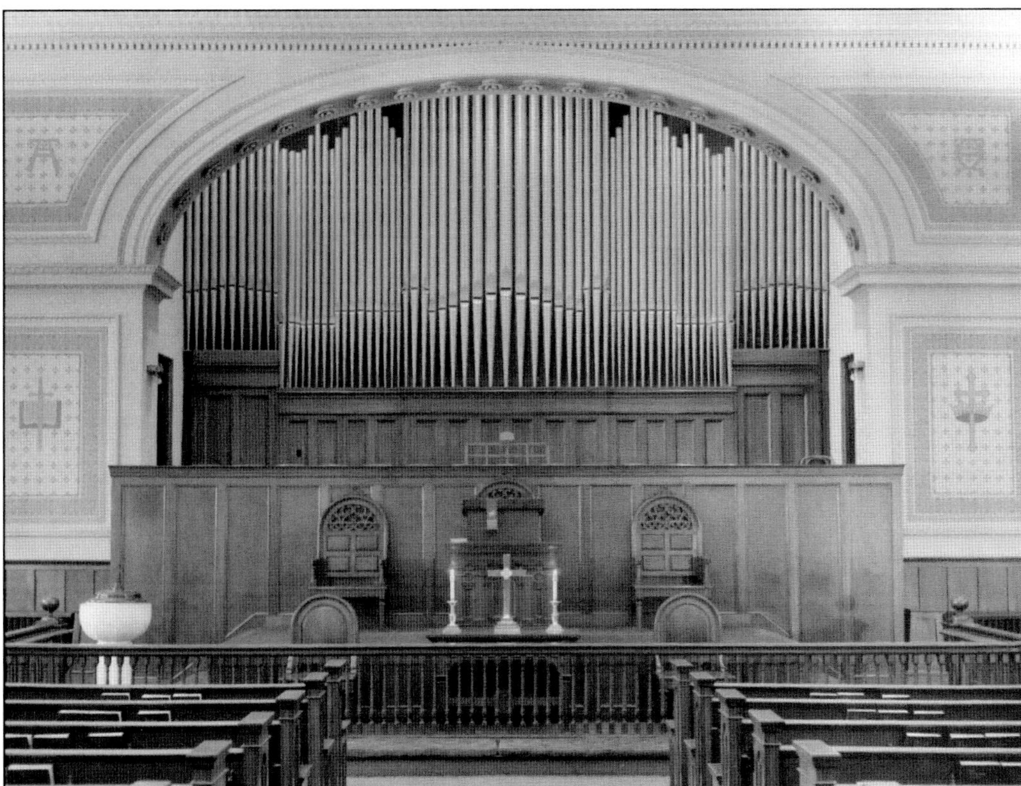

In 1942, Mount Vernon again altered the choir loft, replacing its Hook & Hastings organ with an Austin organ. This view shows the handiwork of plaster contractor and church member Charles Orchard, who gave the original Gothic-inspired sanctuary, with its vaulted ceilings, a Neoclassical "face-lift" around 1912. Other redecorations included new carpeting, wall treatments, and windows from J&R Lamb Studios. (Courtesy of Mount Vernon United Methodist Church.)

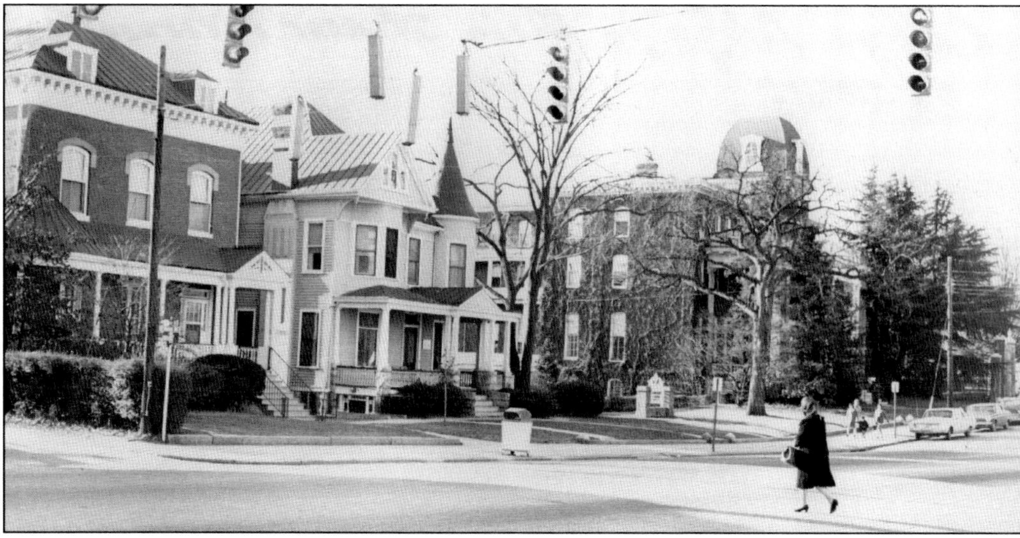

The former Stratford College (now Stratford House) still dominates the block across from Mount Vernon Methodist Church where Main Street divides into South Main and West Main Streets. Stratford's ivy-covered brick Main Hall (right) was built in 1883 when the college moved from the corner of Loyal and Ridge Streets. Contractor Thomas B. Fitzgerald built Main Hall according to the plans of Richmond architect Albert West. (Courtesy of the Danville Historical Society.)

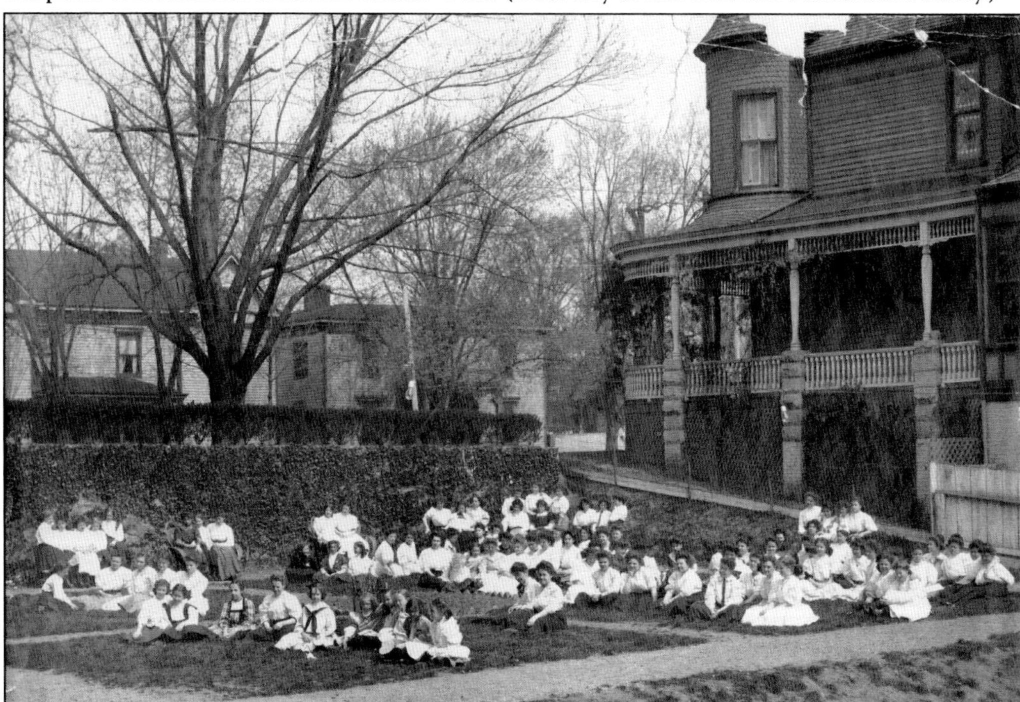

Looking from the former Stratford College campus, this c. 1910 view reveals the original site of Danville's famed Langhorne House. Seen (center) behind the hedgerow, the 1874 dwelling at 1102 Main Street was the childhood home of Nancy and Irene Langhorne. Nancy, the first woman to take a seat as a Member of Parliament, became Lady Astor, while Irene inspired her husband, Charles Dana Gibson, as his model for the "Gibson Girl." (Courtesy of the Langhorne House.)

Three

Around Town

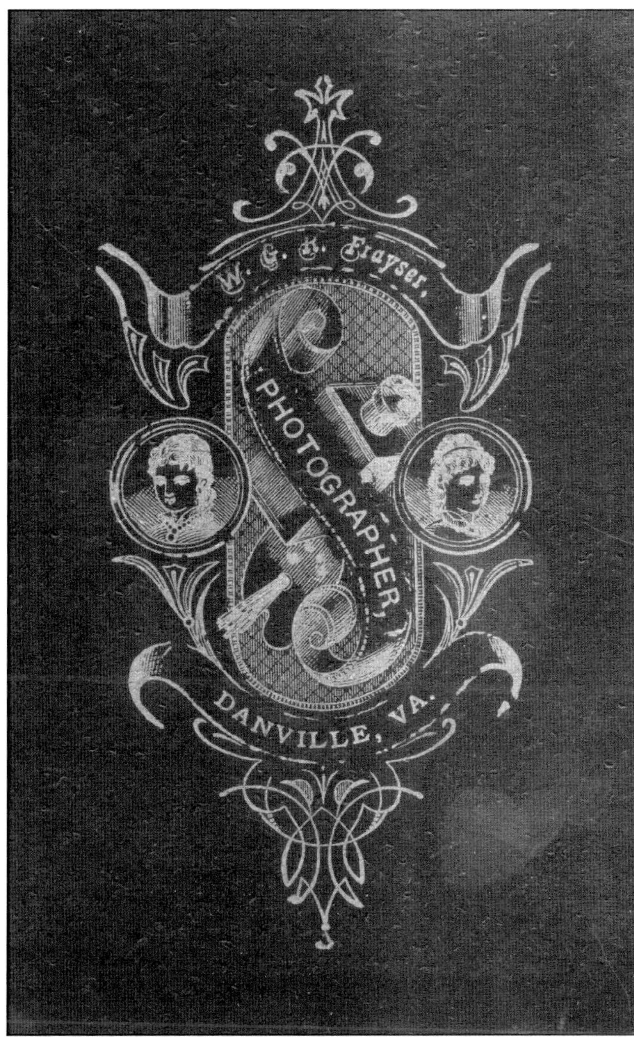

As Danville's population grew, the city added nearby communities to raise its tax base and attract new businesses. Danville annexed Neapolis (North Danville) in 1896, and Schoolfield, the mill village southwest of Ballou Park, in 1951. The reverse of this *carte de visite* identified the studio of Walter G.R. Frayser, an itinerant photographer who lived in Danville from 1887 to 1891. (Courtesy of the Danville Museum of Fine Arts and History.)

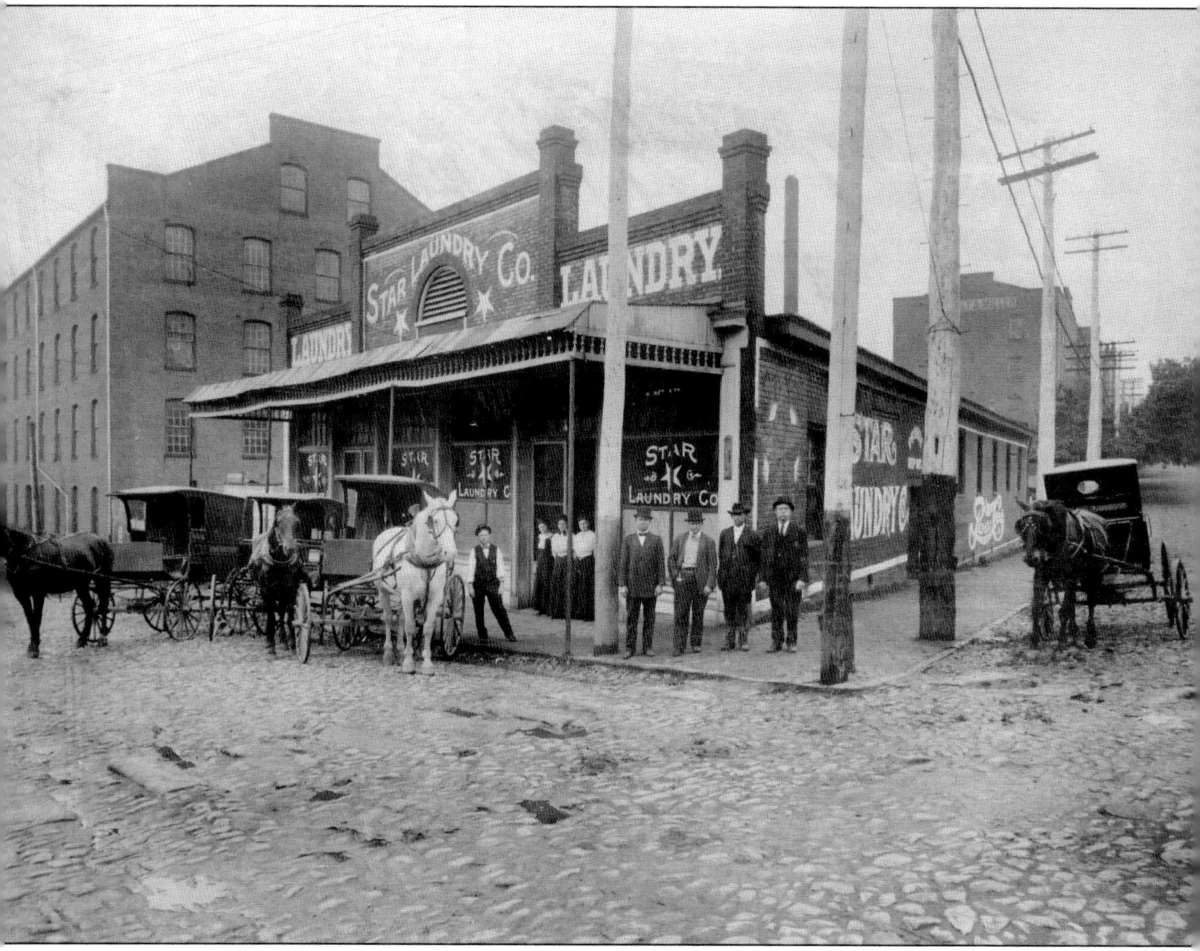

In this c. 1900 photograph, multistory tobacco prizeries along Patton and Lynn Streets, including George E. Tucker & Co. and Gravely & Miller, loom behind Star Laundry, located at 333 Patton Street, just below Danville's courthouse. The photograph shows not only horse-and-buggy transport, but also principals and employees of the firm near the intersection, which was covered in cobblestones and had large pavers marking the "crosswalks." Founded around 1900 by president O. Lewis Roach and secretary-treasurer R.F. Acree, Star Laundry flourished in this location for more than 50 years before moving its headquarters to Riverside Drive in the mid-1950s. After a 1910 fire, this facility was enlarged with a second story, and it maintained a staff of 70 employees. As the firm grew in reputation and size, it oversaw several branches elsewhere in Virginia and in parts of North and South Carolina. (Courtesy of Margaret Winn Dryden.)

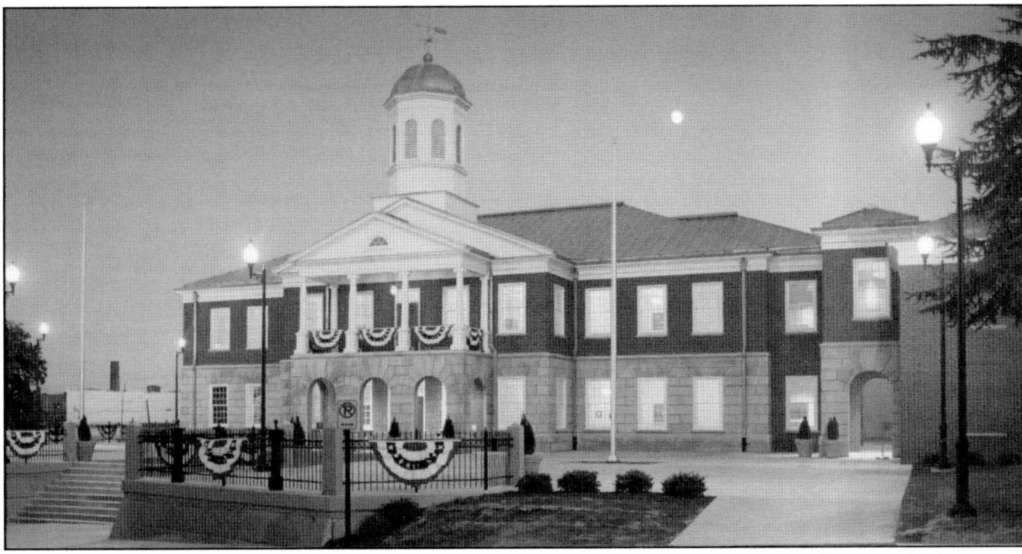

Completed in 1999, the James F. Ingram Justice Center at 401 Patton Street honors the longtime circuit court judge. Its historic facade pays architectural homage to the continuity of this site, which has housed Danville's judiciary for over 140 years. Its inspiration—Danville's first official courthouse, built in 1873 of Renaissance design with a cupola—survived on the lot next door until the Municipal Building was built in 1927. (Photograph by William H. Garrett.)

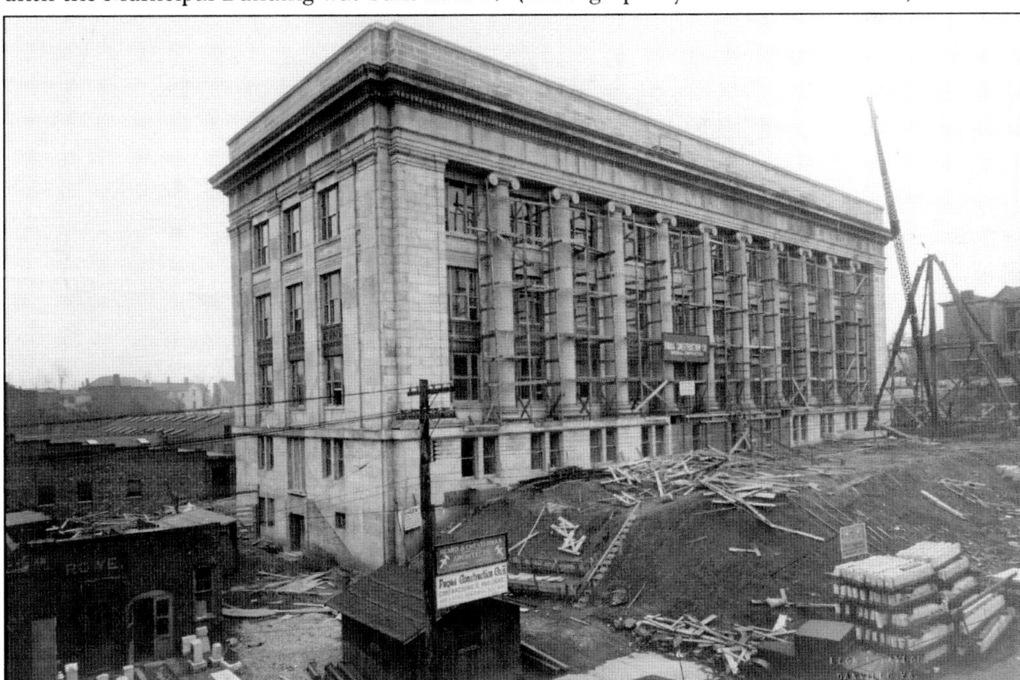

Danville's 1927 Municipal Building, located at 427 Patton Street, combined all city services and judiciary in a building erected on the site of the 1873 courthouse. Built by the Fuqua Construction Company from plans by architects Heard & Chesterman, the Neoclassical-style building, clad in limestone, made use of modern steel framing. The stone monuments at left marked the original home of W.D. Rowe. (Photograph by Leon Taylor.)

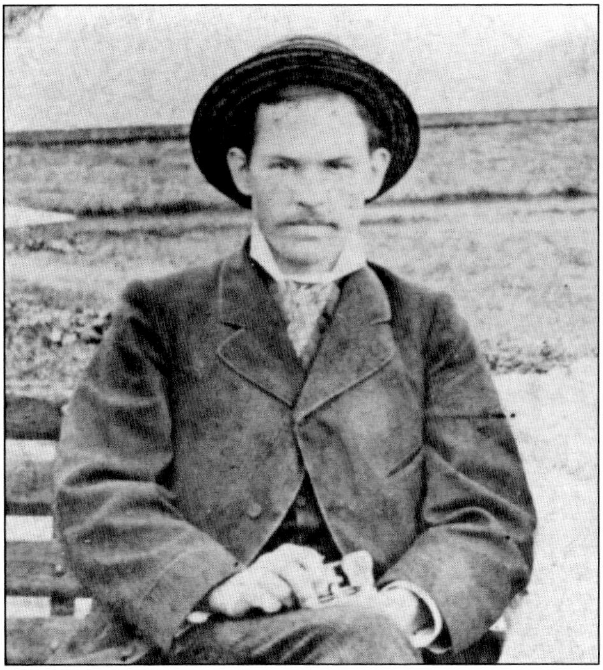

George W. Taylor (left), the father of photographer Leon Taylor, married Katherine Yardy of Pennsylvania in 1878. George Taylor's stone and marble yard on Patton Street, located opposite Union Street just below the old courthouse, may have been Danville's first monument company. After George Taylor's death, William D. Rowe launched his monument business in the same location. (Courtesy of William E. Land.)

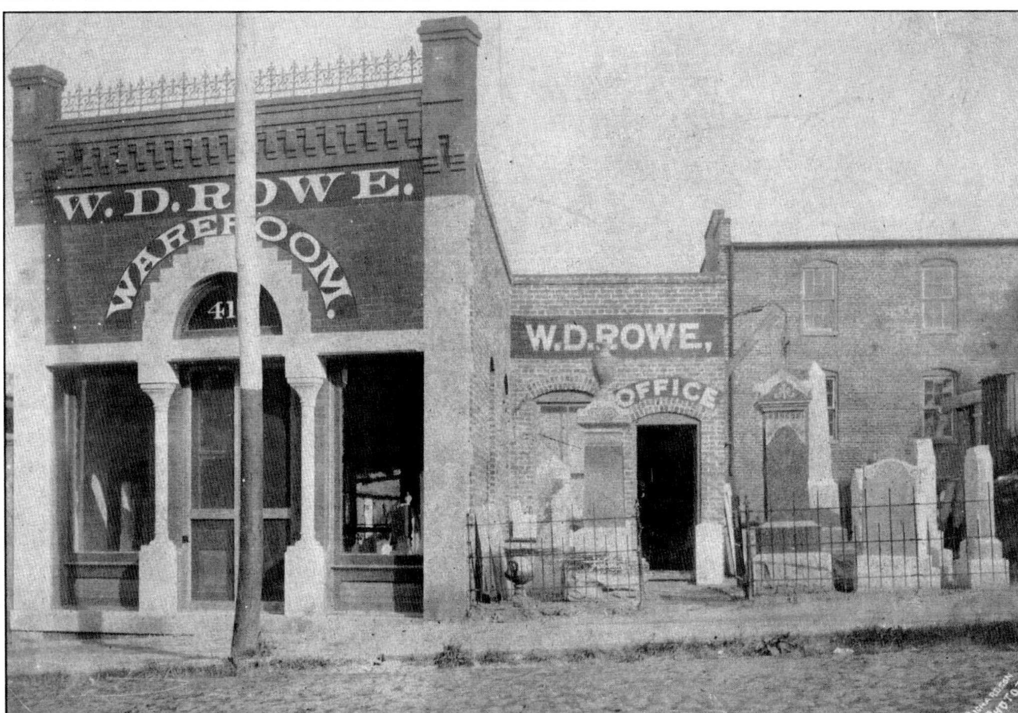

In 1885, William D. Rowe founded the monument business that still bears his name. Occupying George Taylor's old marble yard (now part of the city courthouse plaza), Rowe's outdoor "showroom" flanked the old courthouse and fire station. For 40 years, Rowe managed the business alone, making monuments from the best granite available. (Photograph by F.H. Richardson; courtesy of Edith F. Burns.)

In 1925, E.W. Myers of Blanche, North Carolina, bought an interest in Rowe's firm. Soon after, he became general manager. The two men worked together until Rowe retired in 1936; at that time, because of ill health and age, Rowe sold his share to Myers. (Courtesy of Edith F. Burns.)

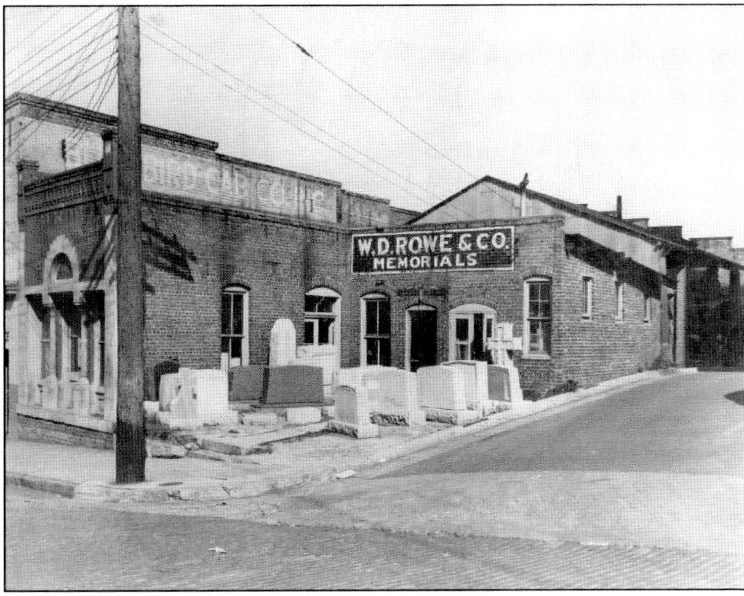

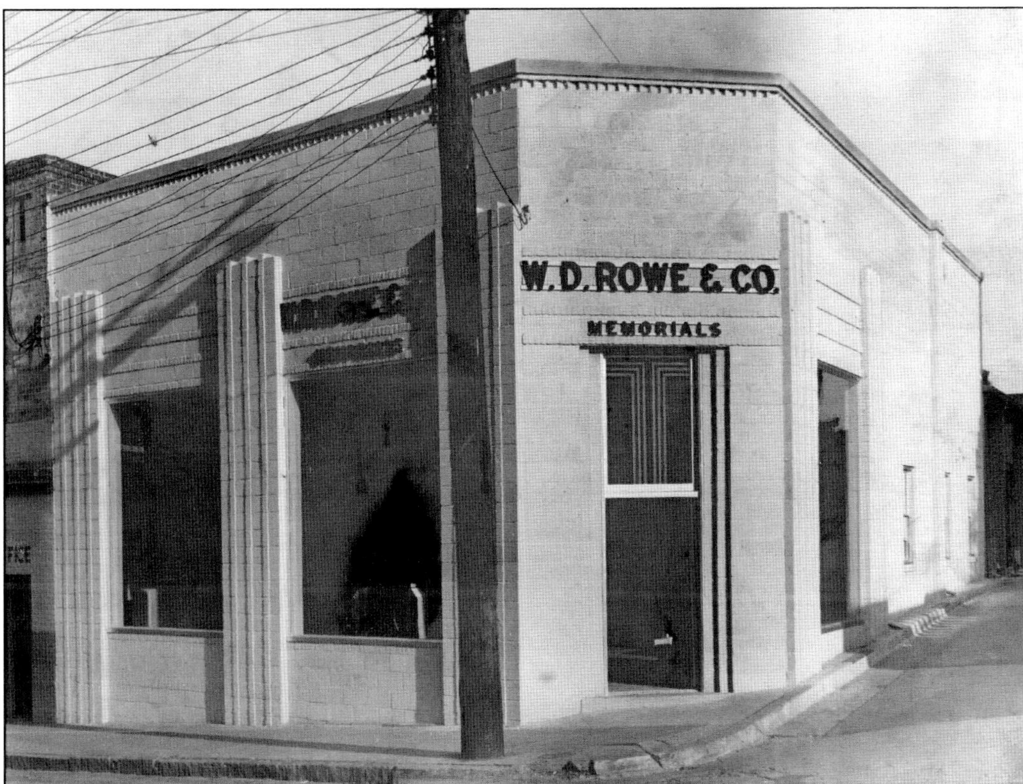

The W.D. Rowe Company grew even more prosperous after Rowe sold his interest to E.W. Myers, who renovated and enlarged the monument company's Patton Street office in 1940. The operation moved to its current North Main Street location in the mid-1950s. The firm provided the life-size statue of Capt. Harry Wooding, the longtime Danville mayor, for the steps of the Municipal Building. (Courtesy of Edith F. Burns.)

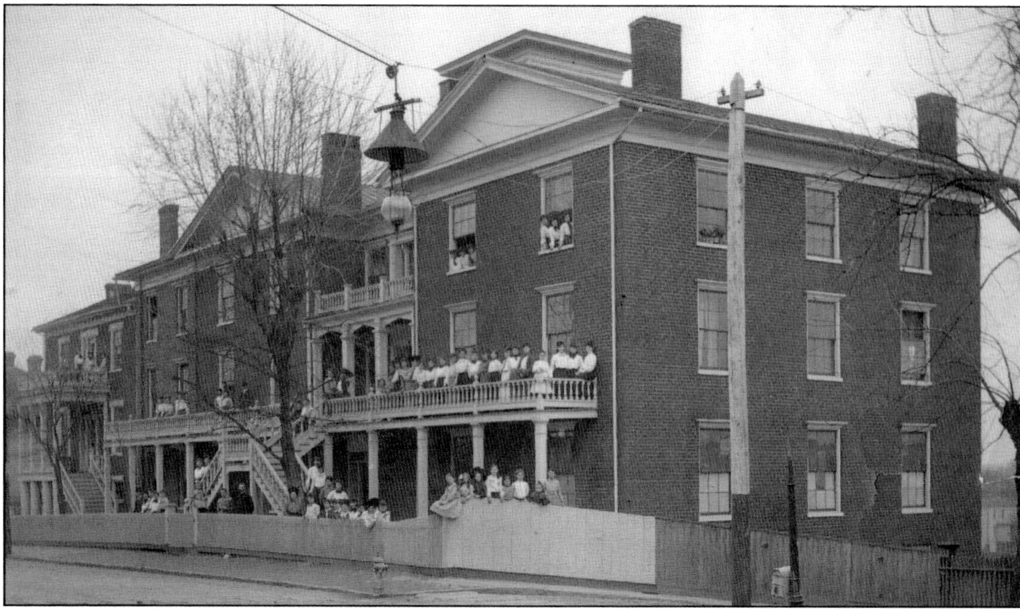

William Isaac Berryman founded Union Female College in 1859 in his own home, to the left of the 1860 school building on the corner of Ridge and Patton Streets (now the site of Biscuitville). Later known as Roanoke Female College, the school became Averett University in 1917 in honor of the eight members of the Averett family who taught there. (Photograph by Leon Taylor.)

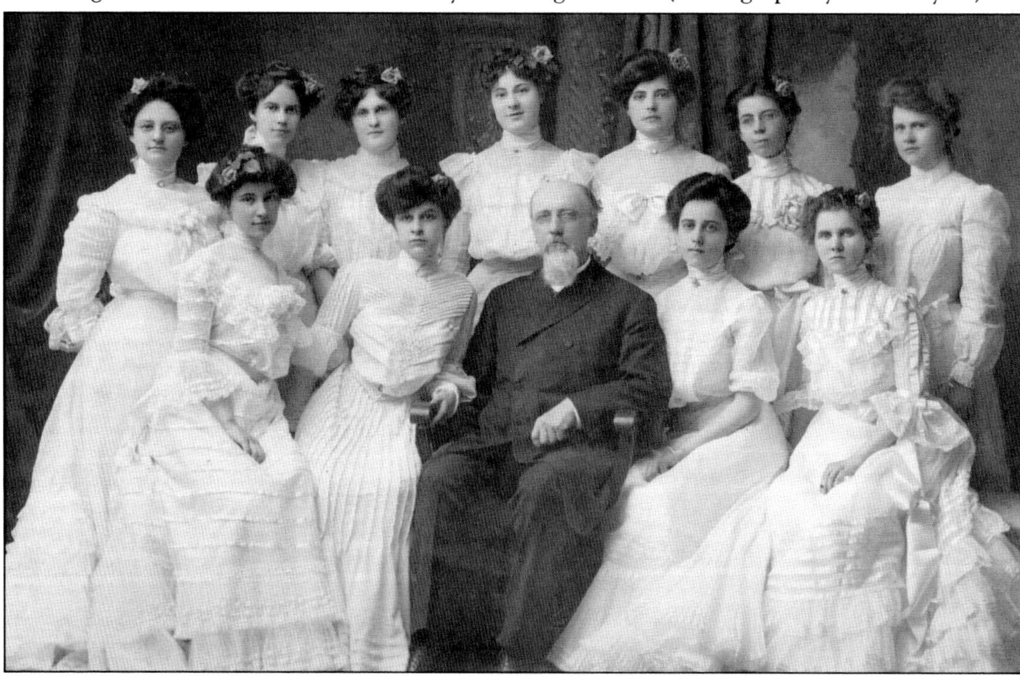

Eutsler Brothers Studio photographed the Roanoke Female College class of 1902. Pictured here are, from left to right, (first row) Myrtle Marshall, Gertrude James, Dr. Charles Fenton James, Dot Richmond, and Mabel McNeely; (second row) Maria Tilman, Carrie Scott, Sophia Grizzard, Anne Mae Roger, Mabel Moore, Mildred Cook, and Pearl Hatcher. (Photograph by Eutsler Brothers; courtesy of Averett University Archives.)

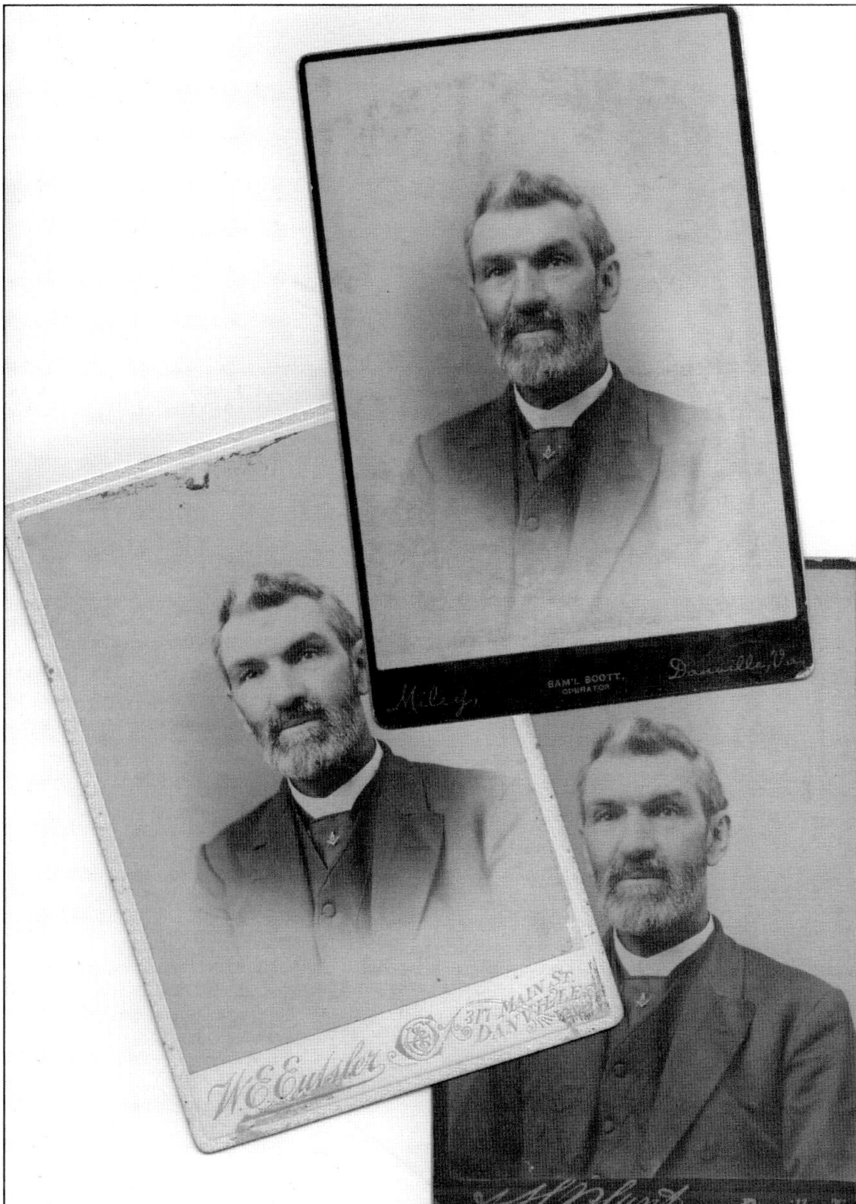

Capt. John "Jack" Taylor Averett came to Danville in 1867 from Ringgold, Virginia, to head the Danville Male Academy. In the early 1870s, school superintendent George W. Dame hired him to be the principal of Danville's first public school. Until the town could provide a suitable building, Captain Averett held classes in the old Danville Female Academy building on the corner of Jefferson and Loyal Streets. A member of the original 1859 Roanoke Female College board of trustees, Captain Averett was named coprincipal of the college in 1873 along with his brother Samuel W. Averett, who left the school in 1887. Captain Averett continued to lead the college until 1892. His identical portraits by Miley, Eutsler, and Blunt suggest that these three photographers must have succeeded each other in the same studio. Blunt probably took the original image, since the later men used a vignette technique (fading around the edges) on their prints. (Photographs by Miley, Eutsler, and Blunt; courtesy of Averett University Archives.)

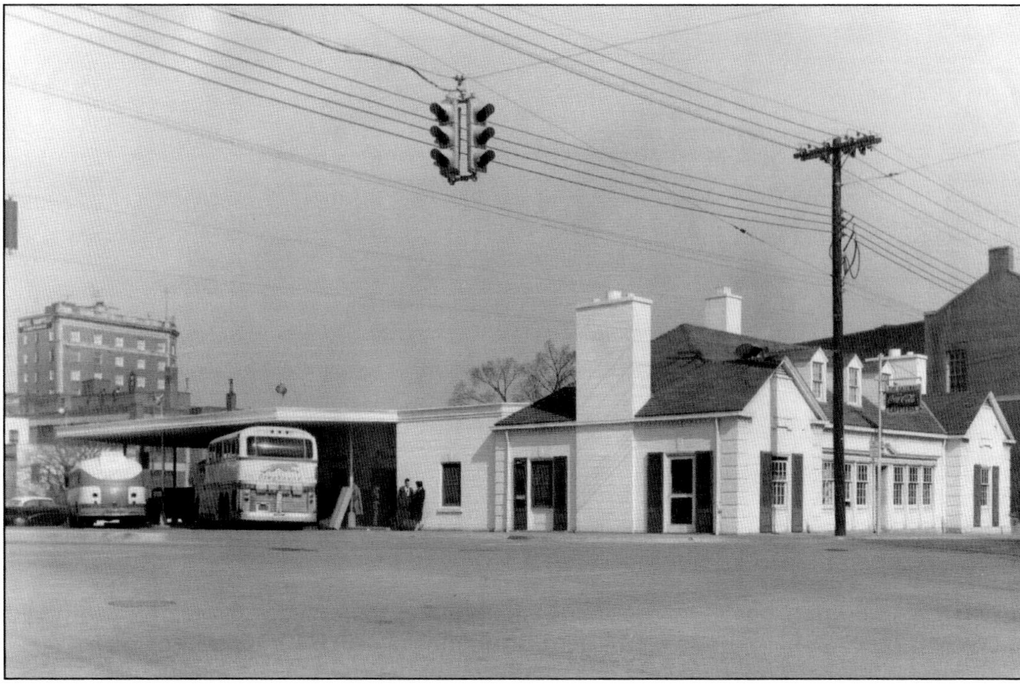

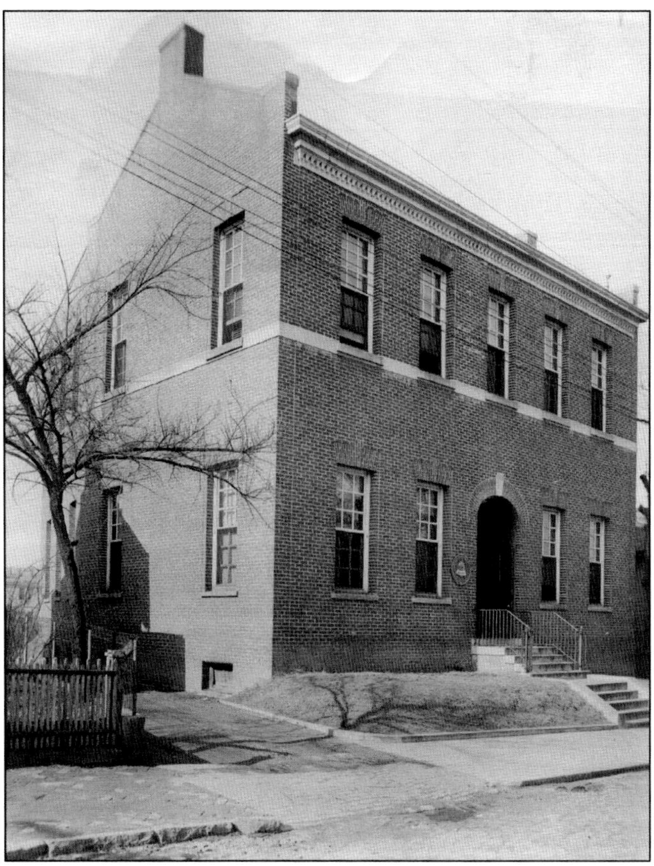

The 1959 photograph above shows the Greyhound bus station at the corner of Ridge and Patton Streets. Constructed on the site of Danville's original First Baptist Church, the bus station later became a bank, and, more recently, a free medical clinic. (Photograph by Dempsey DeHart; courtesy of the Danville Historical Society.)

In 1918, the Chesapeake & Potomac Telephone Company moved from small quarters on Main Street to this new building at 560 Patton Street. Telephone service began in Danville in 1883, and its popularity grew steadily; by 1918, the company had 2,400 customers. In 1957, dial telephones replaced the familiar "number please" models that relied on switchboard operators to assist callers. (Photograph by Leon Taylor.)

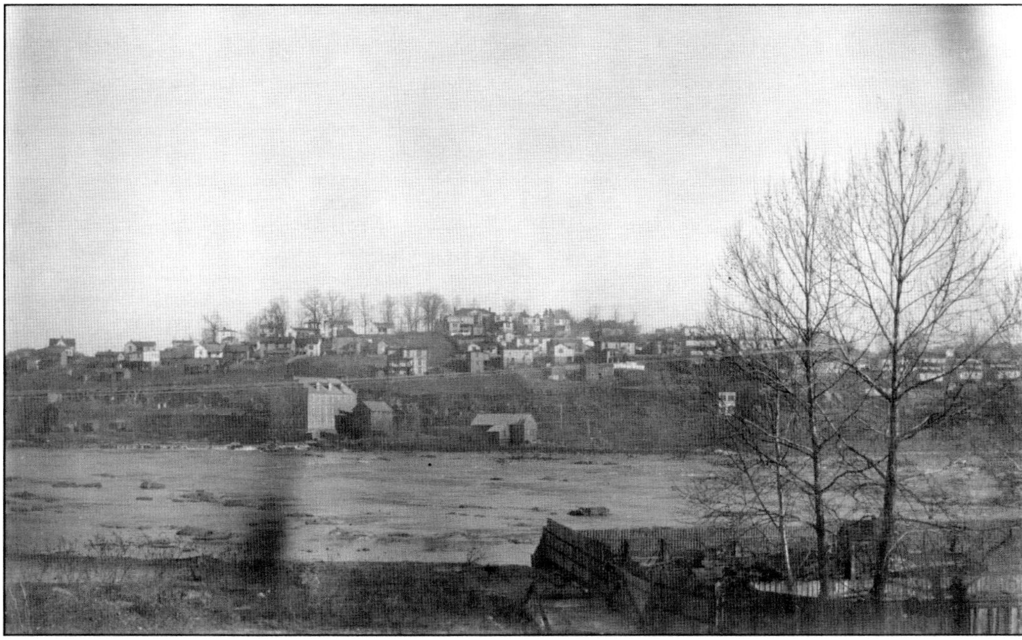

This image, which dates from around 1888, is likely the earliest existing photograph of North Danville hill. An unknown Union soldier imprisoned in Danville during the Civil War returned to the town to record his wartime "home" in pictures, and this image was among them. The antebellum mansion of Col. Leonard Claiborne crowned the pinnacle of the hill, along with large trees. (Courtesy of Bobby Ricketts.)

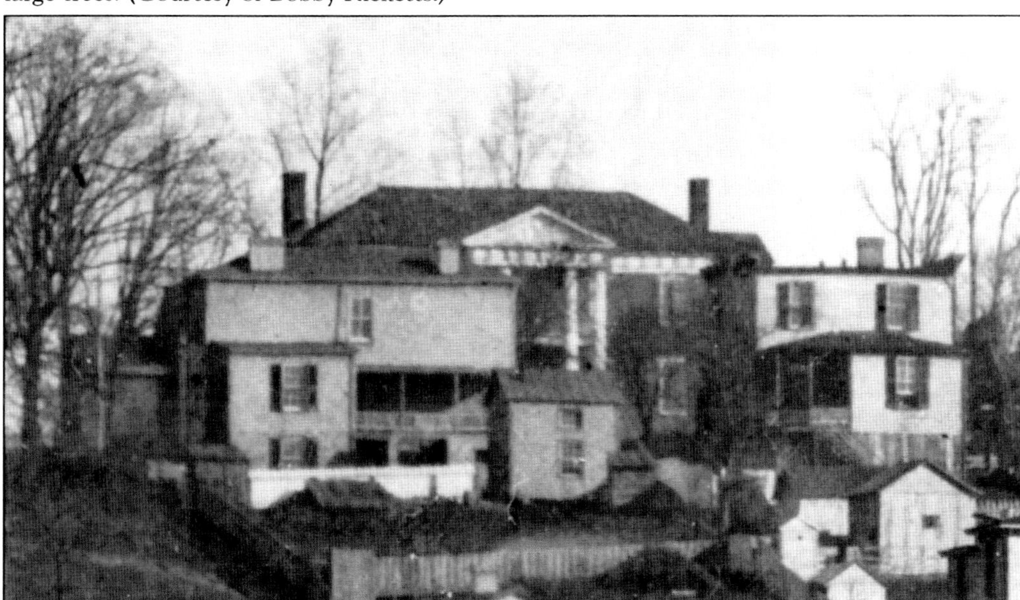

Dominating the skyline of North Danville, the Claiborne mansion (pictured here in a detail from the previous image) sat on landscaped grounds terraced down to the Dan River. Mayor Harry Wooding recalled that, in 1850, it was one of only four houses in North Danville. After Colonel Claiborne's death, the house briefly became a school before it was razed in 1898 for the construction of Bellevue Elementary School. (Courtesy of Bobby Ricketts.)

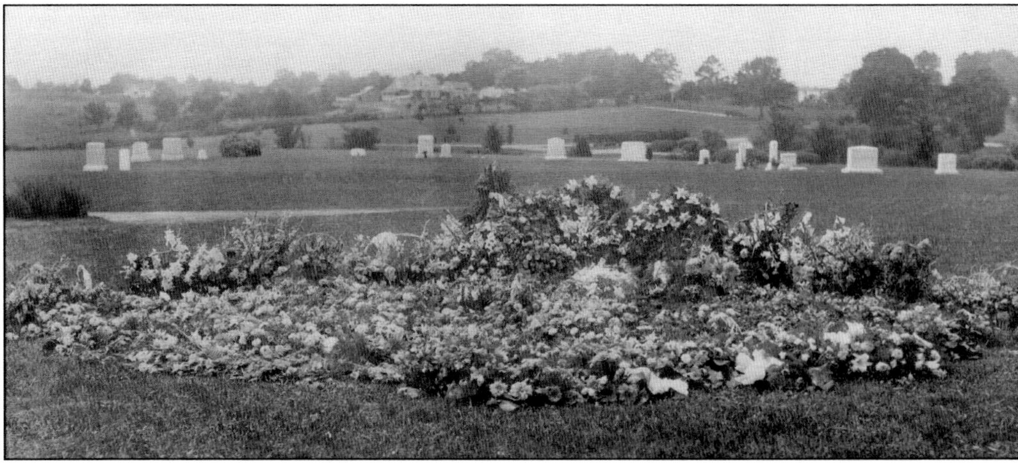

In 1924, the city established Danville's northernmost cemetery, Highland Burial Park, outside the city limits. Today, it covers many acres at the intersection of Highway 29 Business (Piney Forest Road) and North Main Street. Looking toward the northern point of the cemetery, this 1933 photograph shows a practice more common in the past than now: the memorializing of a gravesite. This was the grave of Thomas B. Garrett, an uncle of coauthor Clara Fountain. (Photograph by P.W. Dunford.)

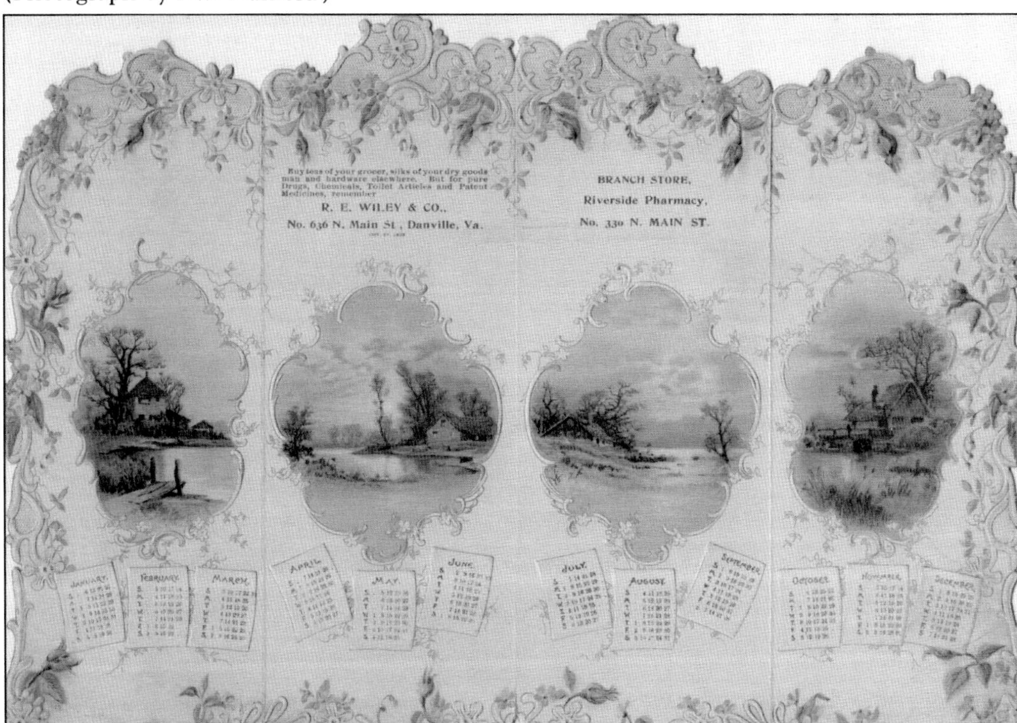

Leonard Claiborne, Richard Yarbrough, Casper Rodenhizer, and Thomas Worsham settled North Danville, the part of the city north of the Dan River. A small village grew around the early flour mill and foundry these men built. R.E. Wiley & Company, a pharmacy at 636 North Main Street, offered this folding calendar to its patrons for the year 1895. (Courtesy of the Danville Historical Society.)

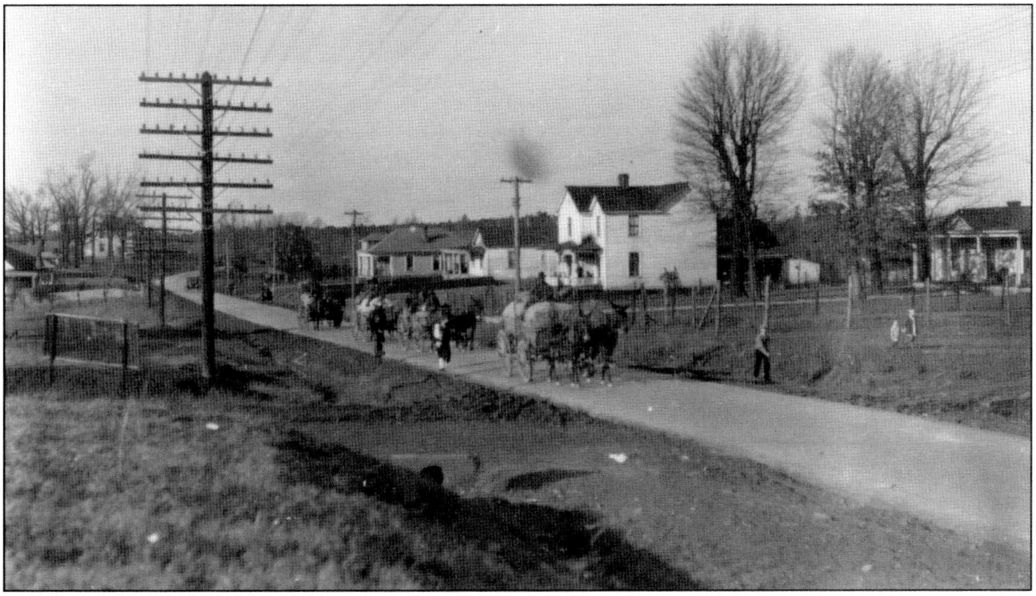

In this c. 1910 image, a caravan of four horse-drawn wagons—each groaning with loads of cured tobacco—struggles south on the old Franklin Turnpike (now North Main Street) between Third and Ficklen Avenues. These wagons were headed toward Danville's tobacco auction houses, either on Craghead or Bridge Streets or to one of many located west of Main Street along North Union Street. (Courtesy of the Virginia State Library.)

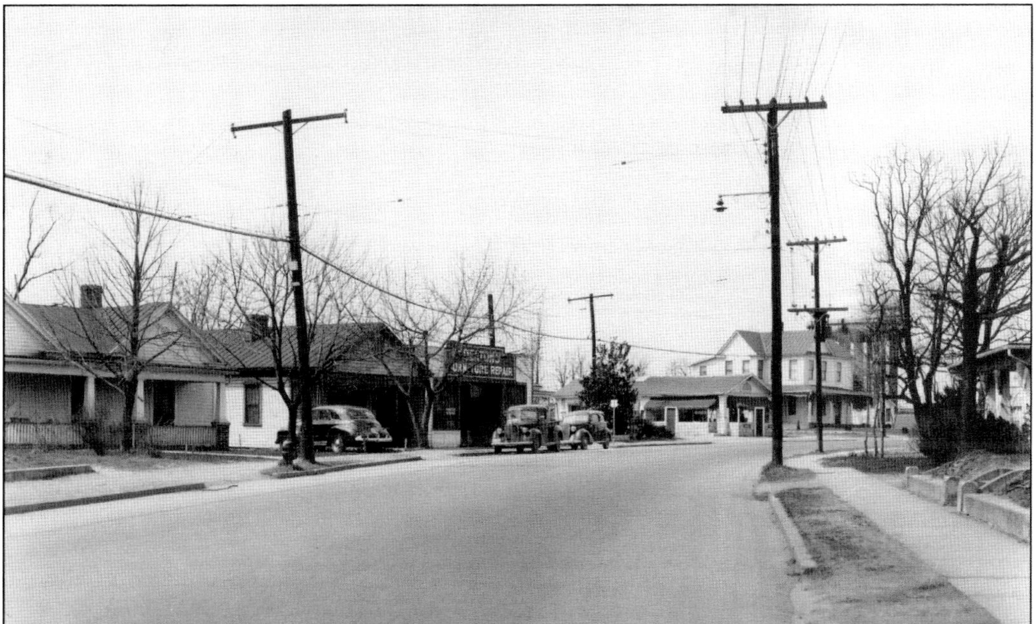

The sign for Deaton's Furniture Repair, long a North Danville fixture, occupied the curve of North Main Street's 2100 block just after World War II. Here, a 1941 Chevrolet sits in a driveway just ahead of a 1937 Ford truck, with a 1934 Chevrolet behind that. In the distance is the two-story boyhood home of Onico Barker, who later went on to become a Danville councilman and a Virginia state senator. (Photograph by William E. Land.)

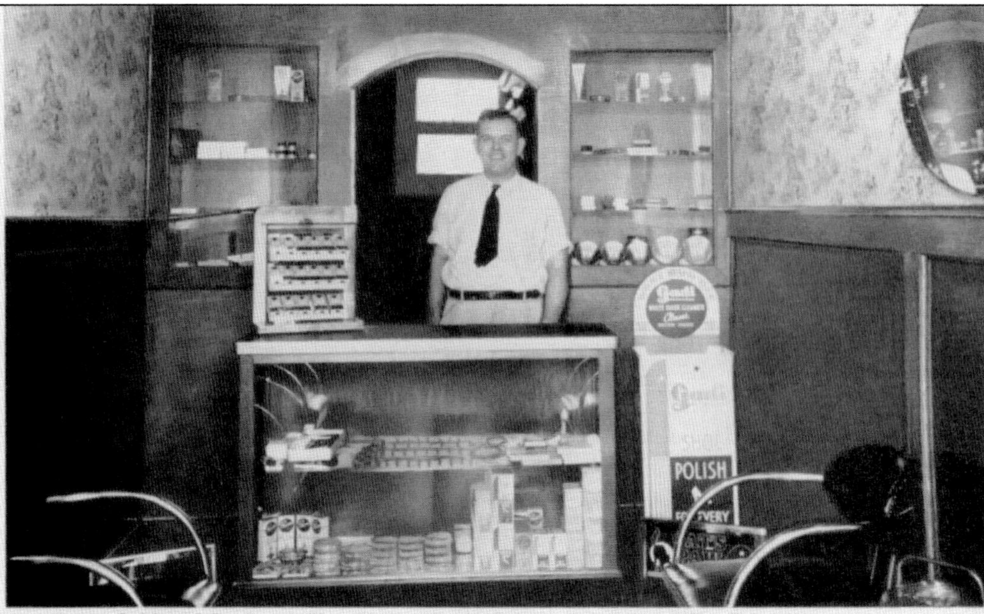

Lobby of Joe Lamb Shoe Shop, 602 North Main Street, Danville, Va., Phone 2953

From 1900 to around 1950, picture postcards provided a visual record of American cities. Photographers produced more than 1,000 views of Danville on postcards sold by local businesses. Often, these postcards provide the only surviving images of places that were later remodeled or destroyed, like Joe Lamb's shoe shop. (Photograph by R.H. Sanford Jr.)

For "Happy Motoring" — Stop at the ESSO Sign

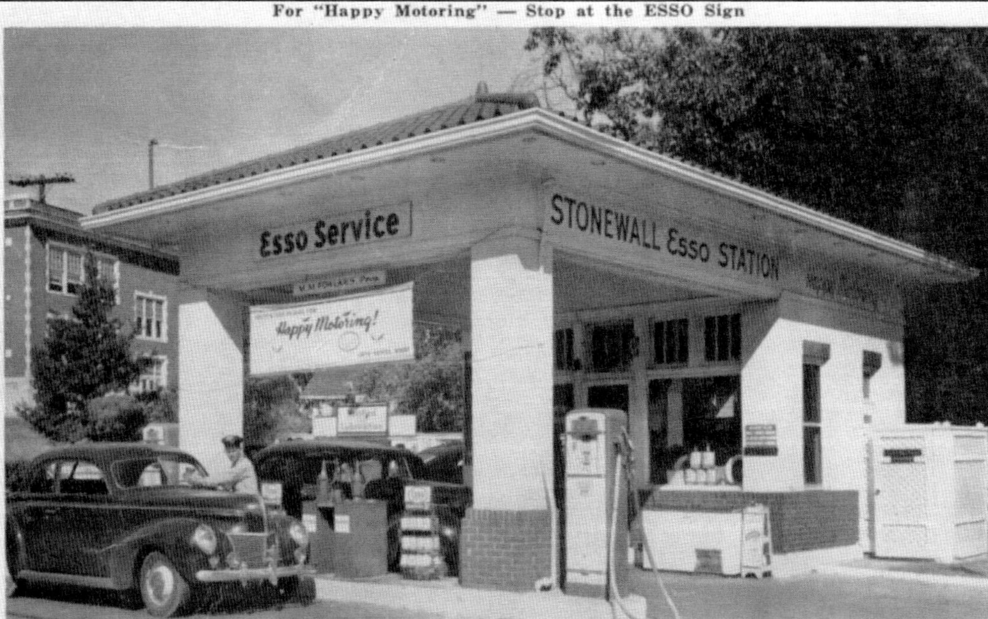

Stonewall Esso Station, 1510 North Main St., Danville, Va.

Robert H. Sanford Jr. of Danville established the Graycraft Card Company, selling postcards of numerous Southern towns. He traveled extensively, taking photographs of public buildings, schools, churches, and small businesses. This Graycraft card shows an Esso Station at 1510 North Main Street that was named for the Stonewall School next door. (Photograph by R.H. Sanford Jr.)

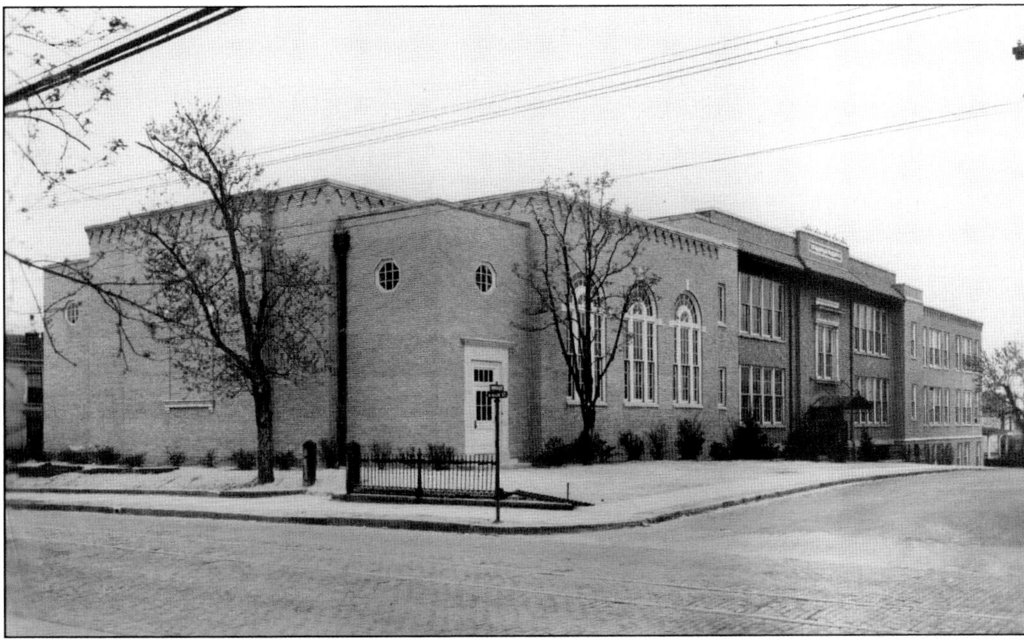

In this c. 1935 photograph, the remnants of gateposts and a cast-iron fence that graced the T.B. Fitzgerald mansion (later an orphanage) stand broken in silhouette against light snow in front of the newly completed gymnasium at Woodrow Wilson Elementary School. Located at 1015 North Main Street, the school's main building, which dates from 1926, joined two other city schools north of the river, Bellevue and Stonewall Jackson. (Photograph by Leon Taylor.)

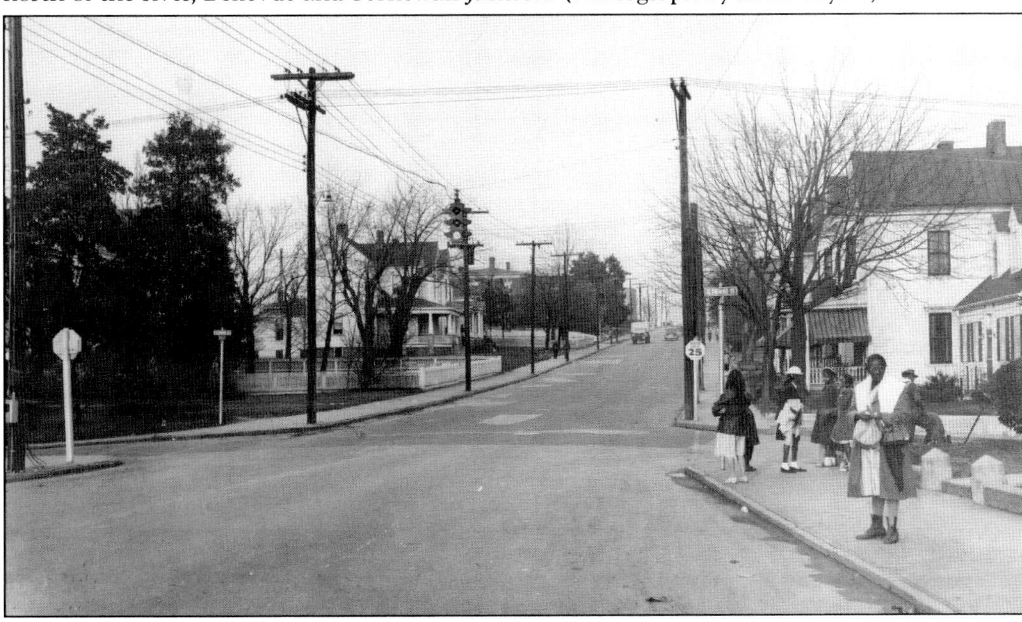

Looking north from North Main Street's intersection with Thomas Street in the late 1940s, trim white picket fences still defined some of the 1880s and 1890s homes of North Danville's founders. At 823 North Main Street, such a fence surrounded the cottage of Carson Sutherlin Davenport, an artist whose early career included painting murals and other works as part of the Works Progress Administration's Federal Art Project. (Photograph by William E. Land.)

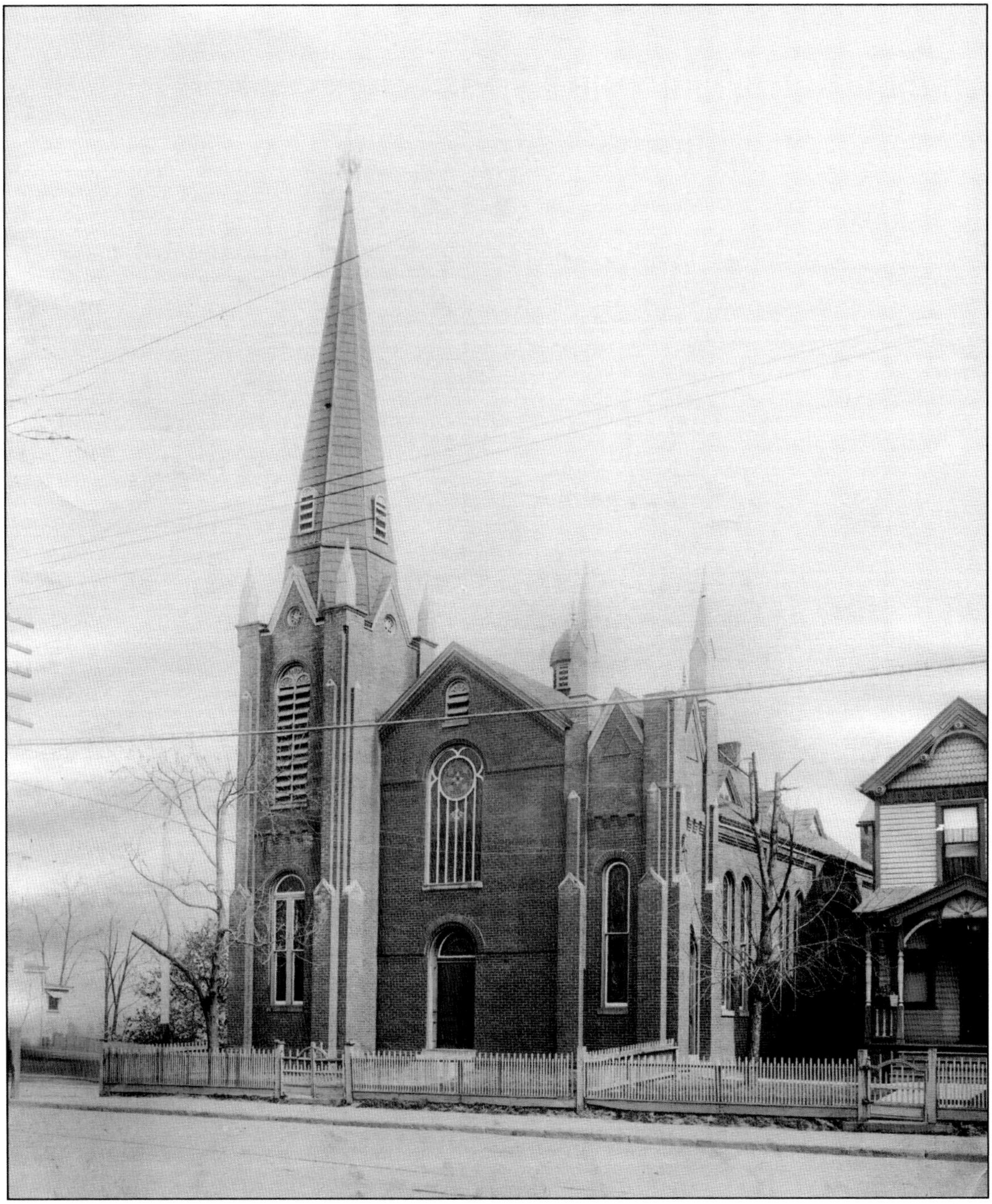

Completed in 1889, Shelton Memorial Presbyterian Church began as a mission of Danville's first congregation, First Presbyterian, founded in 1826. Named for W. Nelson Shelton, a prosperous tobacconist who helped members acquire the corner of North Main and West Thomas Streets for their new Gothic-inspired building, the church also provided a manse (right) for its founding minister, Rev. W.T. Doggett, and his family. Shelton moved to Danville in 1868 from North Carolina to continue his career as a leaf tobacco dealer. He supervised four large tobacco factories on Bridge Street, and he always chose his customers by careful selection. In 1884, Shelton oversaw the construction of his family residence at 723 Main Street, designed by A.L. West and built by T.B. Fitzgerald, where his daughter Alice and her husband, F.X. Burton, also lived. (Photograph by Leon Taylor.)

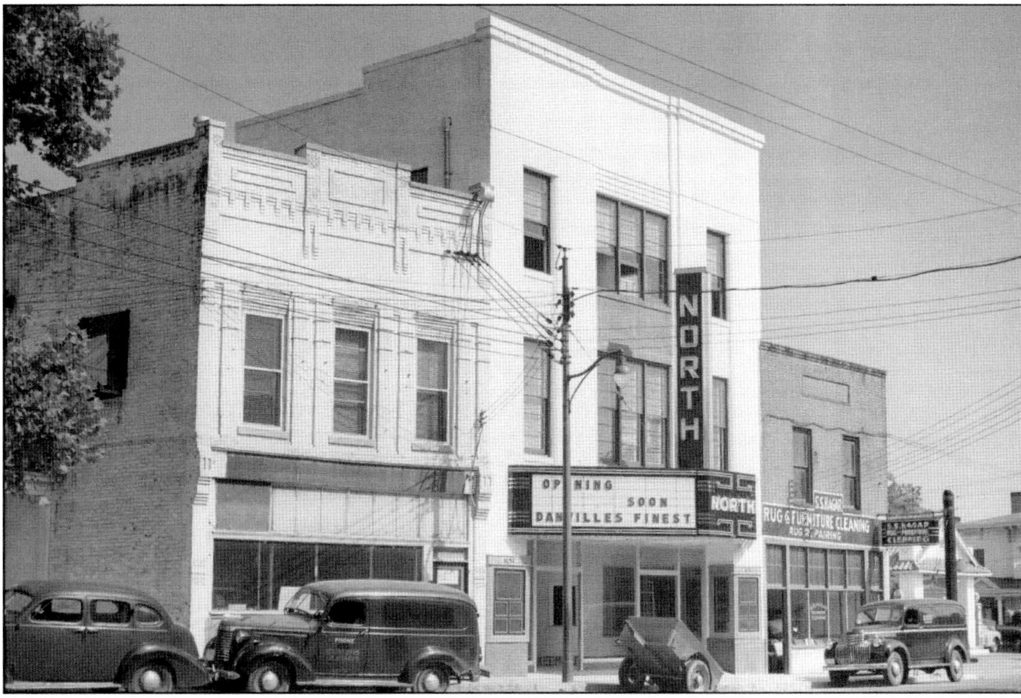

A 1947 stucco face-lift transformed an 1890s storefront and Masonic lodge on the North Main Street hill's summit into the gleaming North Theatre, the city's last movie house. The North's 2005 resurrection followed a $3-million-plus rehabilitation. Today, magician Wayne Alan offers family-friendly fare in the top-notch performance hall. (Courtesy of the Virginia State Chamber of Commerce.)

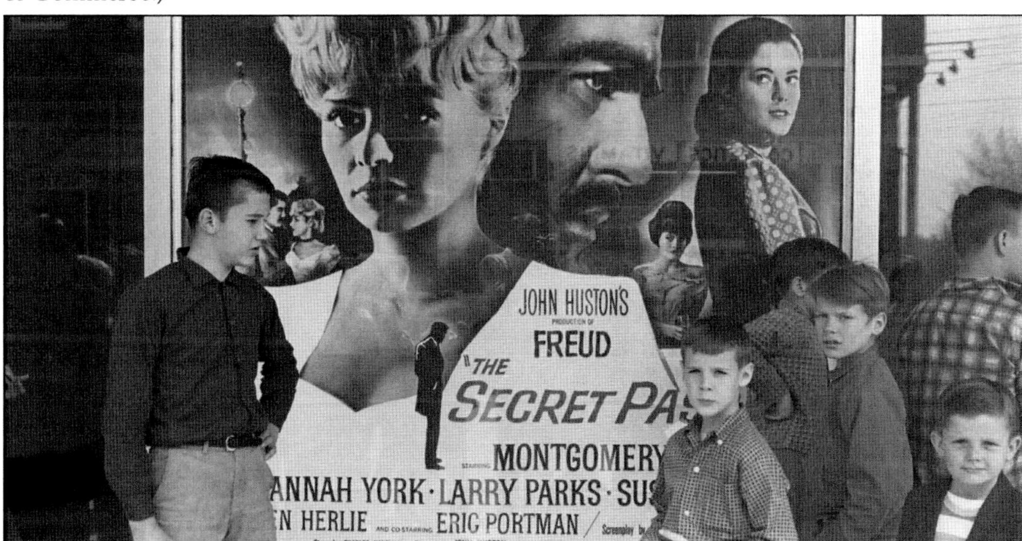

Situated near North Main Street's juncture with Worsham Street, the North Theatre became a favorite place for young people to see the newest releases. Glenn Scarboro began his photography career at age 17 when he was asked by a friend to cover an assignment for him. Scarboro later realized that this random event helped shape his future as an observer of ordinary life. This photograph was taken around 1962. (Photograph by Glenn Scarboro.)

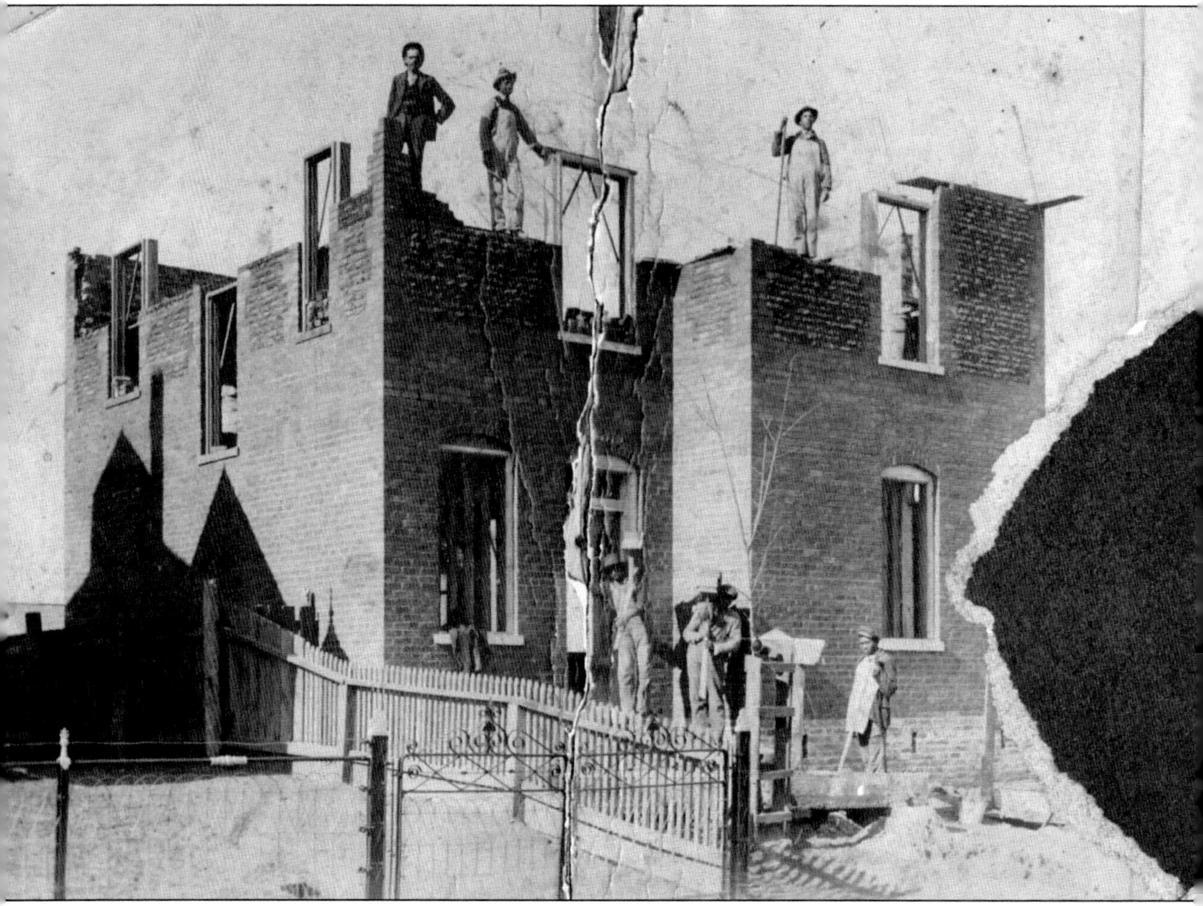

In this c. 1920 image, Robert S. Allen (upper left, in suit) pauses with fellow craftsmen so the camera can record their handiwork, including decorative skintled brick, at 407 Holbrook Street. These skilled masons helped Allen construct his family home, where, in later years, his daughter Ida Mackye Allen lived with her husband, attorney Jerry Williams. Today, the property is included in a self-guided tour of the Holbrook-Ross historic district. Around 1880, developers partitioned building lots along Holbrook and Ross Streets from the estate of Thomas B. Doe. By 1900, these thoroughfares, just off Main Street and north to the Dan River, became the leading addresses for Danville's African American community. The area contained the homes of doctors, lawyers, and educators, as well as merchants, Pullman porters, and chauffeurs. Dozens of the houses and corner stores owned by grocers and other shopkeepers were constructed by their tradesmen neighbors. Some of these men were masons who laid bricks with mortar for the walls of churches and schools. Others were roofers or carpenters who framed and sheathed cottages, bungalows, and American Foursquare–style homes. (Courtesy of Carl Williams.)

Born in Missouri in 1859, Oliver W. Cole married Annie Bell of Virginia in 1895. That same year, he opened Cole Studio locations at both 317 and 427 Main Street. Cole took all the photographs published in the 1913 booklet *Danville, Virginia: Its Interests & Industries.* The promotional publication contained a number of familiar views of city buildings. (Courtesy of Lawrence McFall.)

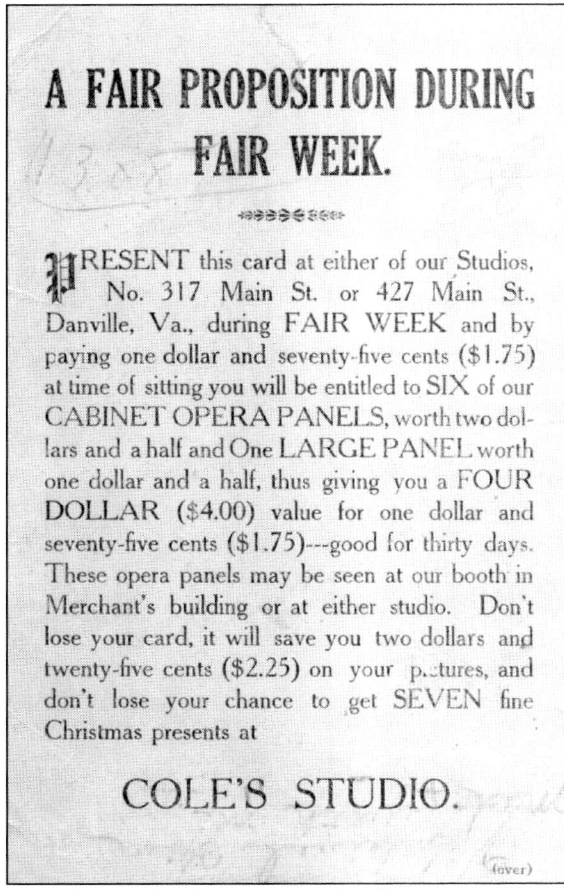

A FAIR PROPOSITION DURING FAIR WEEK.

PRESENT this card at either of our Studios, No. 317 Main St. or 427 Main St., Danville, Va., during FAIR WEEK and by paying one dollar and seventy-five cents ($1.75) at time of sitting you will be entitled to SIX of our CABINET OPERA PANELS, worth two dollars and a half and One LARGE PANEL worth one dollar and a half, thus giving you a FOUR DOLLAR ($4.00) value for one dollar and seventy-five cents ($1.75)---good for thirty days. These opera panels may be seen at our booth in Merchant's building or at either studio. Don't lose your card, it will save you two dollars and twenty-five cents ($2.25) on your pictures, and don't lose your chance to get SEVEN fine Christmas presents at

COLE'S STUDIO.

(over)

On June 18, 1911, a strong storm swept through Danville, causing citywide damage. Oliver Cole took his camera outside and photographed the aftermath, which he then printed on postcard stock in a series of more than a dozen cards. The card below shows a tree ripped from its roots in front of 149 Holbrook Avenue. (Photograph by Oliver W. Cole.)

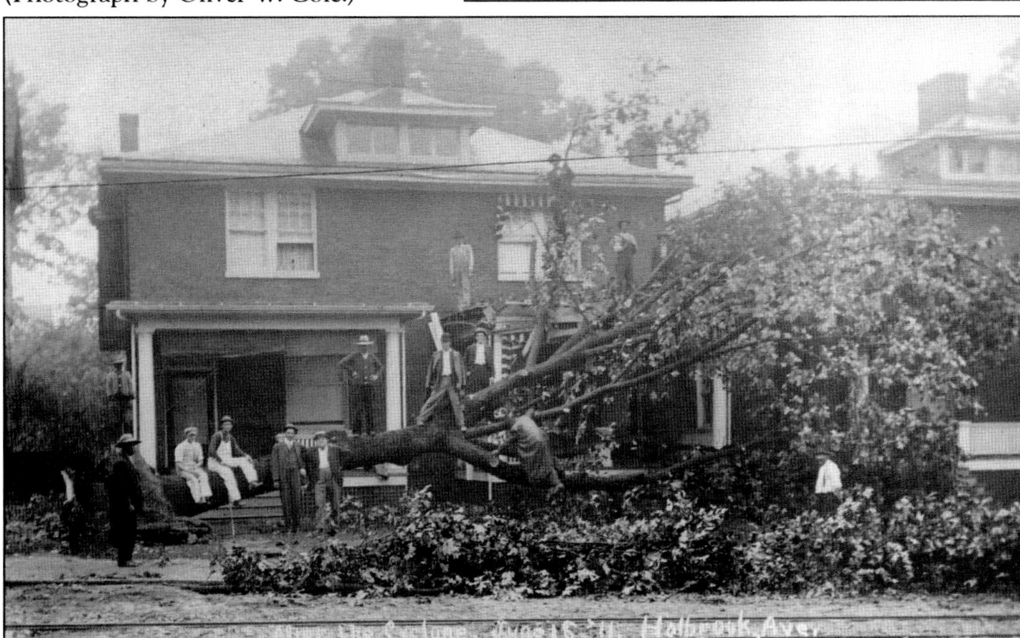

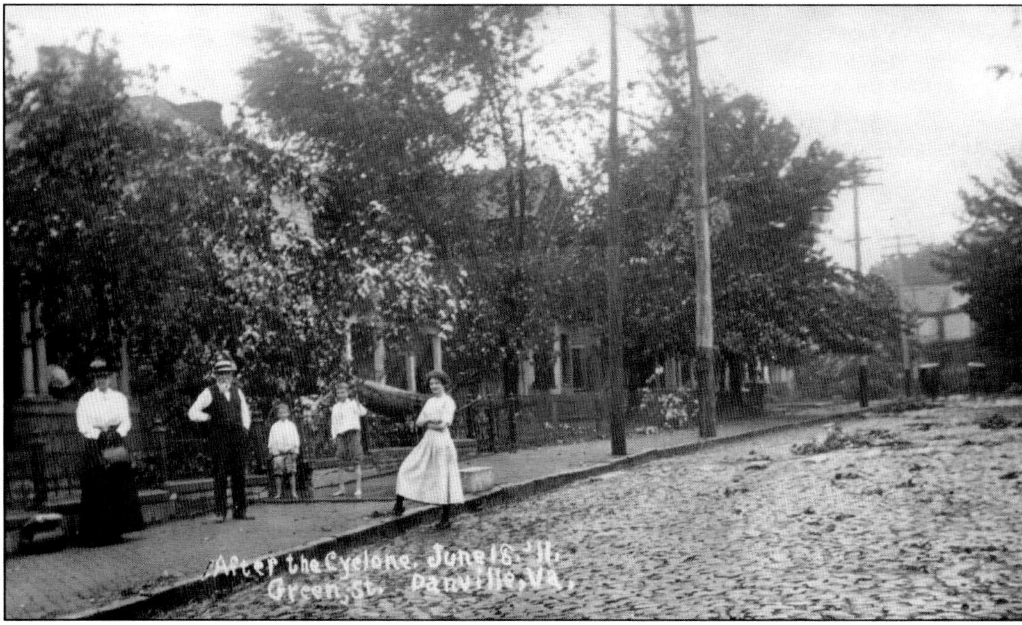

This photograph may show the Thomas A. Fox family; they lived at 879 Green Street, which is pictured here after Danville's notorious June 1911 cyclone. Fox joined the family's business, Fox Funeral Home, a cabinetmaking and undertaking firm established in 1842 and originally based in Halifax, Virginia. Fox Funeral Home, located at 531 Main Street, ceased operations in the 1930s. (Photograph by Oliver W. Cole.)

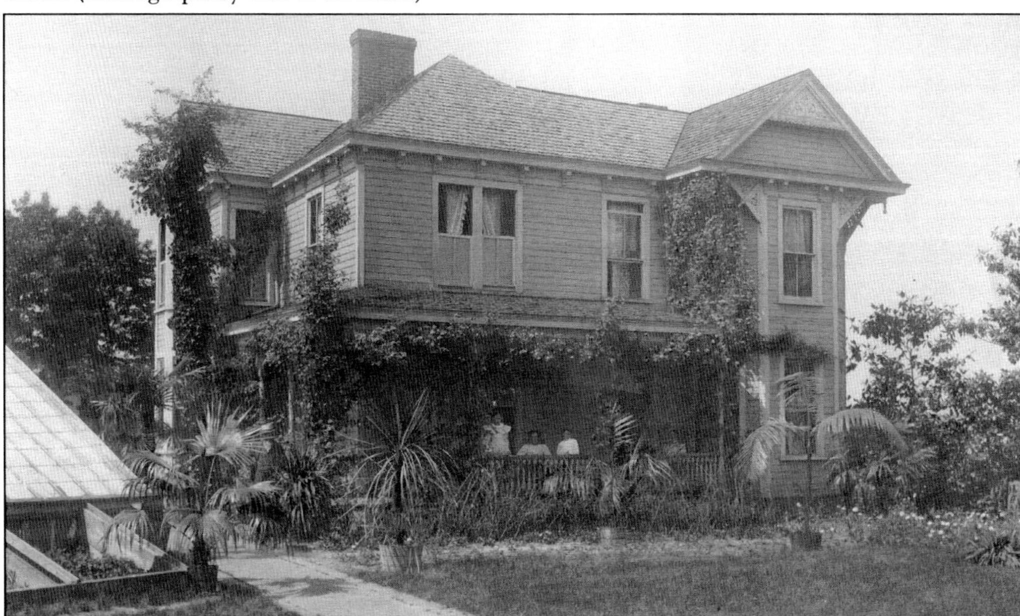

When Henry W. Brown came to the United States from Dorset, England, in the late 1870s, he brought his considerable skills as a gardener to Danville. Tapping his horticultural knowledge, Brown established the Danville Flower Garden in 1883 on Green Street at Chestnut Street. Now known as H.W. Brown Florist, the business operated for many years out of the family home (pictured), which was built in 1894. (Courtesy of Terry Shadrick.)

Emerson R. Loomis and his wife, Mabel McCully Loomis, pose with their infant son, Robert, at their home at 935 Green Street in 1904. Judging from the wealth of photographs in their family album, both Loomises were skilled photographers. After Emerson's death in 1910, Mabel became an assistant to Leon N. Taylor, making her the only known female photographer in the Danville area at that time. (Courtesy of Gary Grant.)

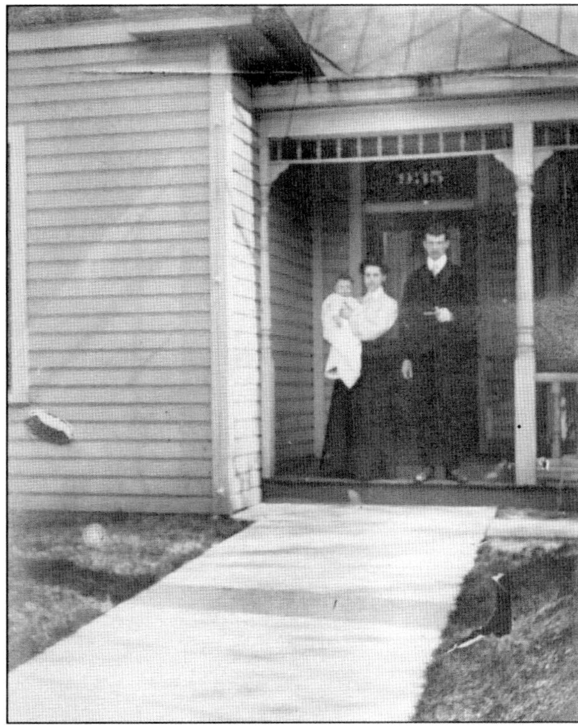

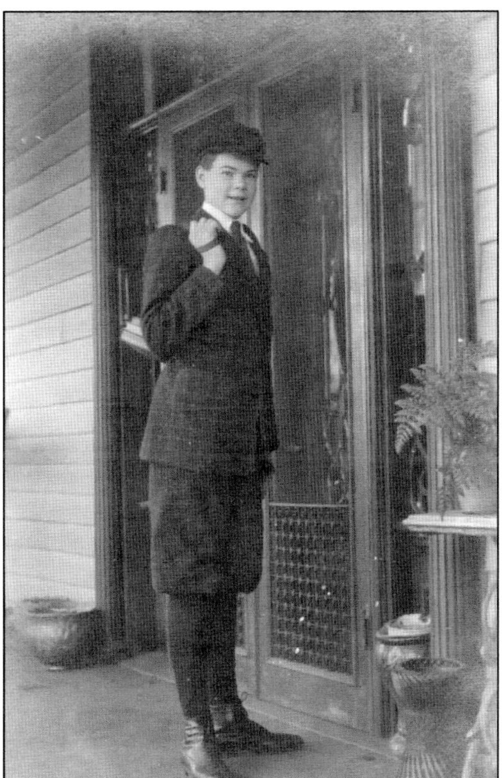

An eager student, Robert Loomis smiles at the camera with his book bag in hand while wearing a tweed suit with knickers and a derby hat. By World War I, he lived with his siblings and his mother, Mabel McCully Loomis (then a widow), at 187 West Main Street, a site now lost to State Route 86. (Photograph by Mabel Loomis; courtesy of Gary Grant.)

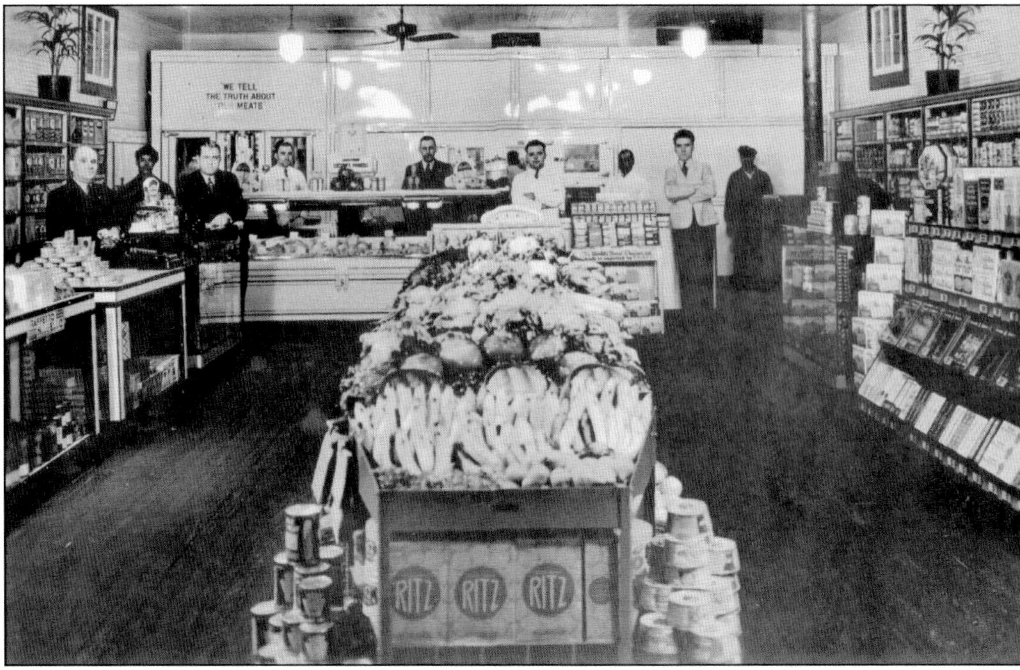

In 1938, founder James M. Church (far left) and his staff at Church Grocery stood proudly in front of the newly-added meat department. Established at 7 Chambers Street in 1921, this "corner" grocer flourishes in the same building today, trading as Midtown Market since 1966. Purchased in 1952 by Bernard C. Grant Jr., the business continues under the watch of his daughter Jan Grant Harris, owner since 2001. (Courtesy of Carson Womack.)

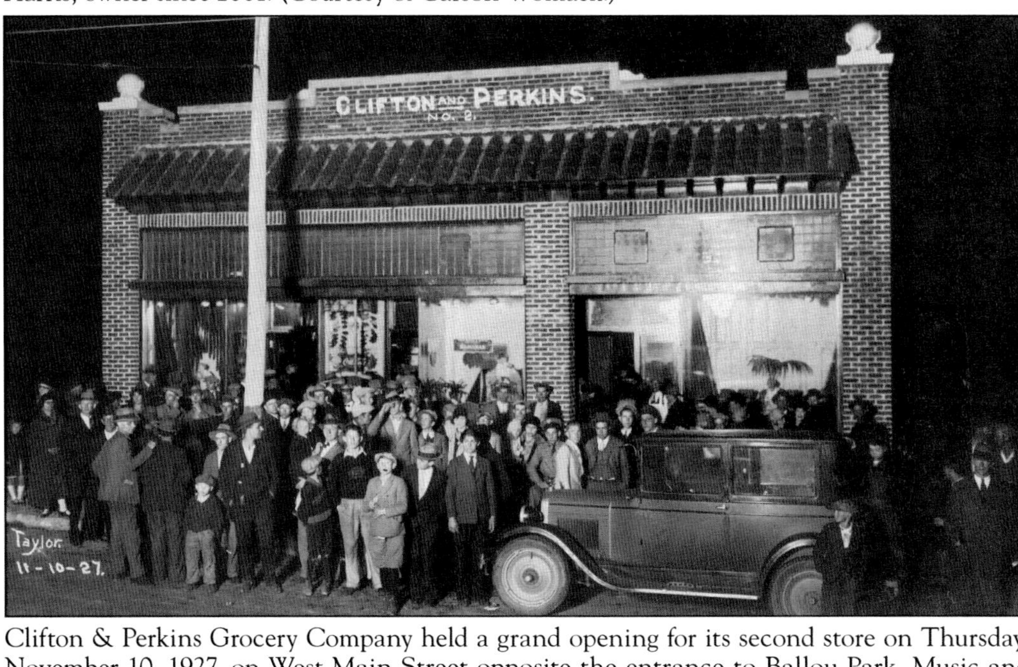

Clifton & Perkins Grocery Company held a grand opening for its second store on Thursday, November 10, 1927, on West Main Street opposite the entrance to Ballou Park. Music and refreshments were free for all guests, who could choose from Velvet Ice Cream, Coca-Cola, Moorefield's cake, and Armour & Company sandwiches. (Photograph by Leon Taylor.)

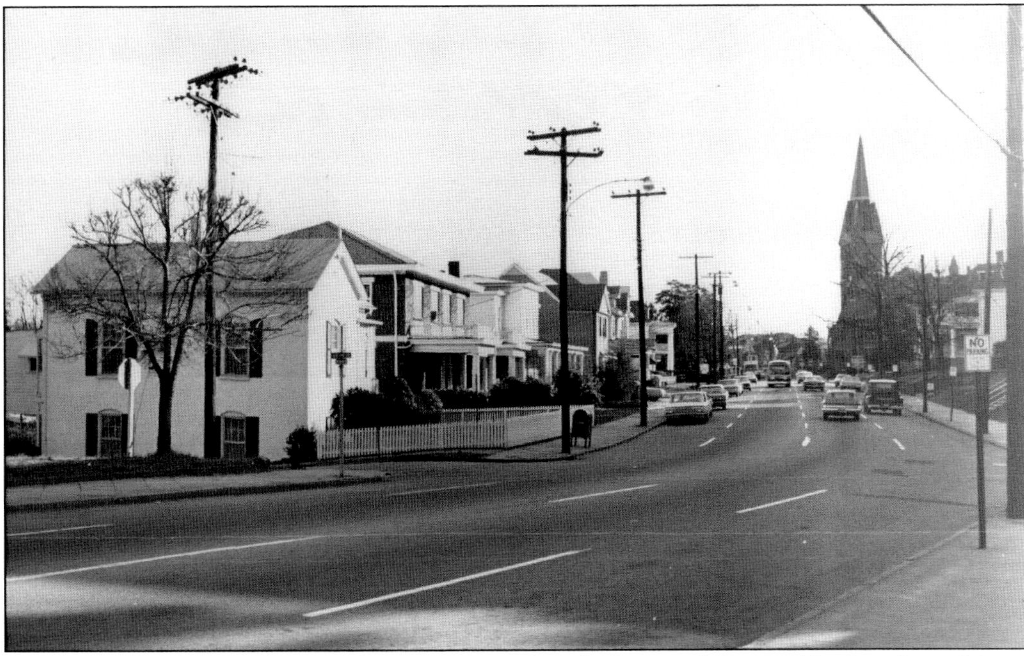

Before the mid-1970s extension of State Route 86 largely destroyed the neighborhood near Mount Vernon Methodist Church, West Main Street's 100 block retained much of its early-20th-century appearance. The collection of eclectic dwellings reflected the town's prosperity after Danville's march westward resumed just after the Civil War. Among the earliest homes was the brick cottage with the picket fence (above, left), which belonged to Pattie Averett, a member of the family of educators for whom Averett University was named. The 1890s brick mansion opposite (below, right), once home to Louis Herman and his family, stood at 179 West Main Street, near Aiken Street. For the first half of the 20th century, devoted customers regarded L. Herman's as the city's leading department store. (Both courtesy of the Danville Historical Society.)

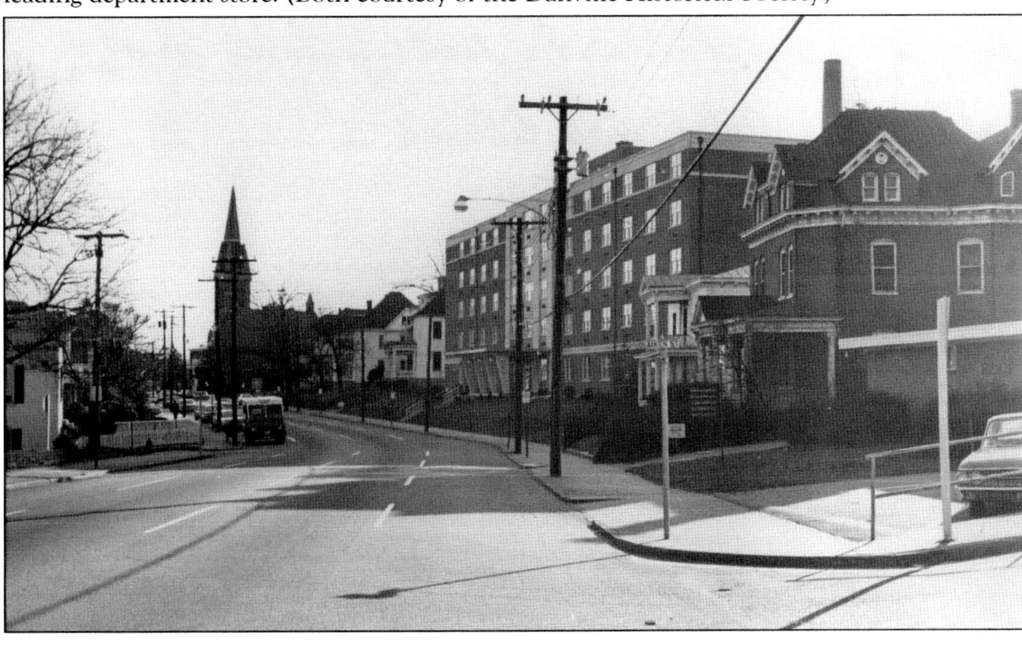

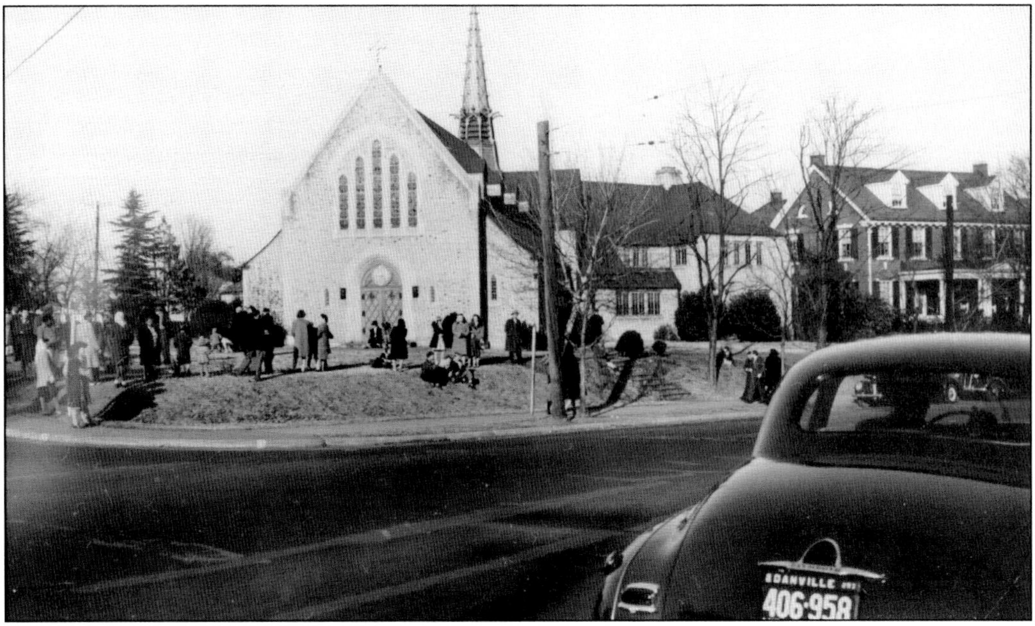

Before Sacred Heart parish was organized in 1878, its charter members first met in a small building not far from where they built their first church at the fork of Holbrook and Ross Streets. About 60 years later, when the growing congregation selected a site for their new, larger church, which was completed in 1939, they chose a similar prominent Y-shaped intersection: 288 West Main Street, at the corner of Randolph Street. (Courtesy of Zoe Edmunds.)

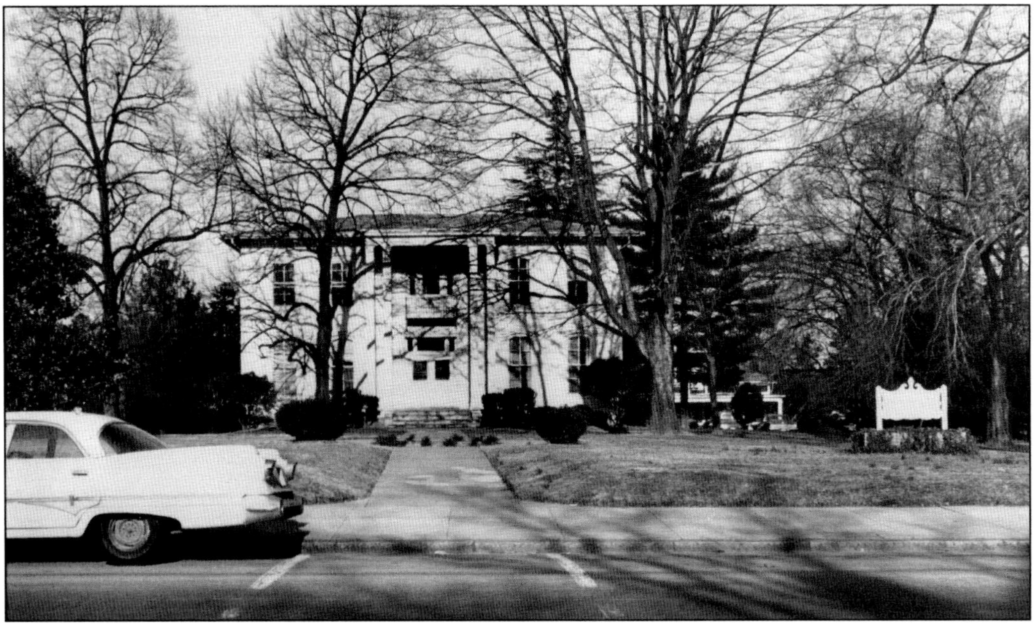

The year 1953 saw the establishment of the city's oldest parochial school, and the first to integrate—Sacred Heart School occupied the house and carriage house of Walter W. Waddill at 344 West Main Street. In 1966, Averett University purchased this property for the construction of its library. Averett's art department continues to use the historic carriage house. (Courtesy of the Danville Historical Society.)

Four

TRANSPORTATION

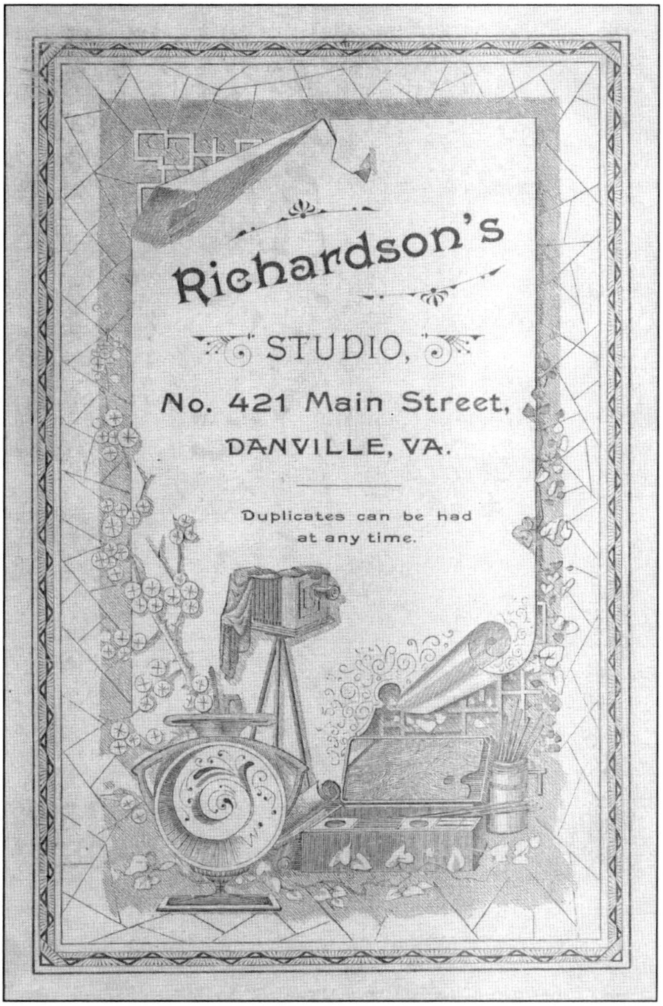

Danville's Main Street ran uphill on an old Indian trail toward a fork in the road separating South and West Main Streets. The earliest settlers had to walk or ride horses. Trains became an option just before the Civil War, and streetcars arrived in the mid-1880s. A decorative advertisement for Frank Richardson's studio was imprinted on the reverse side of this *carte de visite*. (Photograph by F.H. Richardson; courtesy of the Danville Museum of Fine Arts and History.)

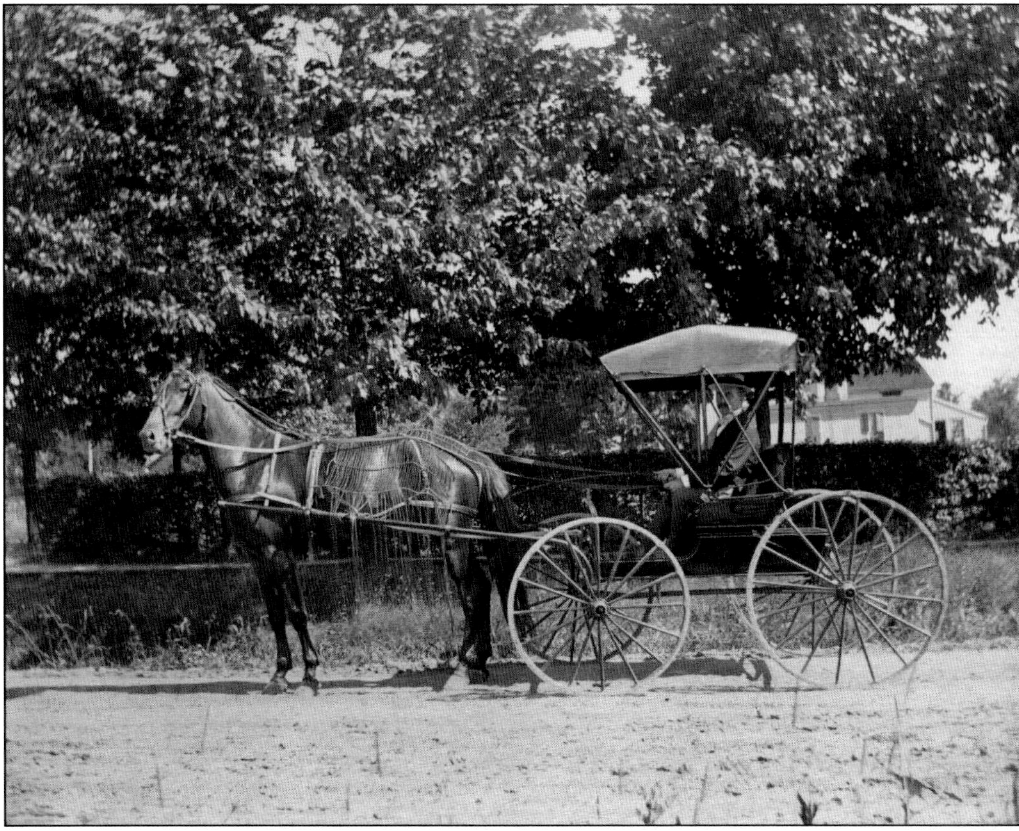

Prior to 1885, when Jesse Roland Noell created Danville's first public bus transportation, only people of means—like this dapper, unidentified gentleman—could afford a smart buggy, pulled by an equally smart horse. Noell's Street Bus Line, consisting of several horse-drawn omnibuses that met trains and conveyed passengers around town, foreshadowed Danville's streetcar system, which rolled on tracks and began in 1886. (Courtesy of the Danville Historical Society.)

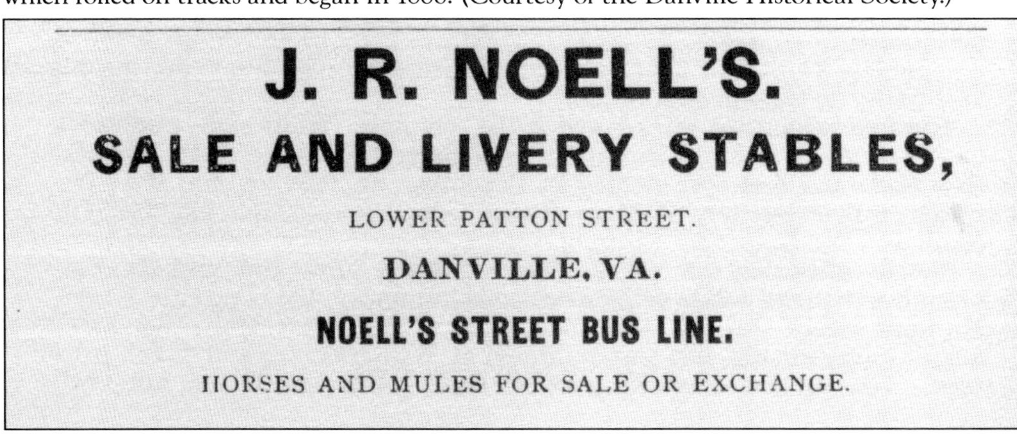

In 1886, the town laid narrow gauge rails from the train station to Mount Vernon Methodist Church, and the Danville Street Car Company was chartered, with mules replacing horses. For two years, 30 mules took turns pulling the town's new streetcars. After a couple of years, the public grew tired of the irregular schedules and the slow pace of cars pulled by mules. (Courtesy of the Danville Historical Society.)

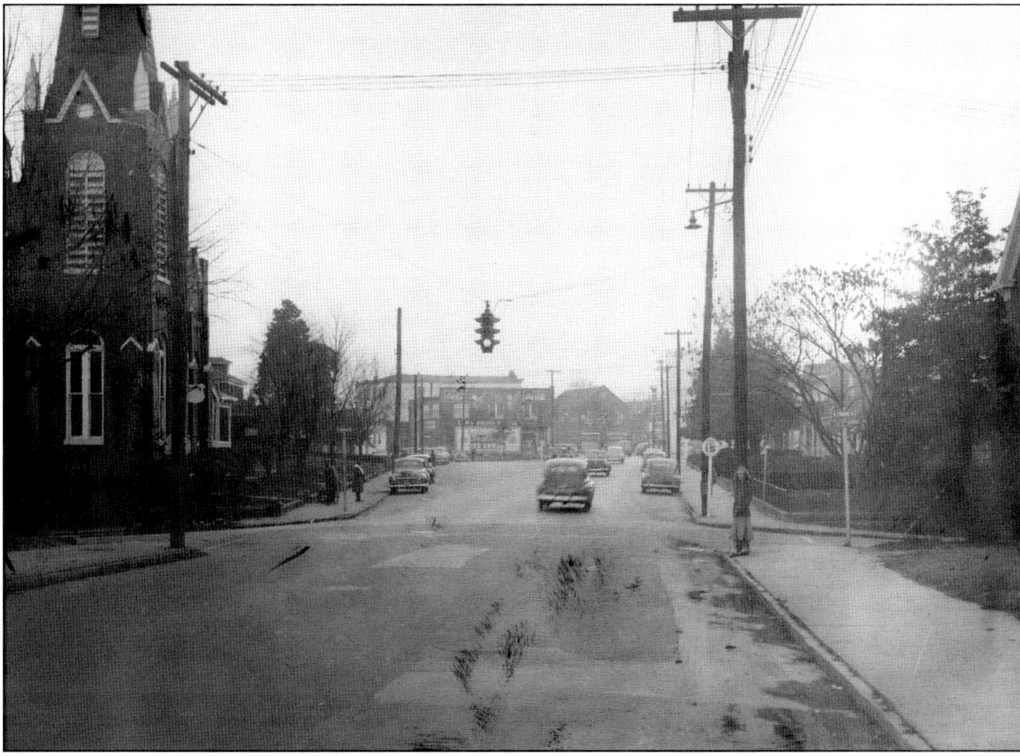

Soon after Danville's 1888 experiment with electric streetcars on tracks proved successful, citizens of North Danville also wanted to reap the benefits of public transportation. In 1891, William H. Buntin led the effort to extend the lines from the river to the top of the hill at Gitt's Switch. Here, in front of Gitt's Drug Store (visible below the traffic light), trolley car drivers reversed directions manually or electrically (by throwing a switch). (Photograph by William E. Land.)

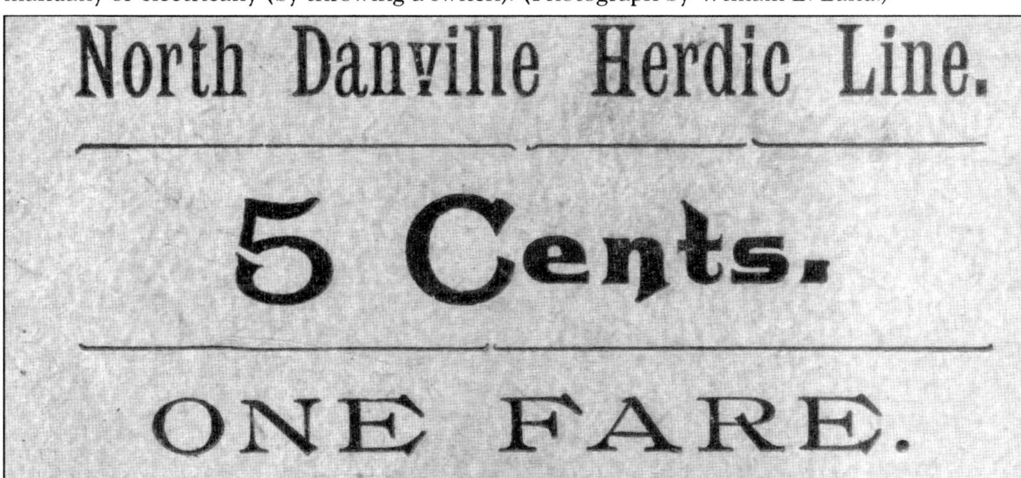

Prior to his investment in bringing electric streetcars to North Danville, William Buntin operated the North Danville Herdic line along Myrtle Avenue, powered by horse- or mule-drawn omnibuses, with a fare of 5¢. Thomas J. Lee, a North Danville mayor, originally built the Herdic line to carry passengers from the Dan River to a point just north of Leemont Cemetery. (Courtesy of the Danville Historical Society.)

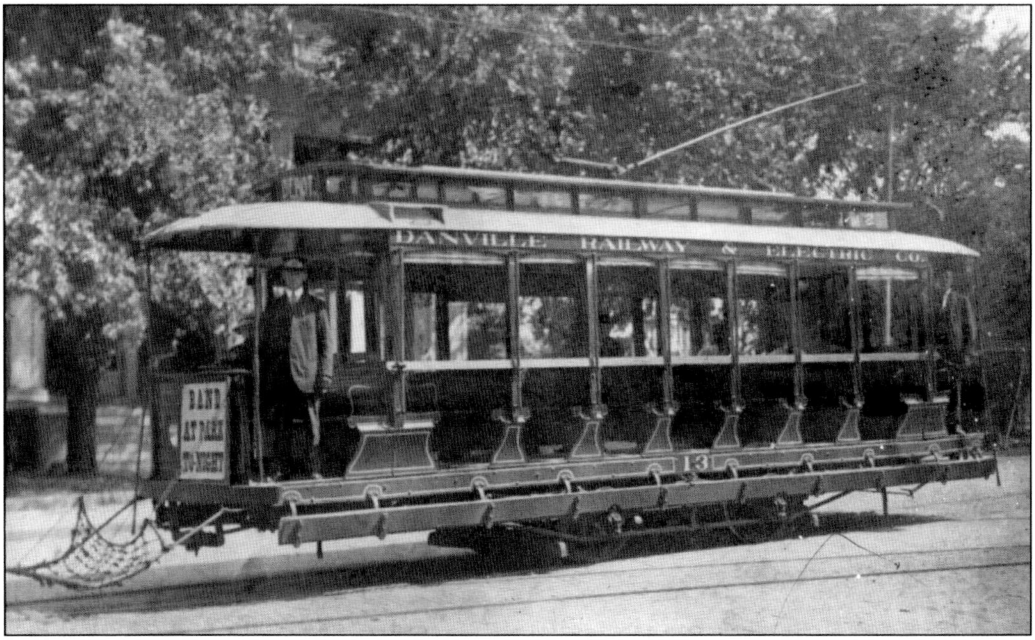

For most of Danville's first century, its citizens traveled by foot, wagon, or horseback. In 1886, mule-drawn streetcars offered public rides on tracks laid from the train depot to Mount Vernon Methodist Church. Danville's first electric streetcars appeared in 1888. The Danville Street Car Company ordered cars from the Lamokin Car Works in Pennsylvania and the Jackson & Sharp Company (J&S) in Delaware. A total of 10 J&S open cars, without windows or sides, provided breezy rides in the summer. (Courtesy of the Allen B. Carter family.)

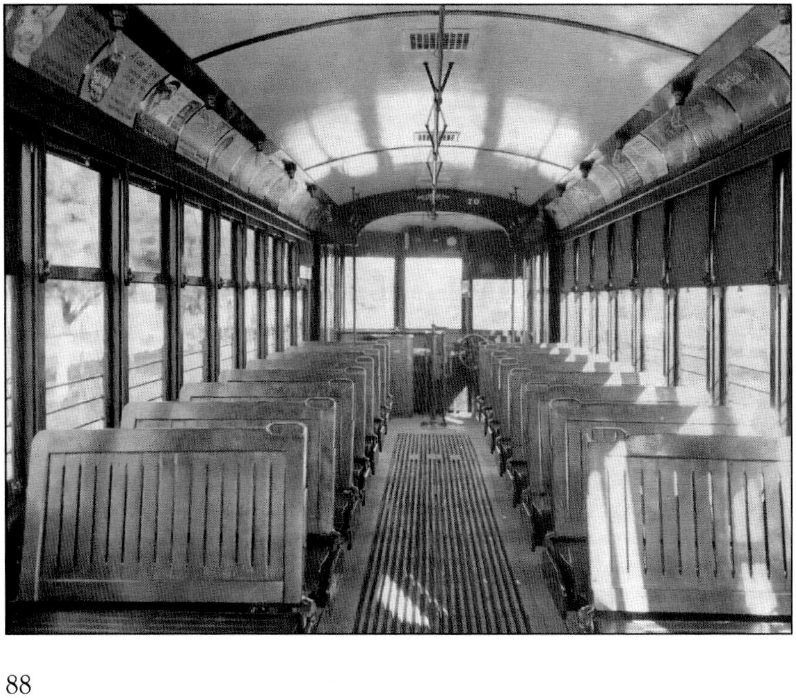

The closed car shown here provided Danville's first customers a no-frills ride without carpets or padded seats. A carbarn on Craghead Street between Loyal and Newton Streets sheltered Danville's electric cars; six of them burned in a disastrous 1891 fire that also consumed the entire carbarn. (Courtesy of Clara Fountain.)

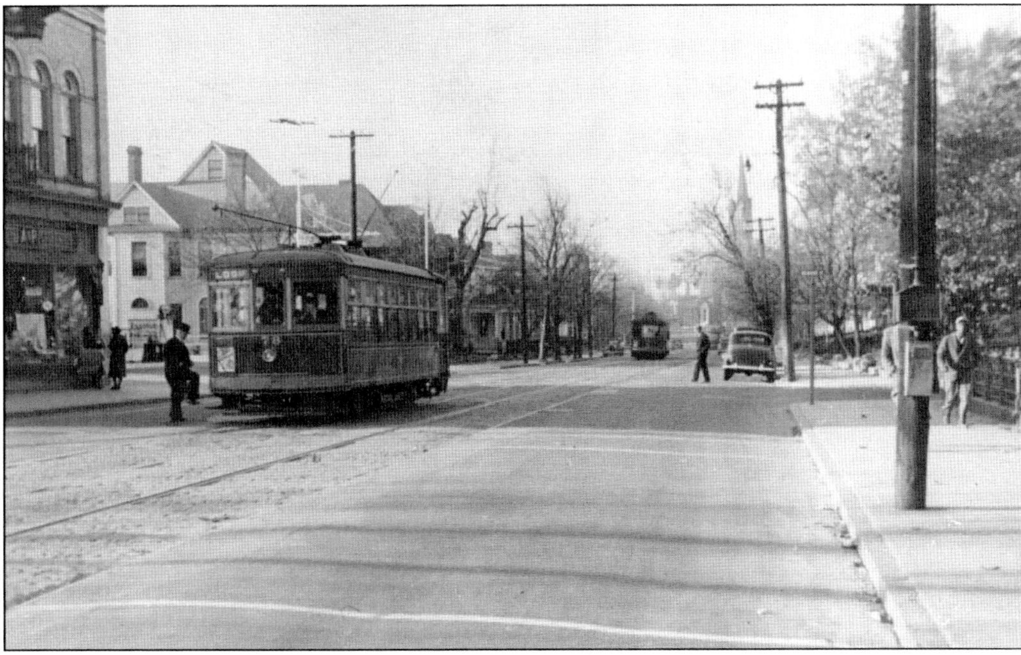

An unidentified photographer captured this passenger boarding a waiting streetcar near Main and Holbrook Streets, with Mount Vernon Methodist Church in the distance. In 1935, the West End pharmacy and grocery occupied the brick commercial building at far left, which survived until the late 1960s, when it was razed to accommodate the expansion of the Esso service station next door. (Courtesy of the Allen B. Carter family.)

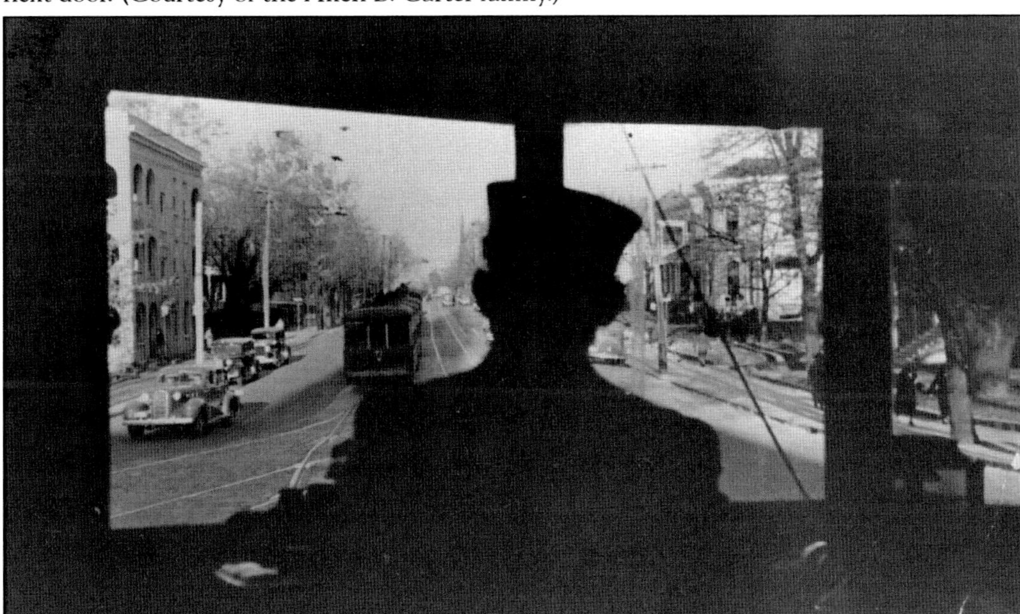

With Mount Vernon Methodist Church at his back, this unidentified driver heads down Main Street towards Broad Street, with the Caswell Apartments at left. At right is the Bethell-Penn House, which stood just beyond Stratford College at Main Street's intersection with Rison Street, which was widened in the 1960s. (Courtesy of the Allen B. Carter family.)

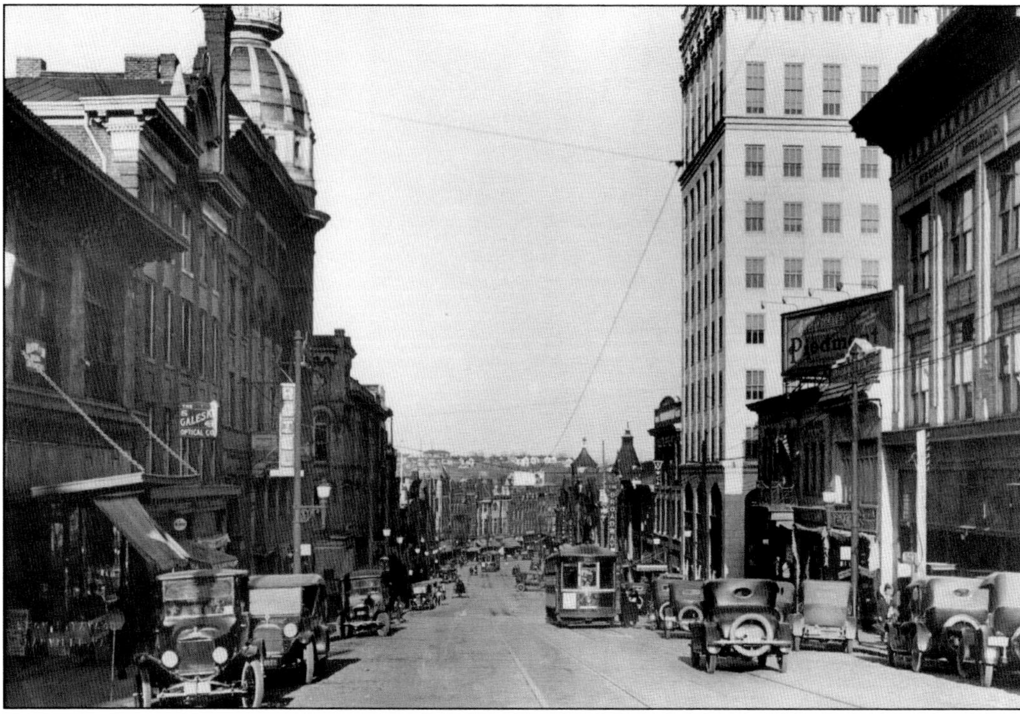

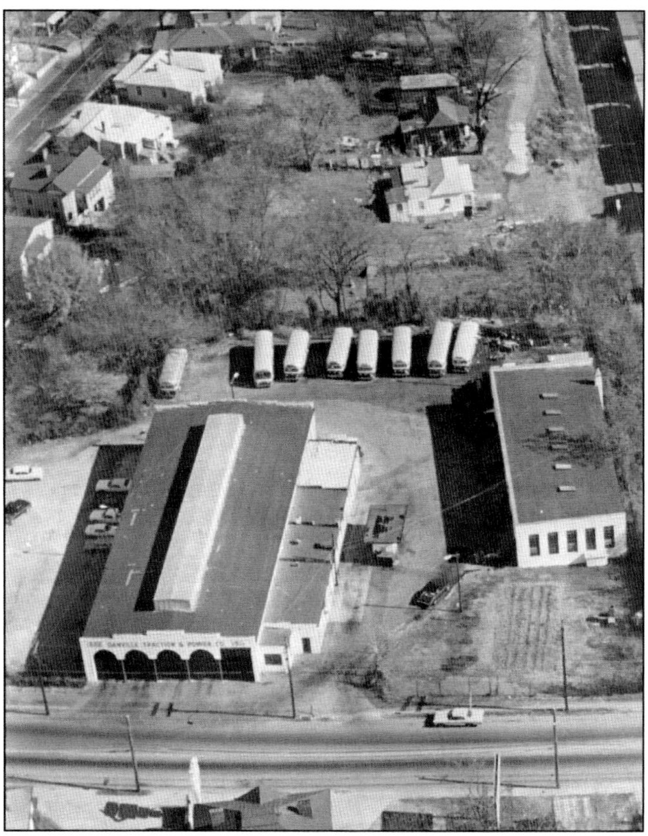

The 1920s Leon Taylor photograph above, framed by the Hotel Burton (at left) and the 1921 Masonic temple (at right), shows downtown Main Street exuding metropolitan energy as an electric streetcar winds down the hill, vying for road space with automobiles. Since the inauguration of its fleet in 1886, Danville's trolleys sported a cream-and-green paint scheme, recalling the colors of the tobacco growing in the fields around Danville. (Photograph by Leon Taylor.)

Established in 1911, the Danville Traction & Power Company moved into the South Main Street carbarn built in 1900 to store and service its electric streetcars (and later city buses). Patrons could take a round-trip sightseeing tour for just 10¢ or reserve an entire car for a party. (Courtesy of the Allen B. Carter family.)

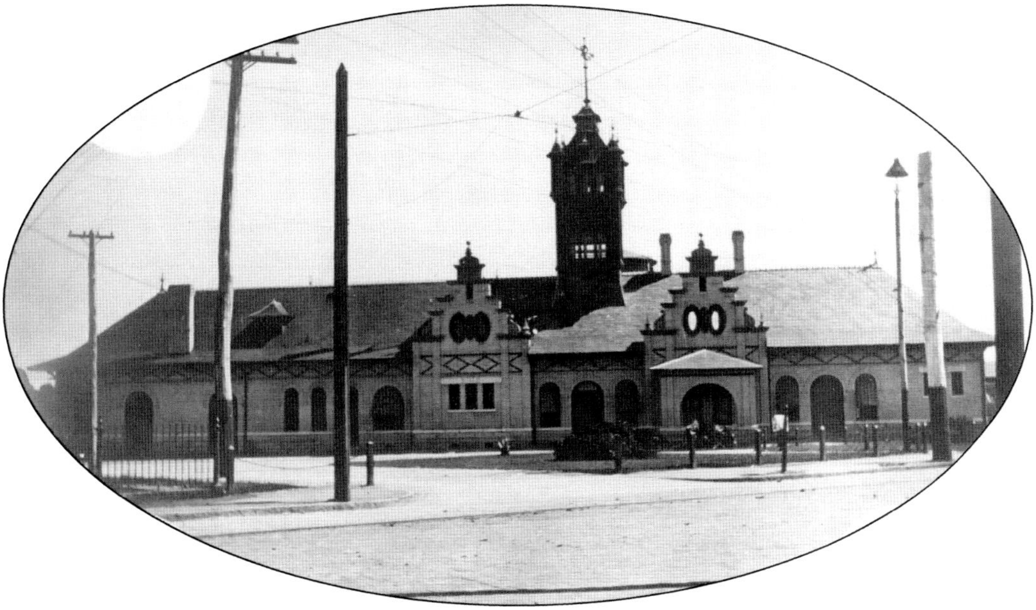

Built in 1899, Danville's railroad station typified the design style of Frank P. Milburn, Southern Railway's architect of record for many years. Reflecting Milburn's affection for Old World style, the structure of Danville's depot has been described as Amsterdam Revival. The depot's contractor, R.B. Graham, used some of the same lot of yellow-buff brick to remodel his house at 879 Green Street. (Photograph by Leon Taylor.)

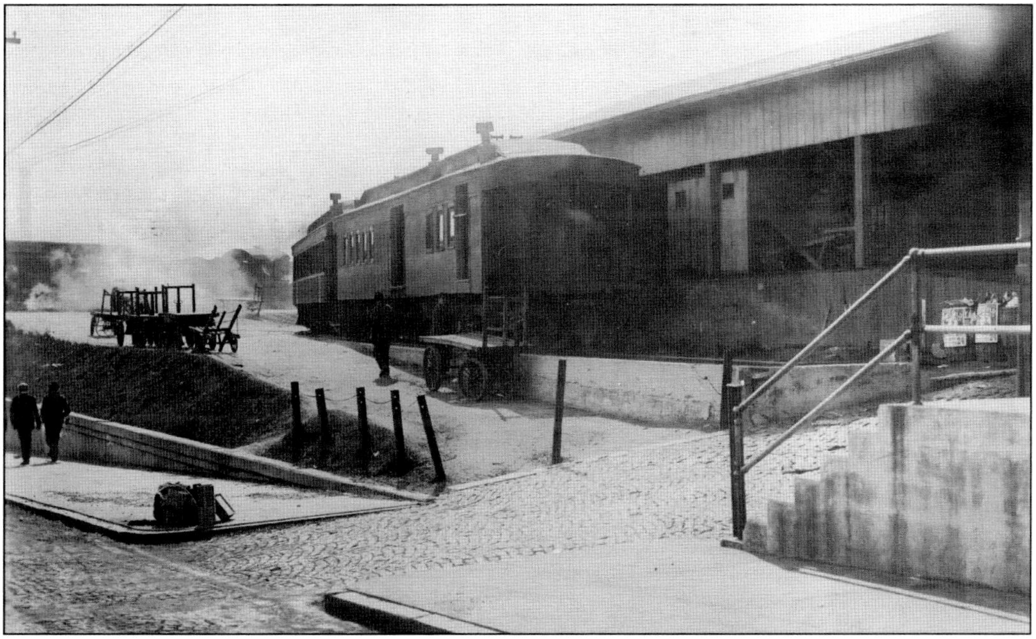

Just across from Southern Railway's Danville depot stood the Danville & Western (D&W) siding yard and its freight and passenger terminal, with access by way of the concrete stairs shown at right. Within sight of Craghead Street's dry bridge, the early-1900s D&W ("Dick & Willie") depot anchored the corner of Deboe Street for almost 100 years until Norfolk Southern Railway had it razed in 1990. (Photograph by Leon Taylor.)

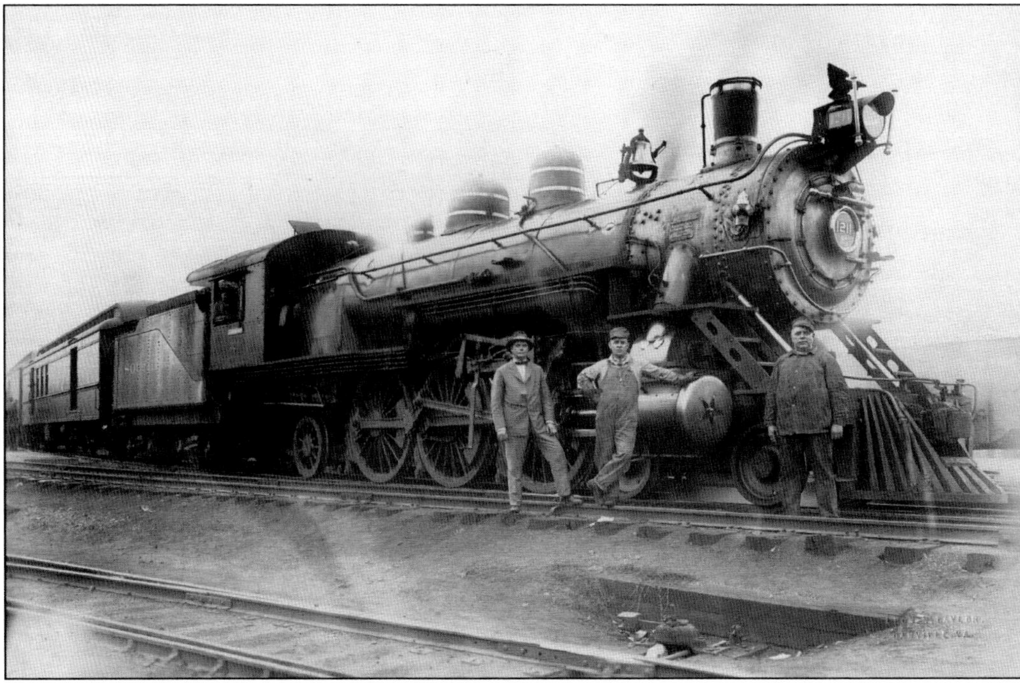

In this c. 1920 photograph, Zachariah Frank Perkinson (far left) stands with two unidentified trainmen beside Southern Railway engine No. 1211 on the tracks at the Danville station. Born in 1873, Perkinson, a North Carolina native, worked for Southern as a general foreman and car inspector. Perkinson, who moved to Danville to find employment, lived with his family on West Thomas Street. (Photograph by Leon Taylor.)

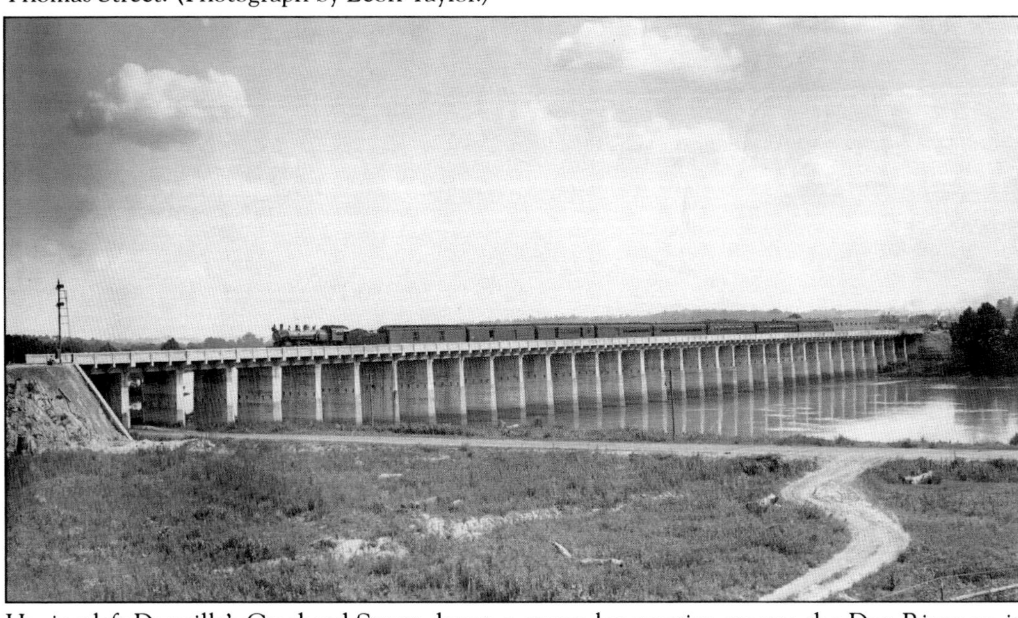

Having left Danville's Craghead Street depot, a steam locomotive crosses the Dan River on its journey toward points north in 1915. As part of its pre–World War I modernization, Southern Railway retained concrete contractors Reed & Lowe to construct new reinforced concrete bridges over Craghead Street and across the Dan River. (Photograph by Leon Taylor.)

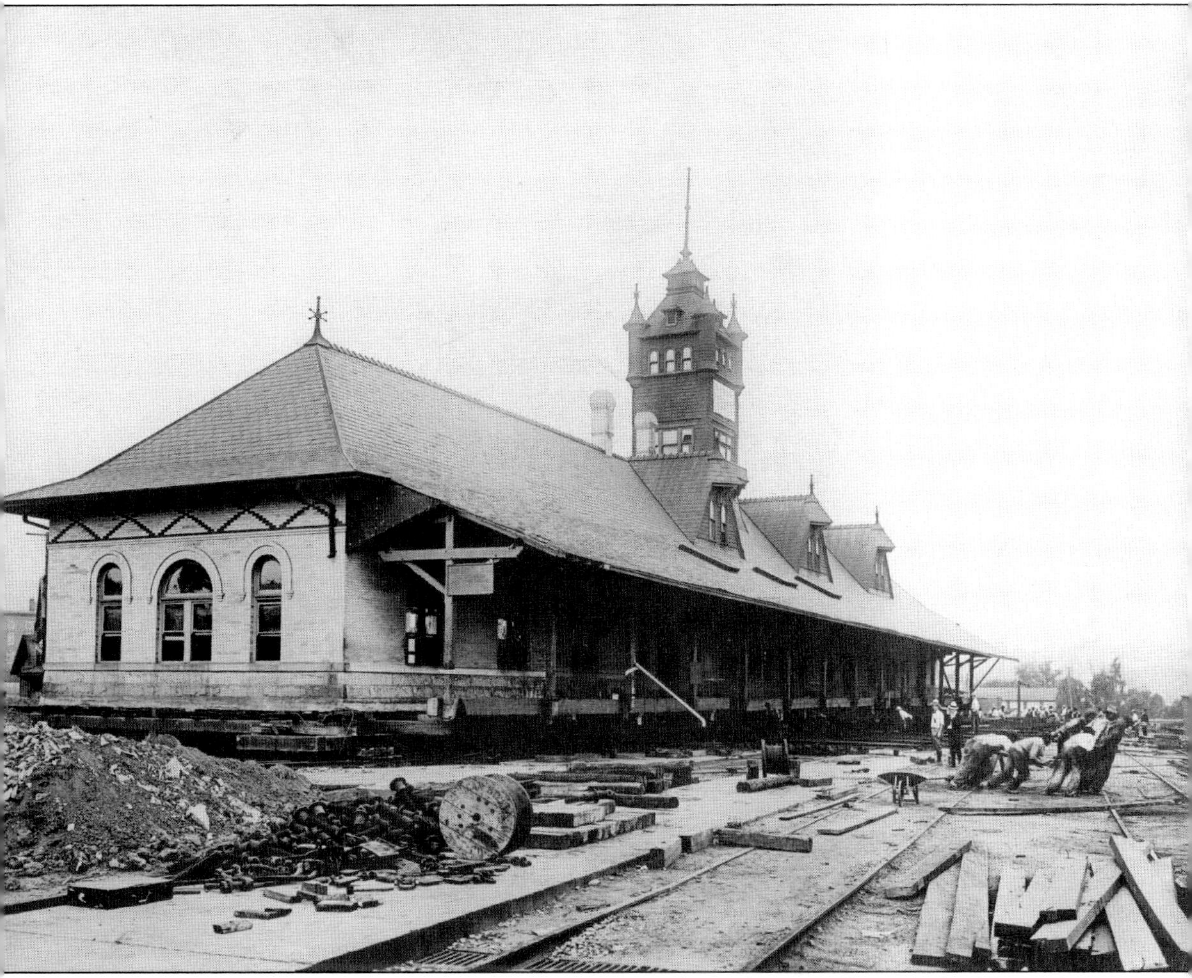

In 1915, Southern Railway upgraded its Crescent line through Danville with double tracks from Washington to Atlanta. Modern concrete bridges over the Dan River and Craghead Street followed a lower, realigned grade farther from the station. Accommodating these new tracks necessitated moving the building some 150 yards east. Using plans by the John Eichleay Engineering Company of Pittsburgh, Danville contractor W. King Anderson employed 12 men and a foreman to relocate the building closer to the new tracks. Mules and stump pullers helped roll the depot to its new foundation so carefully that, according to a report in *Popular Mechanics*, "pigeons nesting in the depot tower were not disturbed." The only other known photograph of this massive undertaking belongs to the Danville Science Center and can be seen in the lobby of the current depot. (Photograph by Leon Taylor.)

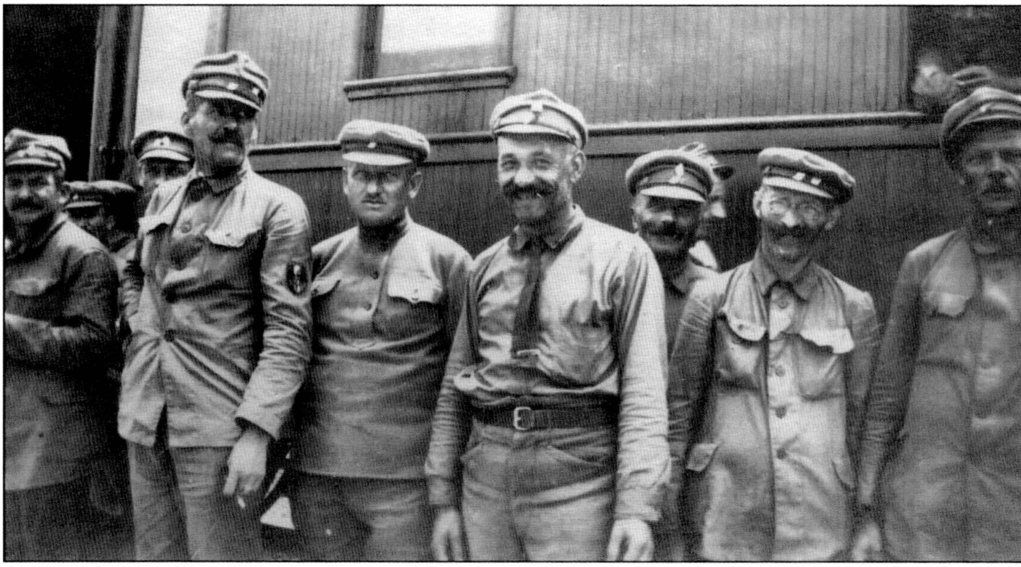

These laughing railroad workers seem to be amused about having their picture taken. Probably brakemen for Southern Railway, this group standing in front of a wooden railcar inspected the train and operated the brakes. They also helped with switching tracks and anything else the conductor needed. (Courtesy of Clara Fountain.)

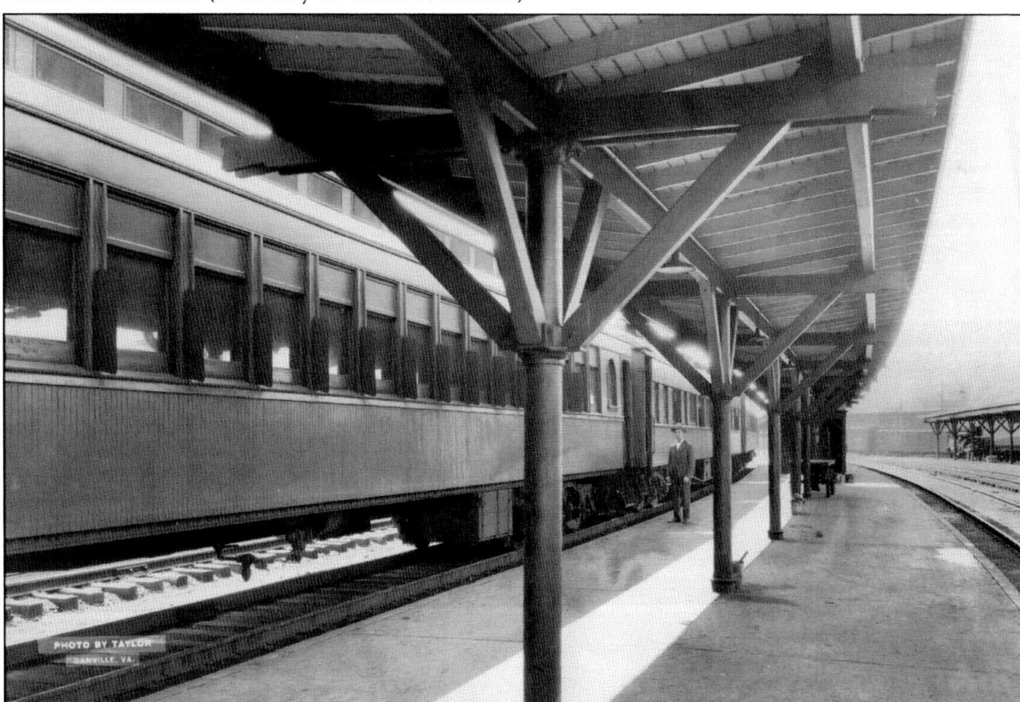

Today, passengers still board and disembark under the shelter of this canopy, which was completed around 1915 when the massive station settled onto its current granite foundation after an arduous, rolling relocation from its nearby original 1899 site. By the time this photograph was taken, and well into the modern Amtrak era, those riding the rails still went from station to train—avoiding crossing the tracks—via an underground stairway. (Photograph by Leon Taylor.)

By 1888, Danville's streetcar system went electric and was manned by drivers like these, dressed in smart caps and uniforms in front of the Danville Streetcar Company office at 309 Main Street, across from Ferrell Furniture. (Photograph by Leon Taylor.)

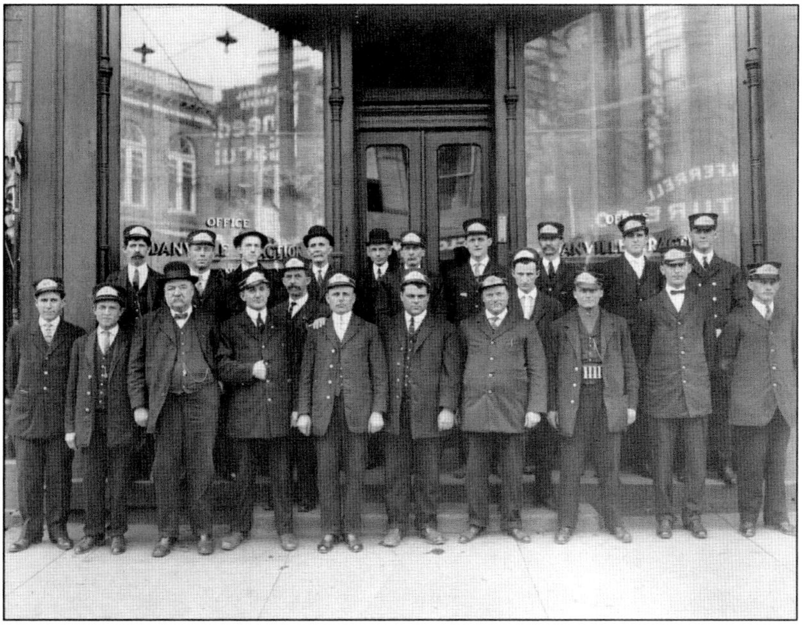

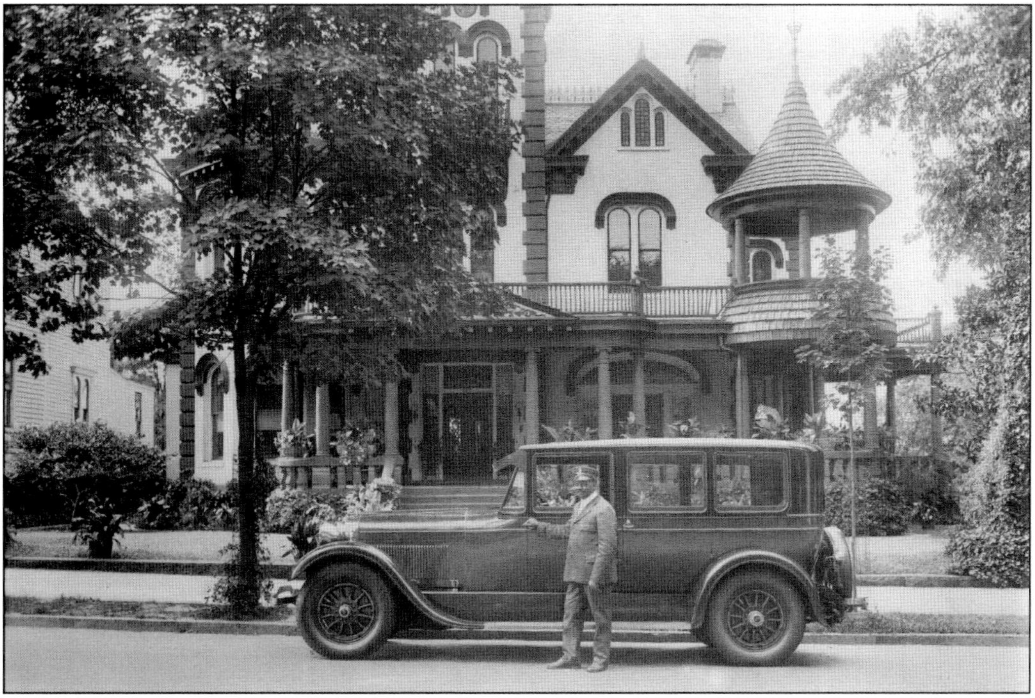

Every aspect of this house at 862 Main Street enhanced the prestige of Penn's Bottom, a section of Millionaires Row between Jefferson Avenue and Chestnut Street where five Penn families built mansions. When Sallie Penn, the widow of tobacconist James G. Penn, bought this seven-passenger Pierce-Arrow limousine in 1927, its $7,000 price tag equaled what a Lamborghini costs in today's market. (Photograph by Leon Taylor.)

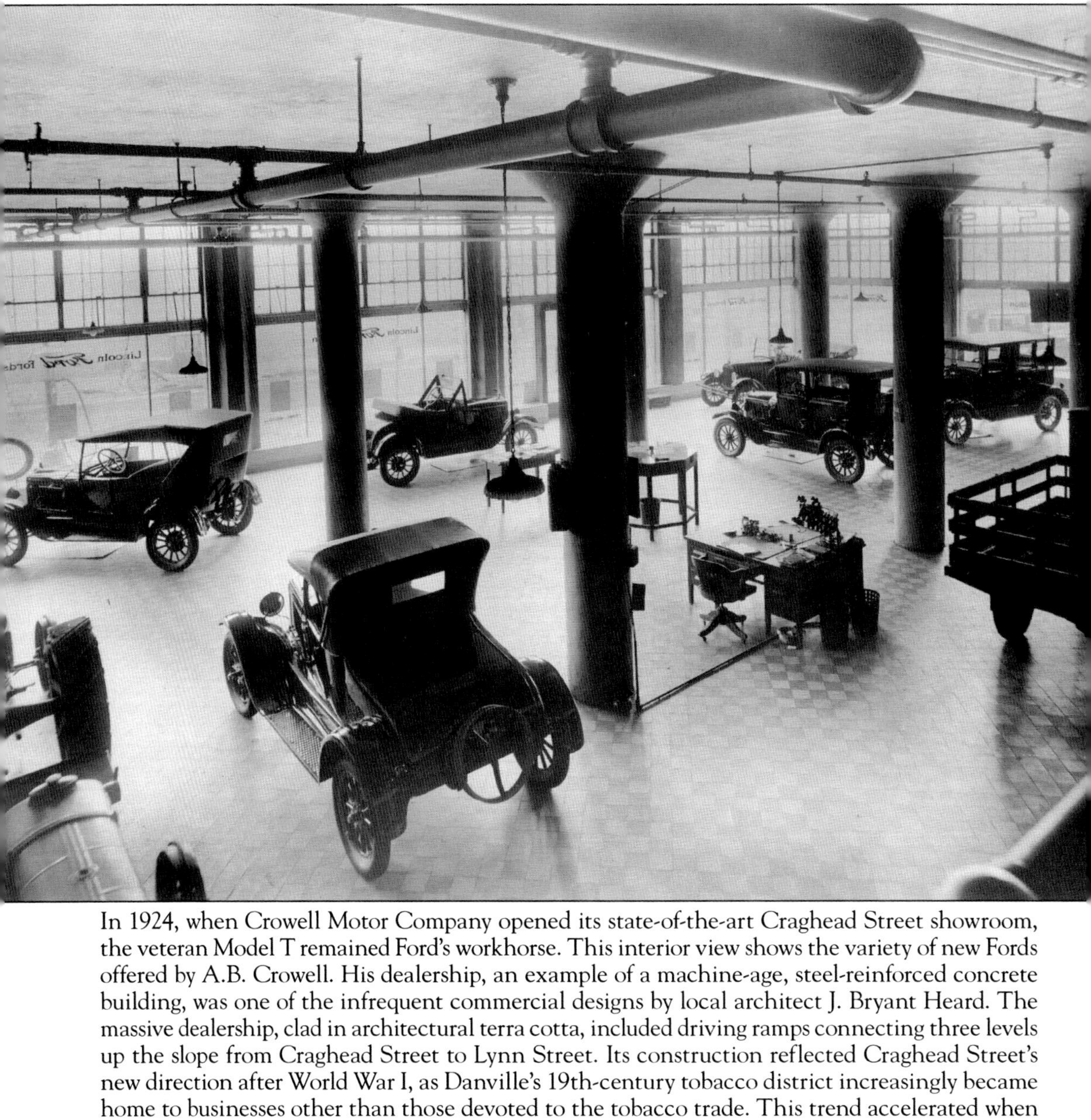

In 1924, when Crowell Motor Company opened its state-of-the-art Craghead Street showroom, the veteran Model T remained Ford's workhorse. This interior view shows the variety of new Fords offered by A.B. Crowell. His dealership, an example of a machine-age, steel-reinforced concrete building, was one of the infrequent commercial designs by local architect J. Bryant Heard. The massive dealership, clad in architectural terra cotta, included driving ramps connecting three levels up the slope from Craghead Street to Lynn Street. Its construction reflected Craghead Street's new direction after World War I, as Danville's 19th-century tobacco district increasingly became home to businesses other than those devoted to the tobacco trade. This trend accelerated when the city paved Craghead Street's cobblestones with smooth asphalt in 1924. Shortly thereafter, a full-page advertisement placed in the *Register* by Craghead Street merchants heralded the street as the city's new business and shopping mecca. (Photograph by Leon Taylor.)

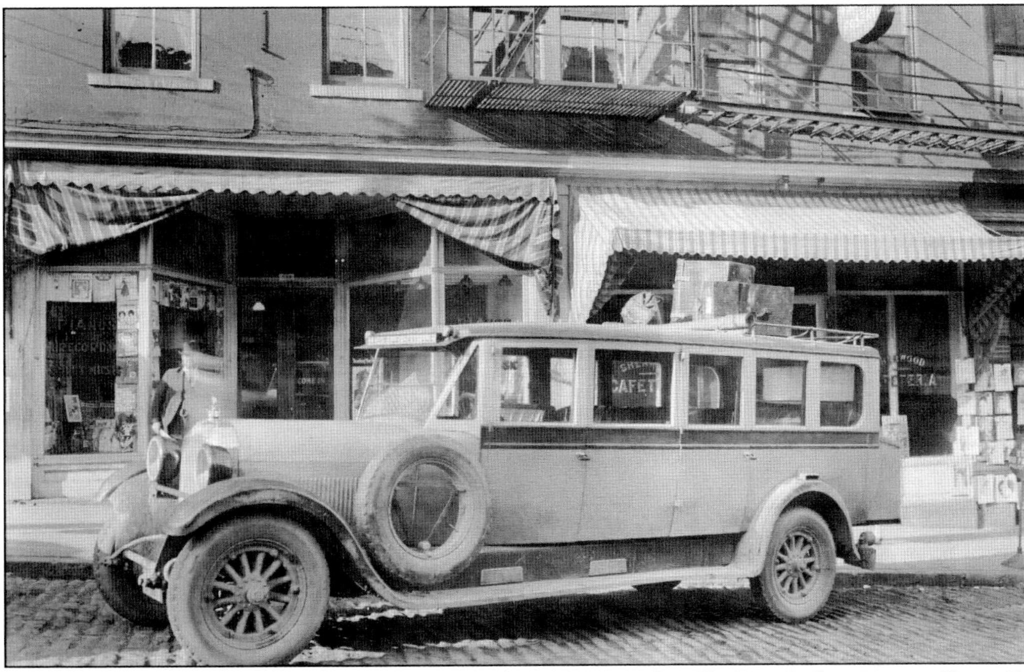

In this 1925 image, a shuttle car traveling round-trip from Leaksville, North Carolina, to Danville sits parked at 542 Main Street, in front of the Morgan Hotel. Just behind the "taxi," two businesses occupied the building's upper end: the Danville Music Company (left) and the Sherwood Cafeteria. The three-story brick hotel building, later known as the Stonewall Jackson, was demolished in 1982 to make way for a bank. (Photograph by Leon Taylor.)

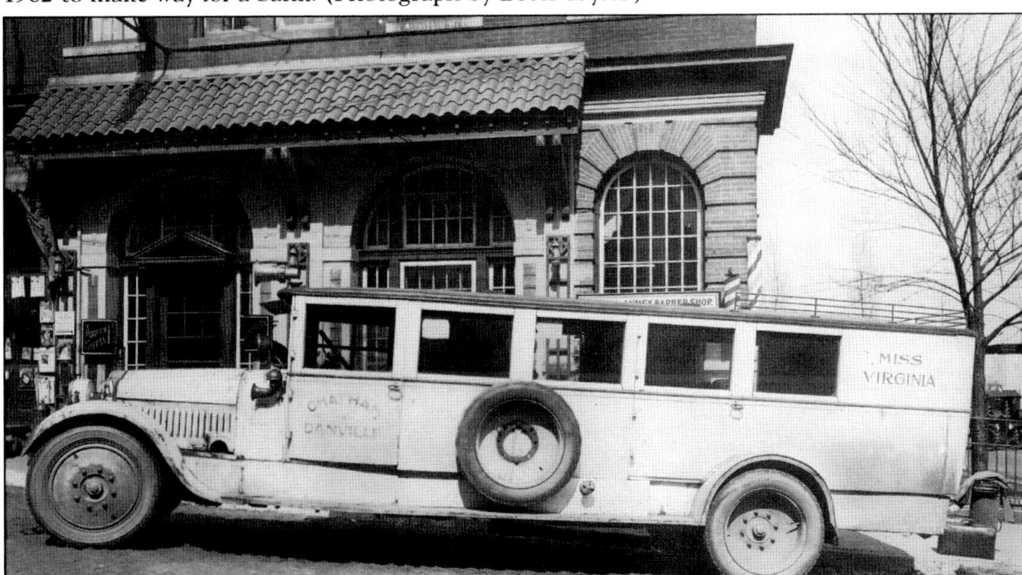

This Chatham-to-Danville shuttle waited for passengers at the lower end of the Morgan Hotel's facade. The "Annex Hotel" sign (at left) refers to another hotel, the Leeland, located just uphill and across the street, which rented the Morgan's lower floor until the Morgan reopened a few years later as the Stonewall Jackson. The Thomas News Company (at far left) sold newspapers and movie magazines. (Photograph by Leon Taylor.)

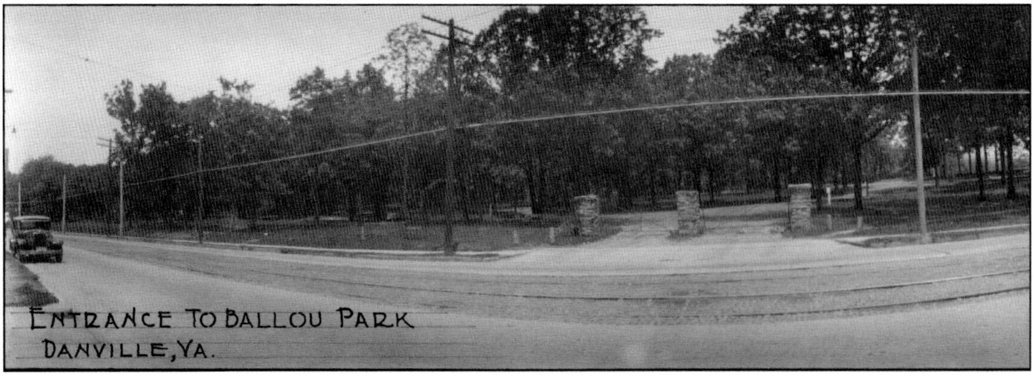

When John J. Hitchcock's health began to fail, his son J. Raymond Hitchcock moved to Danville from Winston-Salem, North Carolina, to help his father and his sister Marian with their photographic studio. From 1934 to 1977, Raymond Hitchcock offered individual portraits and wedding portfolios, but he brought special expertise to group images and panoramic views like this fisheye perspective of the entrance to Ballou Park. (Photograph by Raymond Hitchcock.)

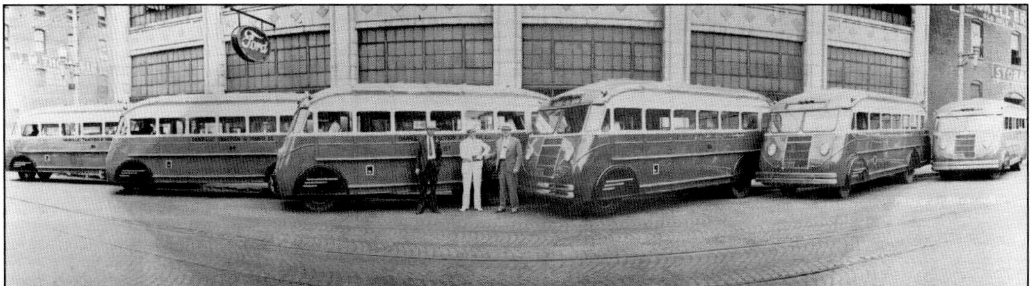

When the Danville Traction & Power Company dismantled Danville's streetcar system in 1938, the firm acquired new rubber-tired rolling stock. Raymond Hitchcock took this photograph—of Danville's first buses in front of the Crowell Ford Company on Craghead Street—using a Kodak Cirkut camera that rotated to allow the photographer to stand close to his subject and pan from one side to the other. (Photograph by Raymond Hitchcock.)

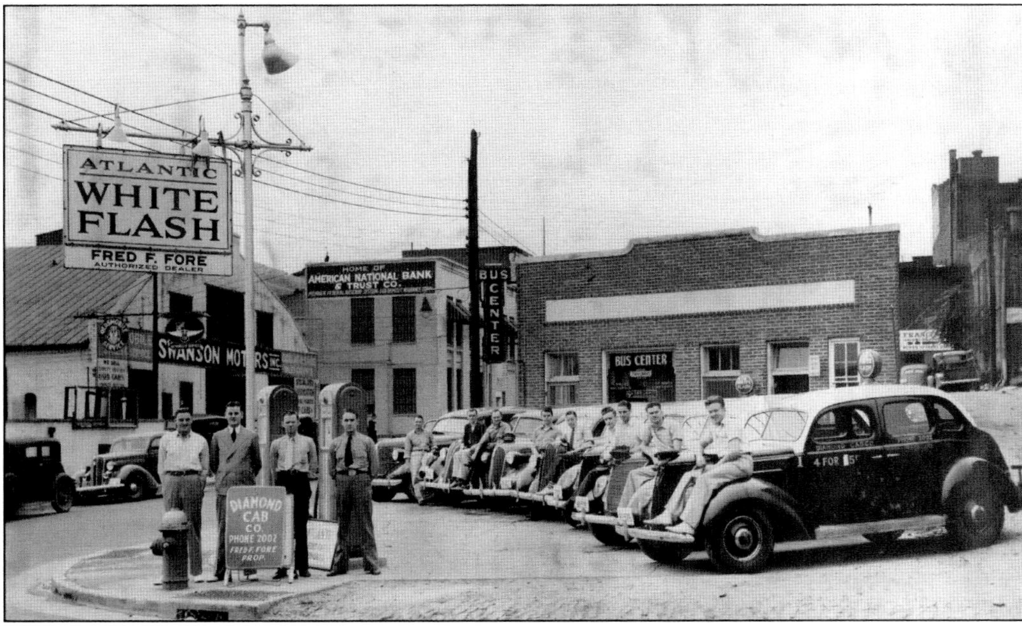

In the 1930s, Danville's Trailways bus station anchored the corner of Spring and Market Streets immediately across from Swanson Motor Company, a local dealer for Oldsmobile, Cadillac, and LaSalle. Here, the Diamond Cab Company's fleet and drivers stand ready to meet arriving buses and drive travel-weary patrons to their destinations. (Photograph by Leon Taylor.)

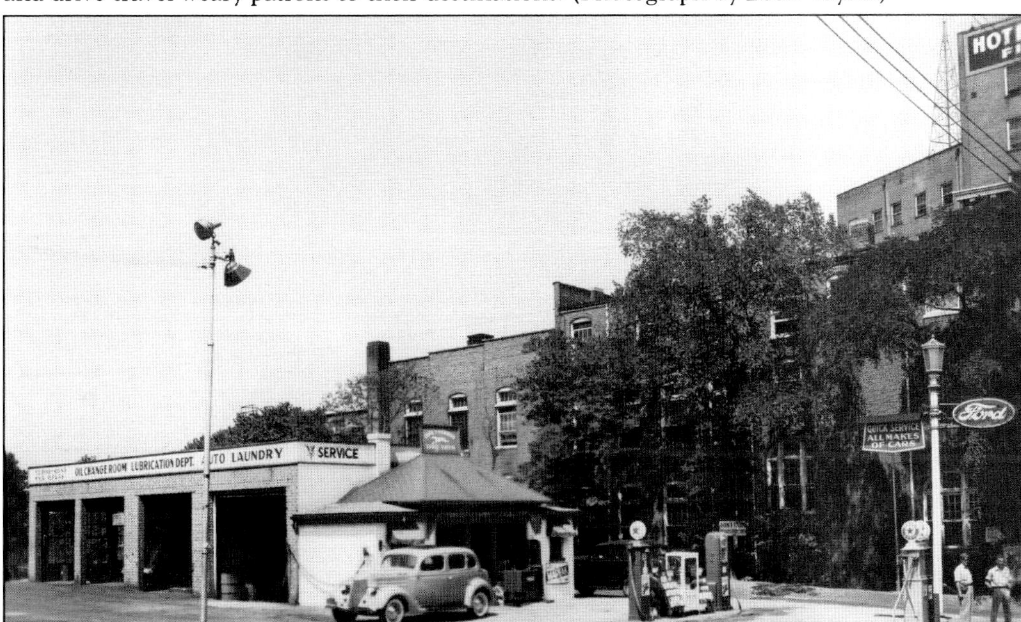

The city's early Greyhound service station occupied a narrow lot just uphill from Hotel Danville. Travelers found the location convenient to several nearby hotels, as well as to an array of restaurants and other downtown businesses. Both Greyhound and Trailways built larger facilities in the mid-20th century: Greyhound on Patton Street at South Ridge Street in the 1940s, and Trailways just up Main Street in the 1960s. (Photograph by Leon Taylor.)

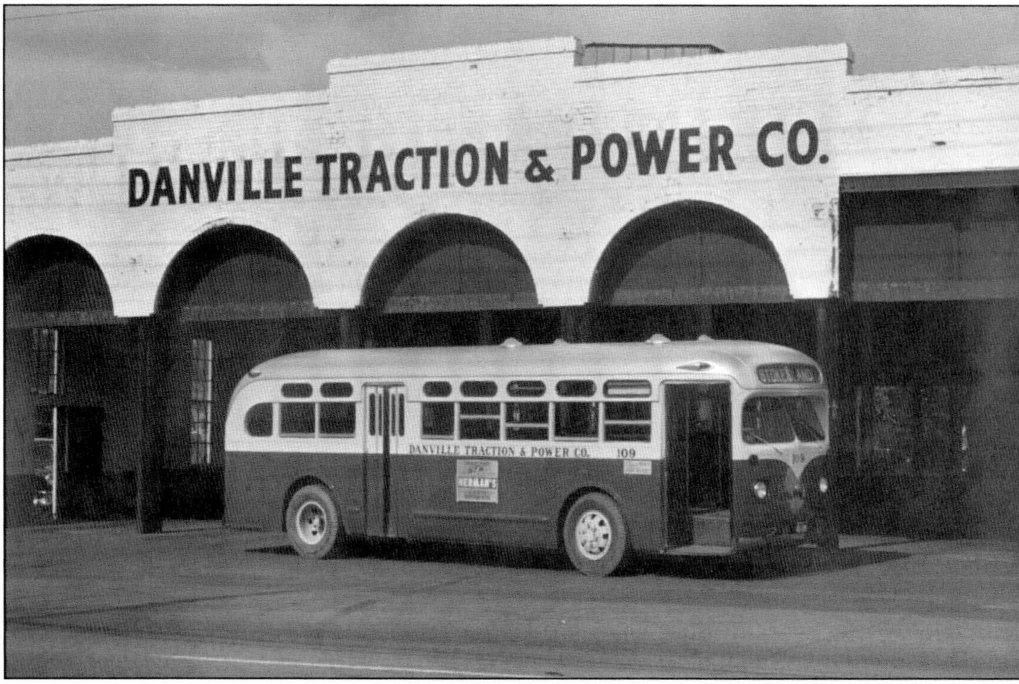

In 1900, the Danville Street Car Company constructed a carbarn on South Main Street at Stokes Street. Enlarged a few years later, it eventually housed 34 electric streetcars and provided enough space for company offices, as well as maintenance and repair areas. The business had formerly operated out of an old building on Craghead Street. (Courtesy of Jane Carter.)

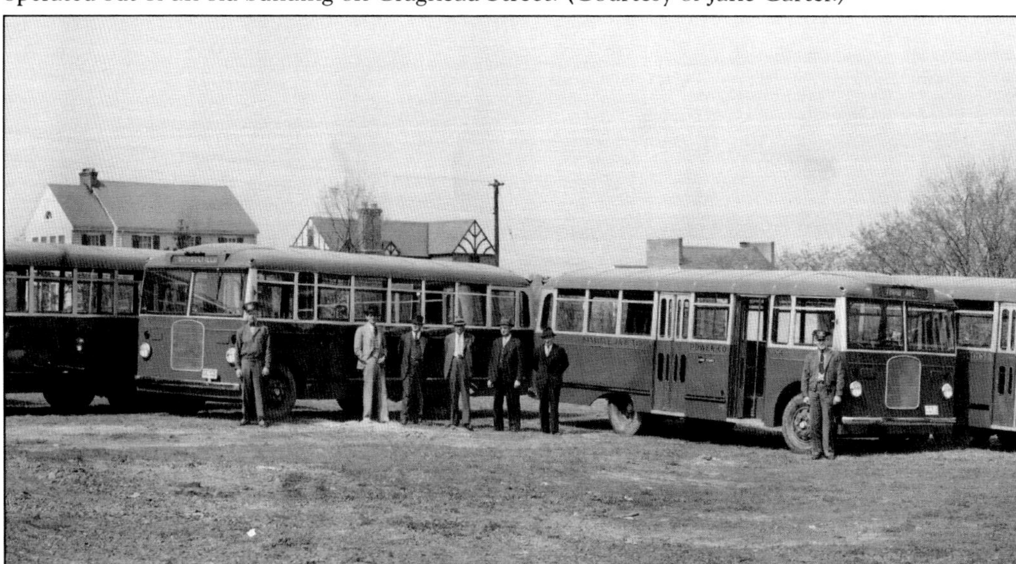

By 1938, streetcar transportation gave way to public buses and private automobiles not dependent on tracks and prescribed routes. The Danville Traction & Power Company stored their fleet of modern buses in the carbarn on South Main and Stokes Streets. Newspapers of the day extolled the greater comfort and reduced noise the new buses afforded to passengers. (Courtesy of Jane Carter.)

Five

MISCELLANY

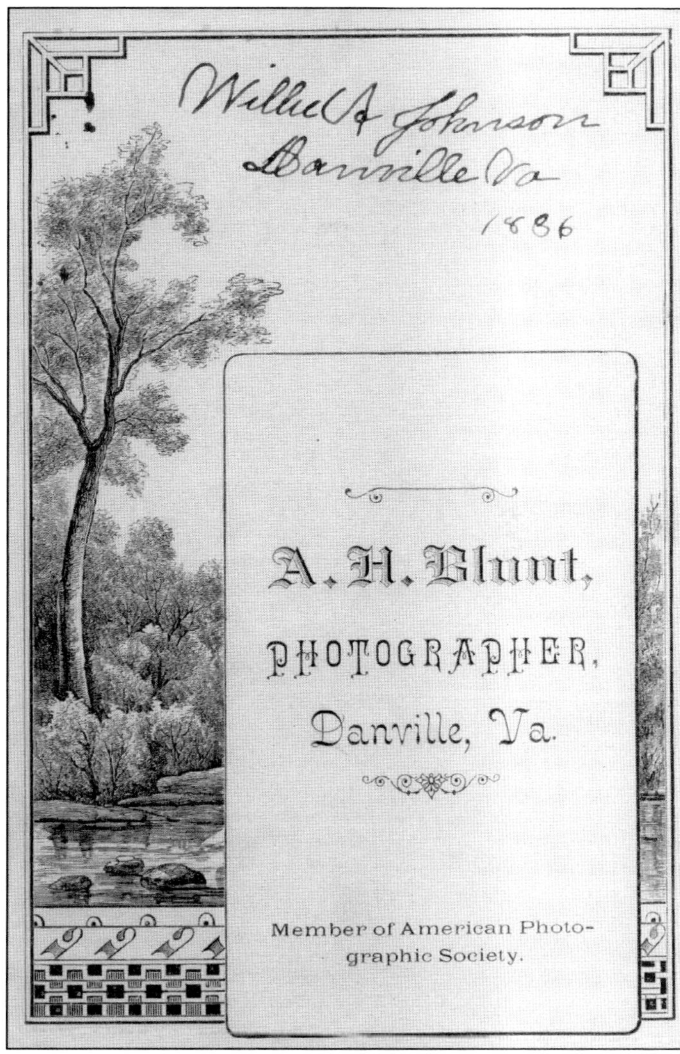

By the mid-1880s, photographers took advantage of the larger size of cabinet cards to advertise on the backs, as shown here on the reverse side of a portrait. From 1879 to 1886, Anthony H. Blunt enjoyed a popular business in Danville. He then moved to Richmond, where, years later, he took his own life in 1912. (Courtesy of the Danville Museum of Fine Arts and History.)

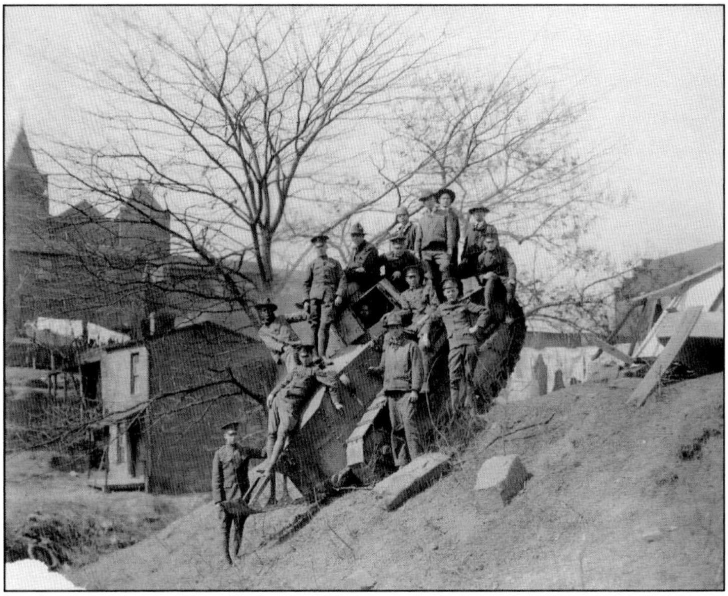

For the fifth anniversary of the end of World War I, Danville held an Armistice Day celebration on November 11, 1923. Here, a local tank company waits above Spring Street, just behind the old YMCA, in preparation for the patriotic parade. A speech by New York senator Royal S. Copeland and music by the Riverside & Dan River Mills Band, led by professor Joseph Vezzetti, preceded the parade. (Photograph by Leon Taylor.)

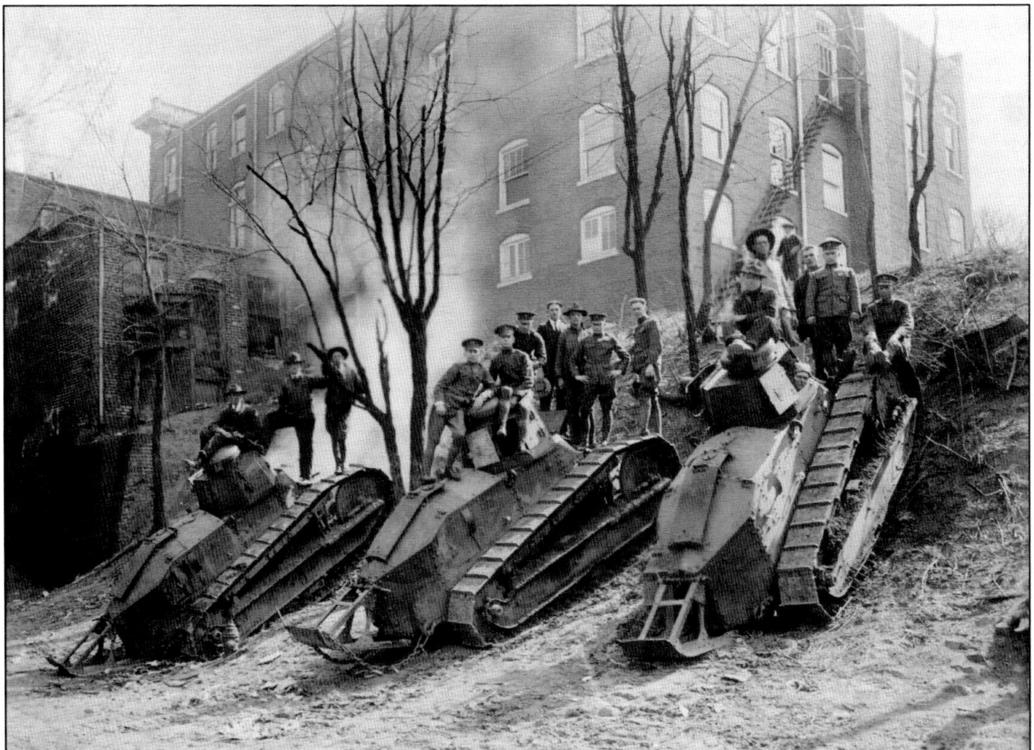

The Armistice Day parade participants included Danville Military Institute cadets, who presumably also manned the tank company behind the YMCA, as well as local companies of the National Guard, Army nurses, Confederate veterans, and members of the American Legion. Other groups participating in the parade included Boy and Girl Scouts, a hospital company, high school and college students, members of the Daughters of the American Revolution and United Daughters of the Confederacy, and Red Cross workers. (Photograph by Leon Taylor.)

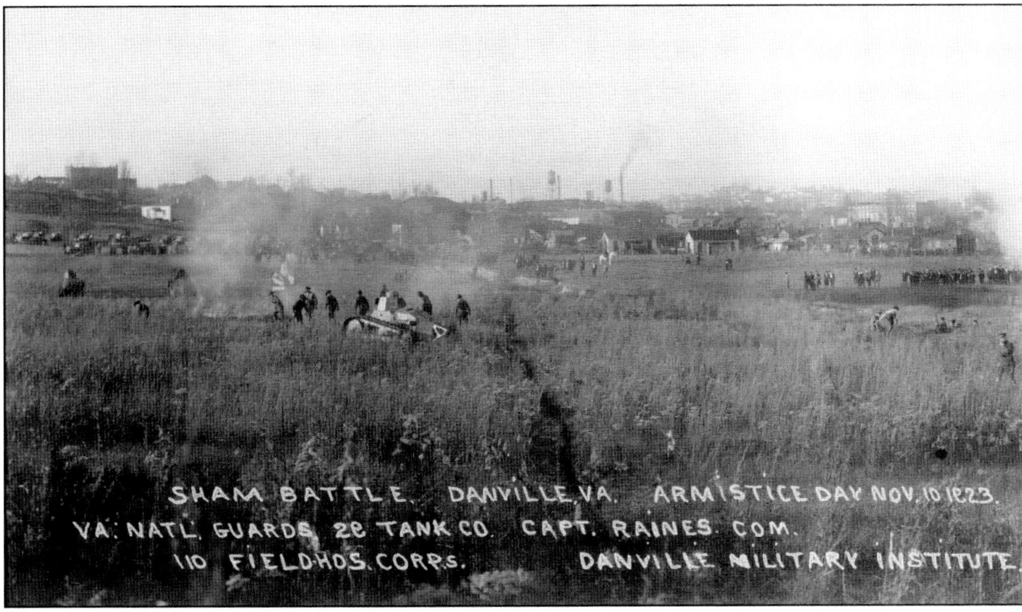

On November 10, 1923, units from the Virginia National Guard and Danville Military Institute staged a sham battle at the old fairgrounds beyond the railway station. Beginning at 3:30 p.m. and lasting about an hour, this spectacular reenactment was something new to Danville, and thousands gathered to watch. Two open streetcars requested by the American Legion transported female students from Averett and Stratford Colleges to the scene. (Photograph by Leon Taylor.)

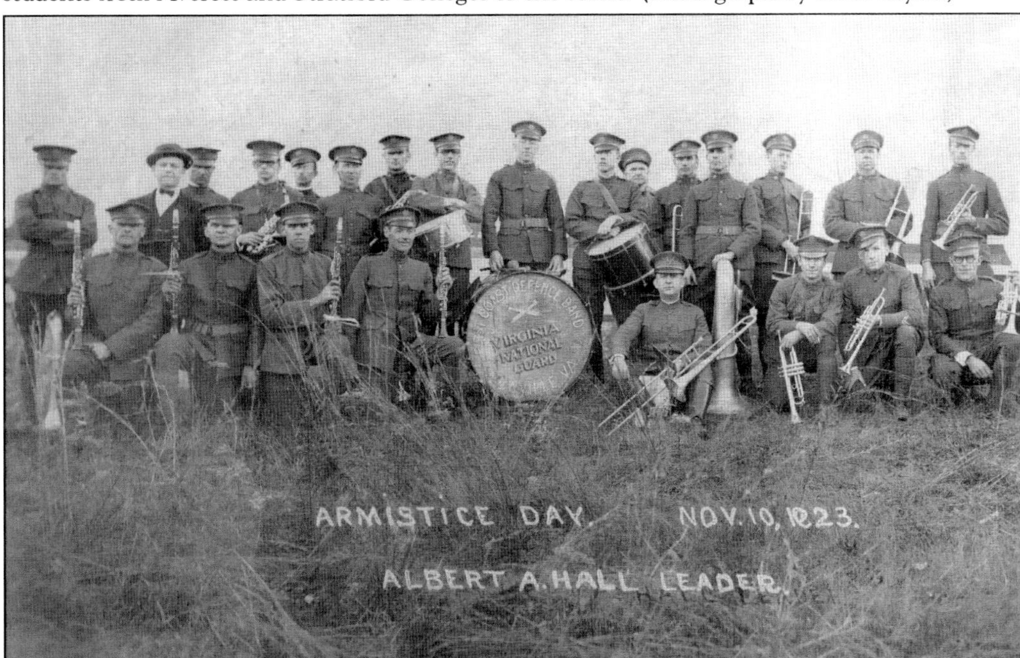

A flare from the "enemy" stronghold opened the battle. The enemy opened fire, and, after several skirmishes, the attacking forces gained the upper hand. A final flare announcing the Allied victory concluded the event, followed by a rendition of the national anthem by the Virginia National Guard band under the leadership of Albert A. Hall. (Photograph by Leon Taylor.)

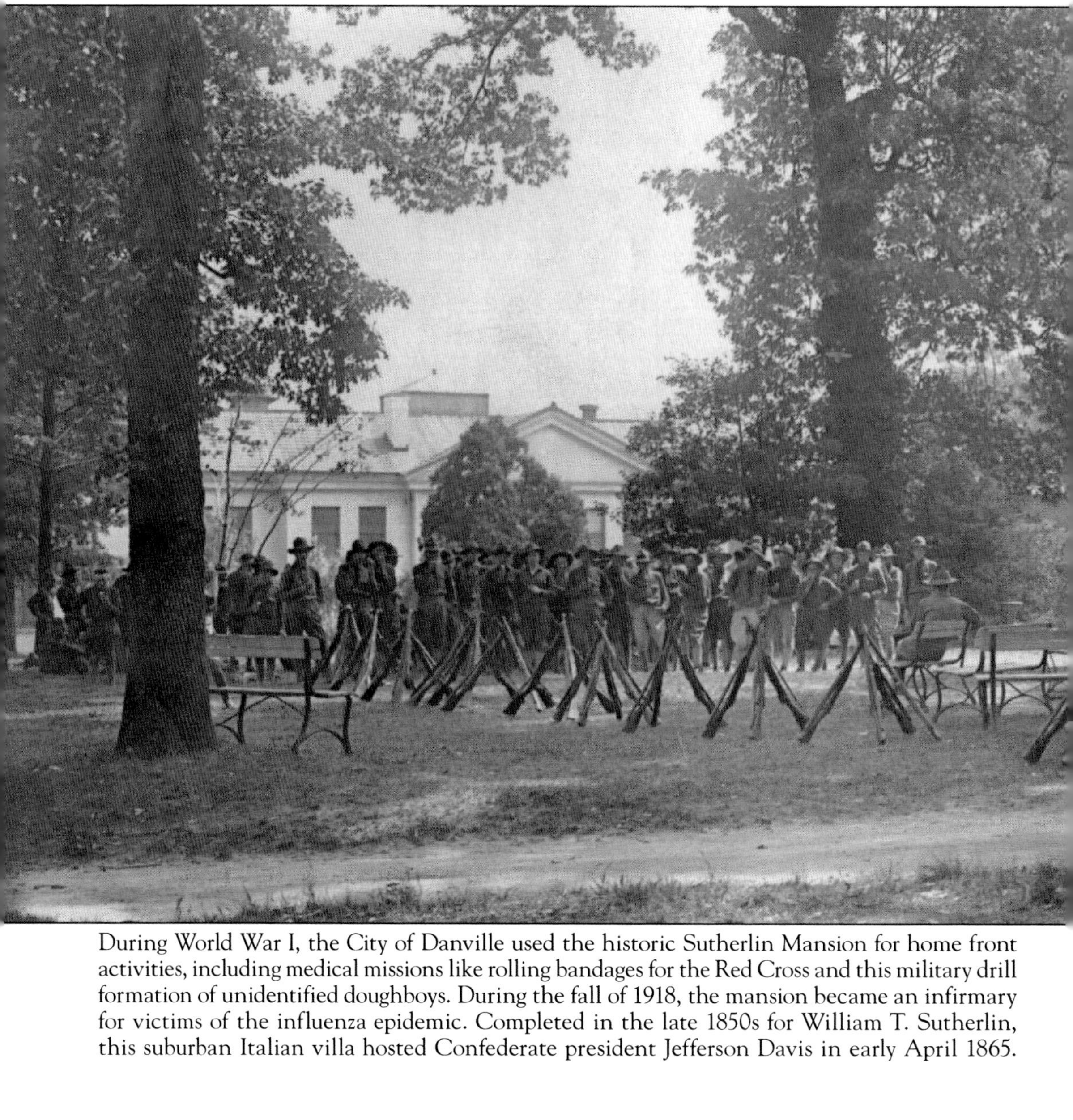

During World War I, the City of Danville used the historic Sutherlin Mansion for home front activities, including medical missions like rolling bandages for the Red Cross and this military drill formation of unidentified doughboys. During the fall of 1918, the mansion became an infirmary for victims of the influenza epidemic. Completed in the late 1850s for William T. Sutherlin, this suburban Italian villa hosted Confederate president Jefferson Davis in early April 1865.

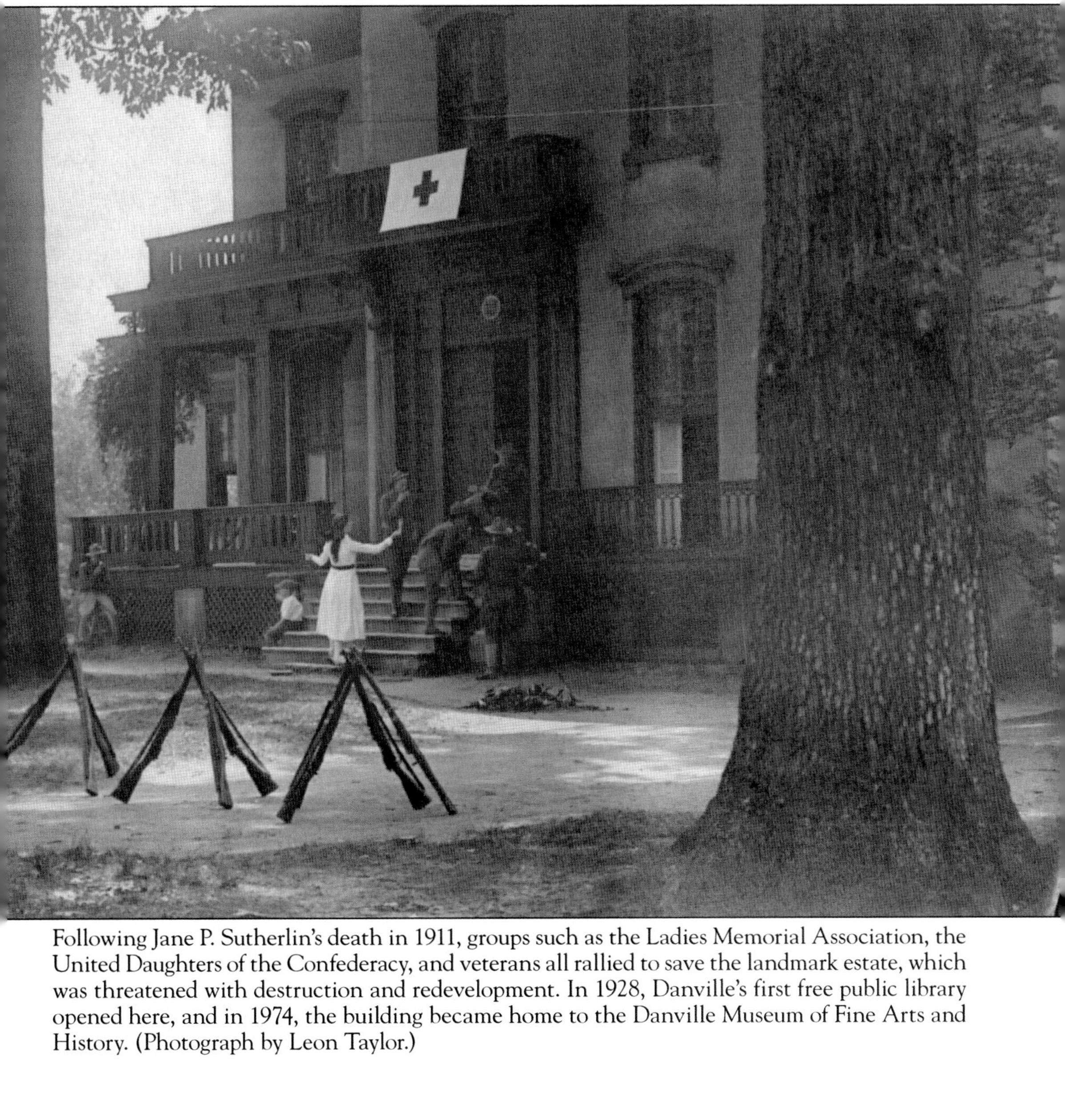

Following Jane P. Sutherlin's death in 1911, groups such as the Ladies Memorial Association, the United Daughters of the Confederacy, and veterans all rallied to save the landmark estate, which was threatened with destruction and redevelopment. In 1928, Danville's first free public library opened here, and in 1974, the building became home to the Danville Museum of Fine Arts and History. (Photograph by Leon Taylor.)

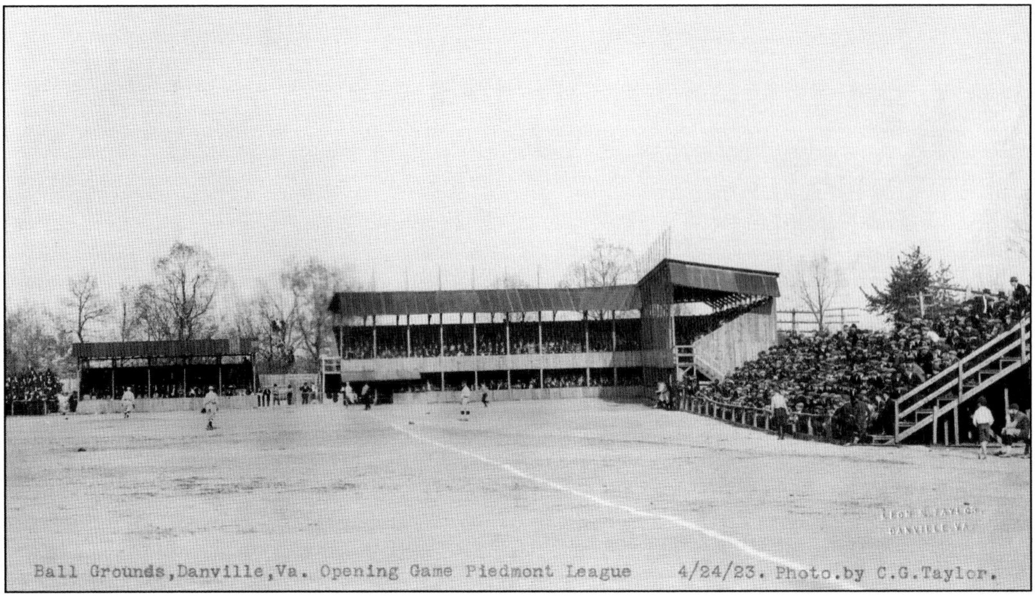

April 24, 1923, ushered in the fourth season of minor league baseball for Danville's Piedmont League club. The Danville team, led by owner/manager Herb Murphy, won their first game against High Point. Clinton G. Taylor, who worked for his brother Leon Taylor, photographed the opening game. After Danville mayor Harry Wooding tossed the first ball, umpire Joseph Ferguson shouted to the crowd, "Play ball." (Photograph by C.G. Taylor.)

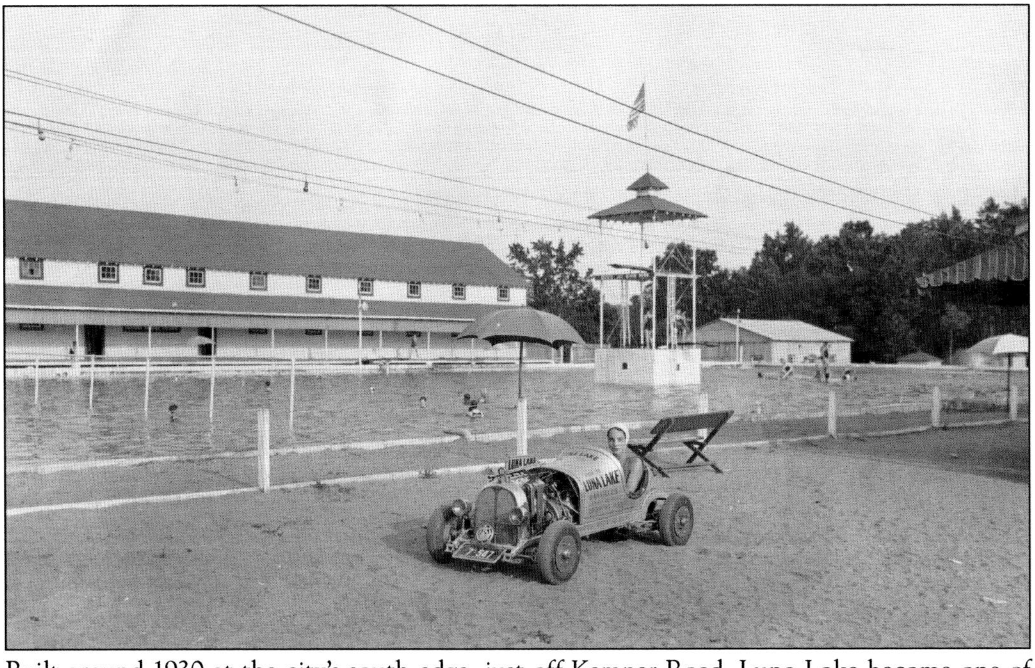

Built around 1930 at the city's south edge, just off Kemper Road, Luna Lake became one of Danville's popular recreational complexes. A high diving platform, coupled with the pleasures of its famed food pavilion, delighted bathers who crowded around Luna Lake's large swimming pool summer after summer. Even after the bathhouse burned down in 1948, the pool remained a favorite spot until its demise in the 1960s. (Photograph by Leon Taylor.)

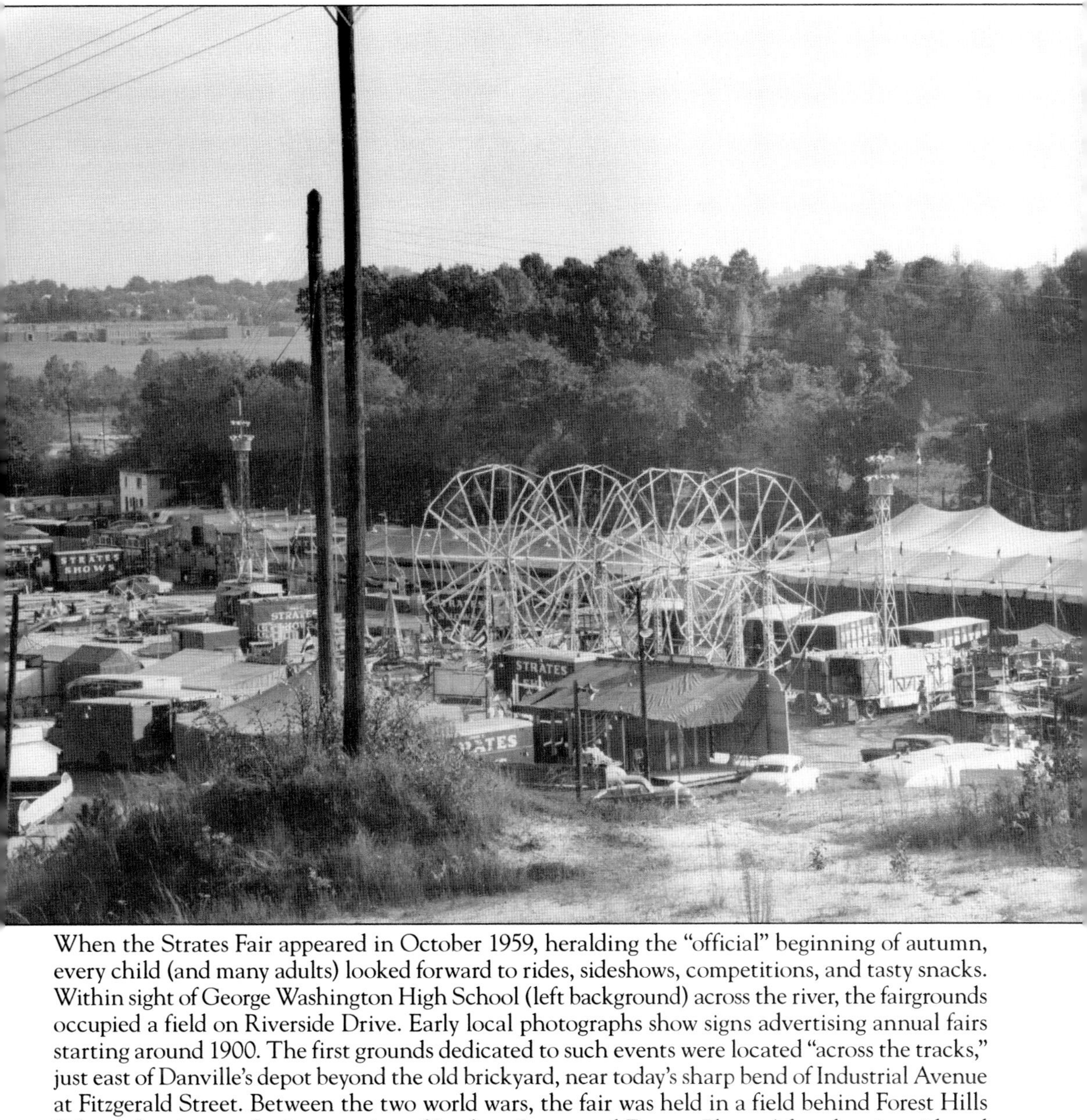

When the Strates Fair appeared in October 1959, heralding the "official" beginning of autumn, every child (and many adults) looked forward to rides, sideshows, competitions, and tasty snacks. Within sight of George Washington High School (left background) across the river, the fairgrounds occupied a field on Riverside Drive. Early local photographs show signs advertising annual fairs starting around 1900. The first grounds dedicated to such events were located "across the tracks," just east of Danville's depot beyond the old brickyard, near today's sharp bend of Industrial Avenue at Fitzgerald Street. Between the two world wars, the fair was held in a field behind Forest Hills School that is now the intersection of Lockett Street and Fenton Place. After the city widened River Street into Riverside Drive in 1947, annual fairs were held at the junction of Riverside and Old Piney Forest Road until 1970, when Central Boulevard cut through that property, part of which later became King's Fairground Plaza (shopping center). Today, the combined Danville-Pittsylvania County fairgrounds stretch over many acres well east of the city on State Route 62 toward Milton, North Carolina. (Photograph by John Tate; courtesy of the Danville Historical Society.)

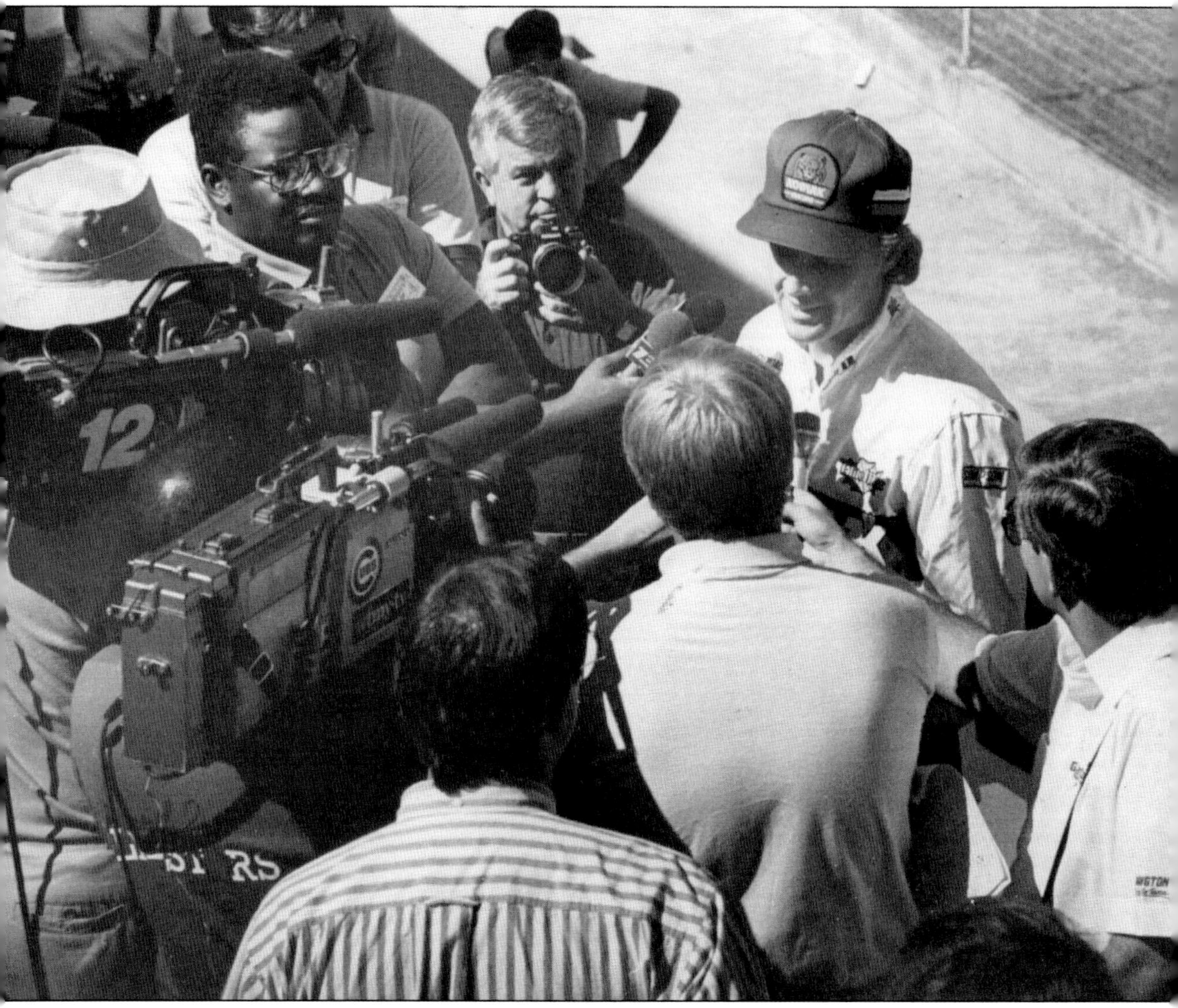

In this 1980s image, NASCAR racing legend Rusty Wallace fields questions from the press at the Martinsville Speedway. Veteran newspaper photographer Leon Townsend (center, holding film camera) focused on Wallace with his trusty camera while area television affiliates from Winston-Salem and Greensboro, North Carolina, rolled tape for upcoming evening news telecasts. Townsend followed every local news story for more than five decades. He had a keen eye for a perfect shot to go along with a story, and he would go to any length to get it right. Near the end of his career, Townsend compiled a 50-year collection of his photographs for the *Register & Bee*, which they published in 2004 as *Decades on the Dan*. In the pictorial book, Townsend included numerous images of local people, notable places, and historic events in and around the Danville community. (Photograph by Richard T. Davis.)

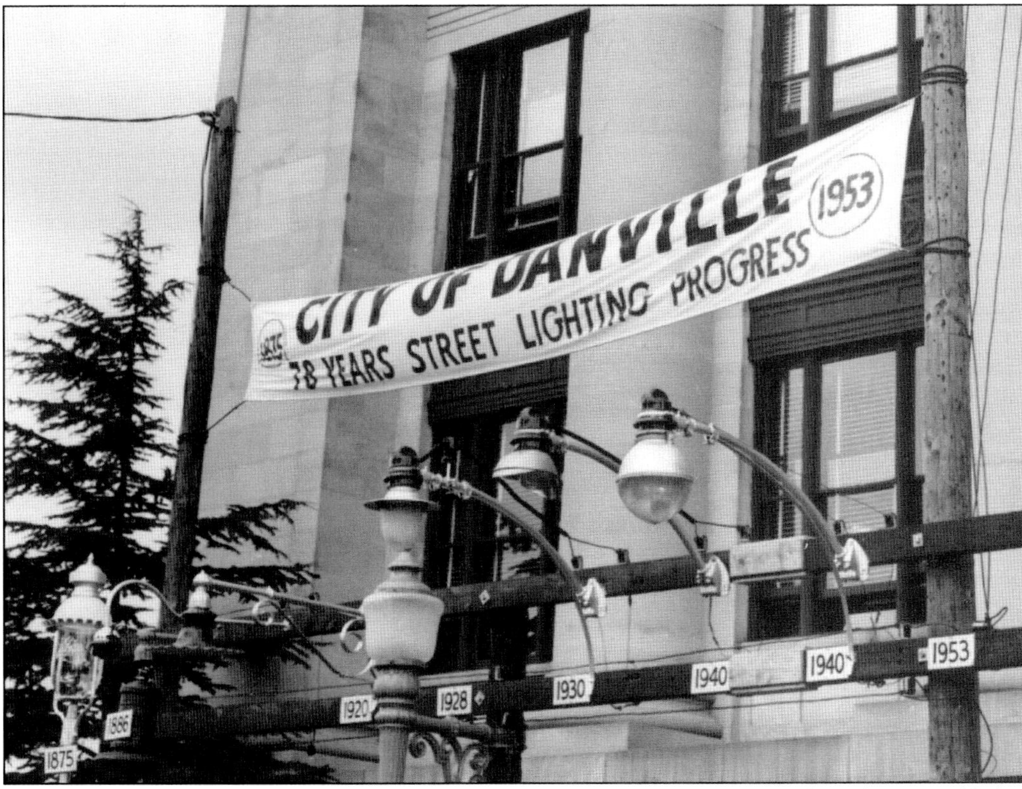

Danville celebrated "78 Years of Street Lighting Progress" on June 5, 1953, when the city added its first mercury-vapor lights on Main Street. Installed from the North Main Street hill to Schoolfield Drive, these high-intensity lights offered six times the illumination of previous lamps. A display in front of city hall showed examples of streetlights through the decades, starting with the open-flame gaslights of 1875. (Photograph by Arnold Turner.)

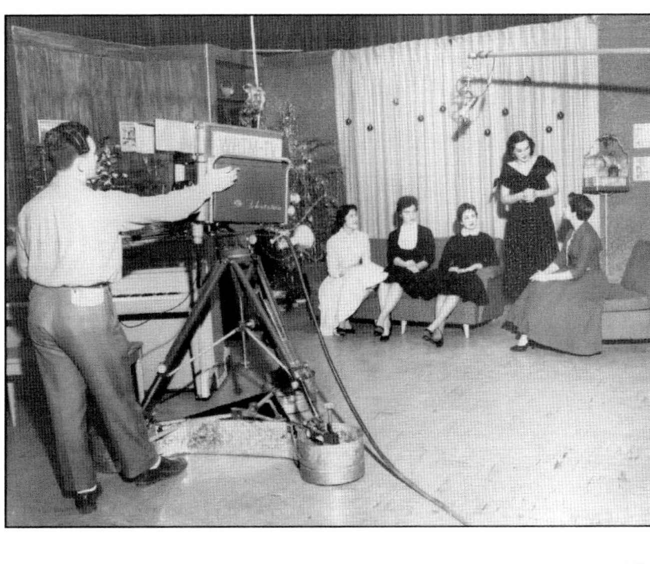

Television's moving images offered an exciting alternative or enhancement to traditional still photography. Averett College's longtime theater director, Elizabeth Smith, hosted *Birdcage*, a talk show on WBTM's short-lived television experiment. Broadcast from the radio station's then-new Grove Street studios, UHF Channel 24 never attracted a national network affiliate during its short run from February to December 1954. (Photograph by John Tate; courtesy of the Danville Historical Society.)

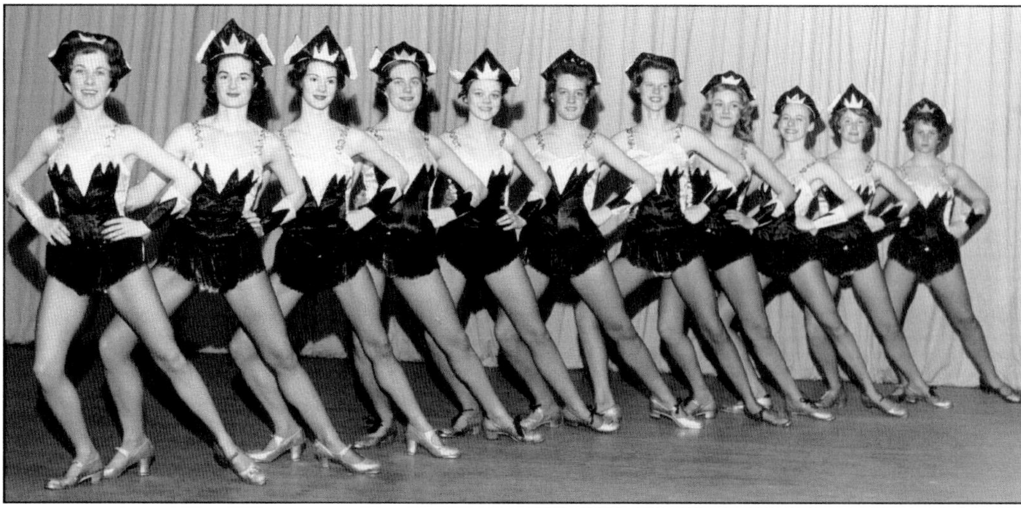

Anne Boyer brought dancing to Danville when she opened a studio on Watson Street in 1937. Pictured in 1960 standing in position for their line dance are, from left to right, Lucy Gayle Cousins, Meredith Wilson, Linda Wilson, Joan Smart, Florence Tompkins, Anne Mayo, unidentified, Carol Hogg, Judy Pointer, unidentified, and Debbie Smith. Every student hoped to be included in a number with high kicks. (Photograph by Carl Furgurson Jr.; courtesy of Meredith Gravely.)

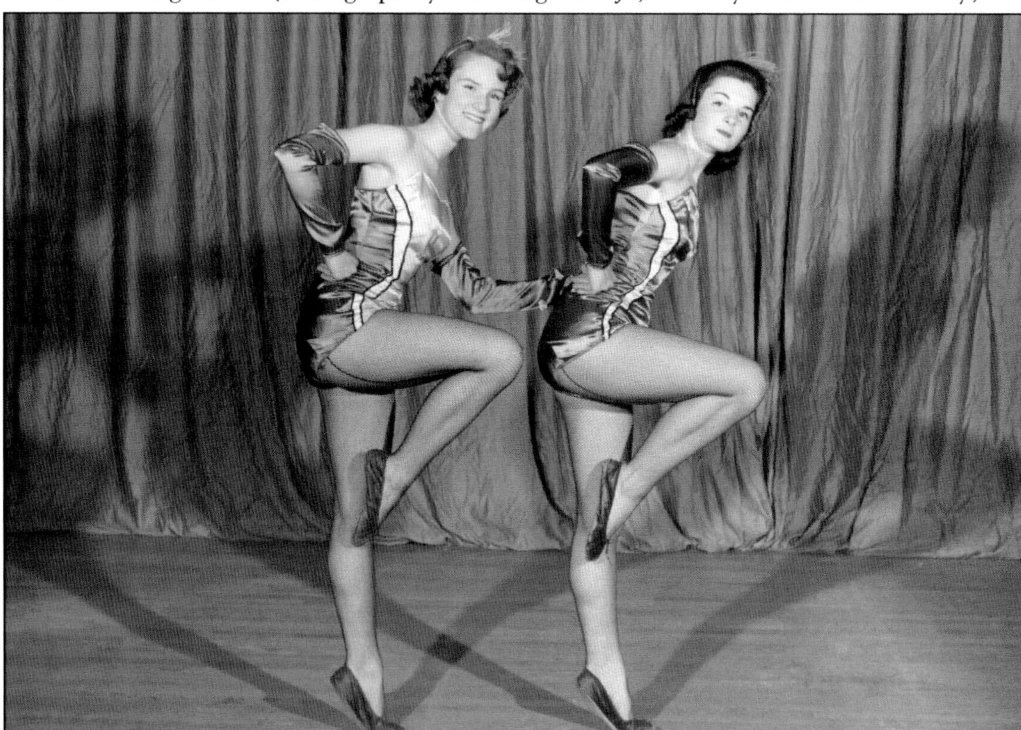

Jane Williams (left) and Meredith Wilson pose in dancing costumes for the Anne Boyer dance recital of 1960. When Boyer retired in 1973 after a lengthy career instructing pupils from the entire community, two of her former students— Martha Fowlkes and Meredith Wilson Gravely—continued her work with studios of their own. (Photograph by John Williams; courtesy of Meredith Gravely.)

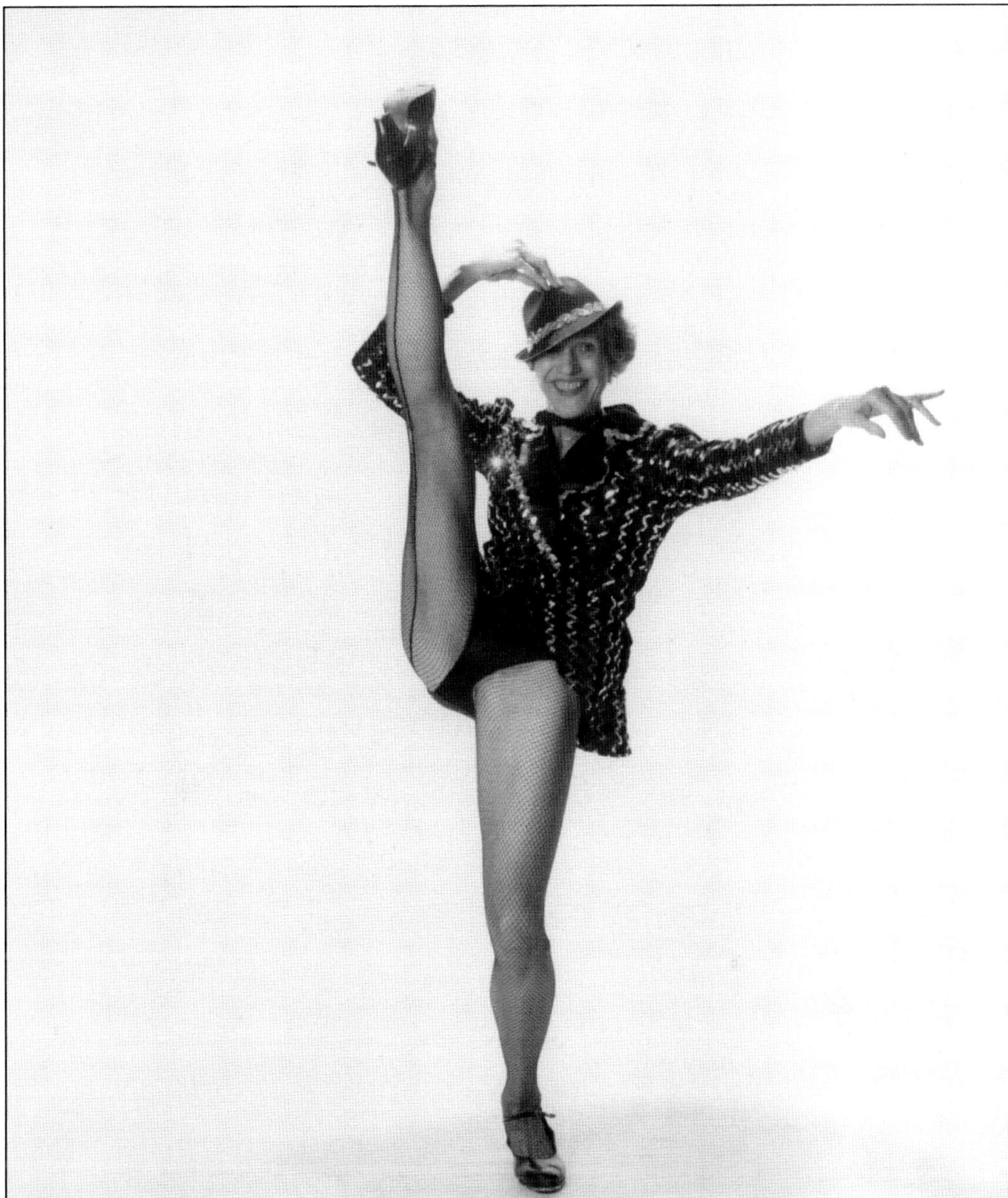

A native of Danville, Martha Ann Houlton was the daughter of Ruth and Fred O. Houlton, a tile setter living on Edwin Court. In 1951, Martha married William Temple Fowlkes Jr. at Mount Vernon Methodist Church. From 1954 to 1956, the couple resided in Tehran, Iran, where Bill Fowlkes was employed by the US Department of State as an assistant attaché at the US Embassy. During those years, Martha learned the intricacies of exotic belly dancing. Martha Fowlkes began her illustrious dance career at the age of eight as one of Anne Boyer's pupils. She went on to perform with the Rockettes in New York City. Martha took over the Boyer studio on Watson Street in 1974 and taught until 1990, when she moved to Riverside Drive. After 28 years of teaching, she retired and sold the studio in 2001 to Ann Pflugshaupt and Lisa Michaels Jones. (Photograph by Mike Compson.)

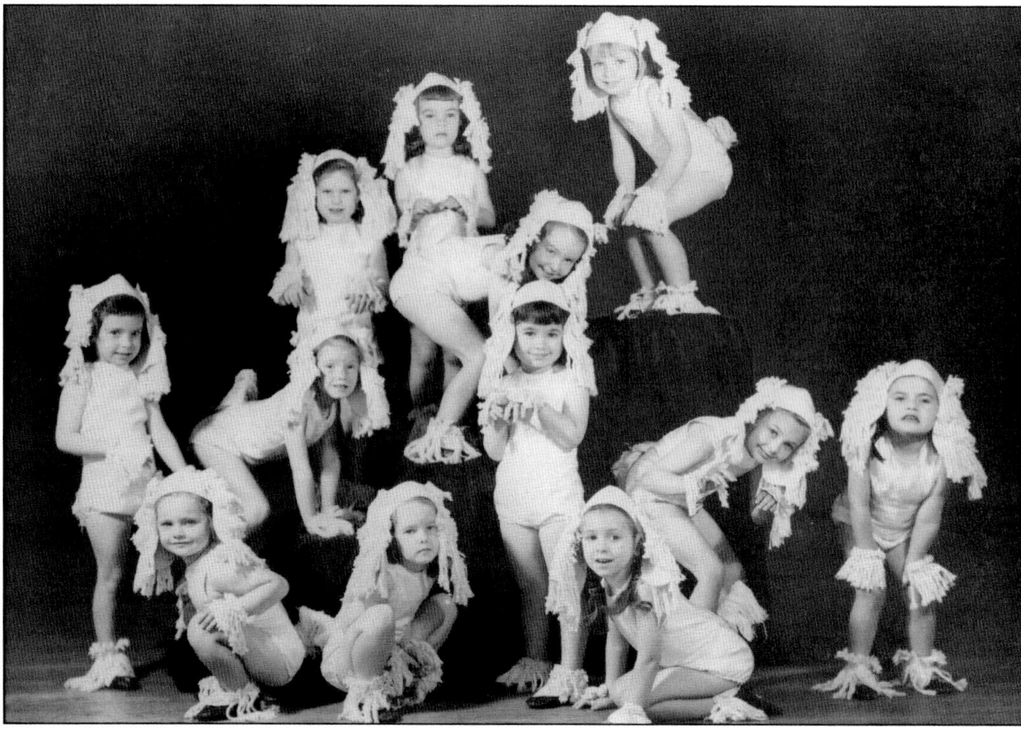

Anne Boyer's School of the Dance presented a delightful recital every spring. These young girls, dressed as cocker spaniels, were just one of the acts in her 1946 show, "Pied Piper of Pittsylvania." From left to right are (first row, on the floor) Patsy Riley, Clara Garrett, and Lettie Hiller; (second row) unidentified, Mildred Millner, Betty Lou Giles, unidentified, and unidentified; (third row) unidentified; (fourth row) unidentified, Libby McMann, and Gracie Turbeville. (Photograph by Raymond Hitchcock.)

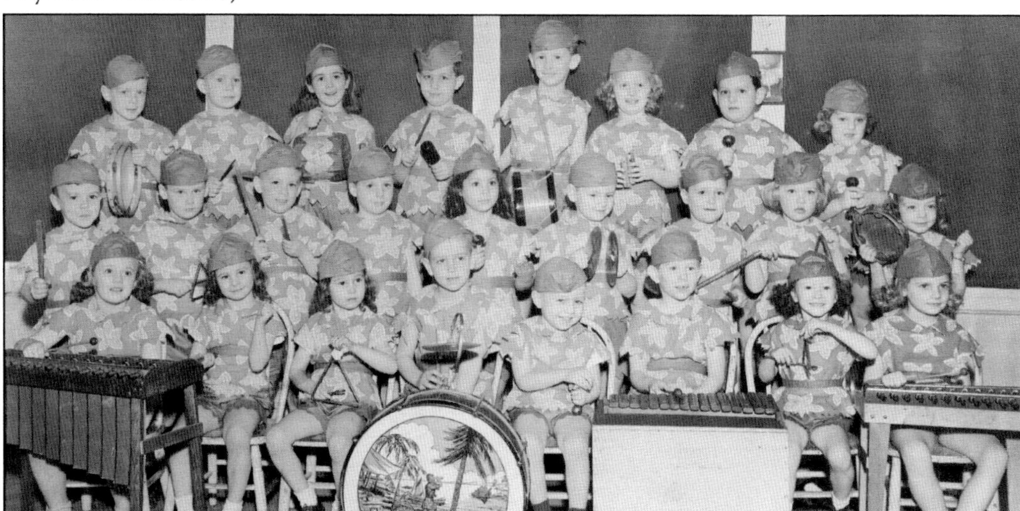

One of Danville's oldest preschool groups was the Peter Pan Kindergarten, managed for decades by Eva S. McKinzie in her home at 237 Randolph Street. At the end of each year, the children entertained parents and friends with a musical revue. The class of 1947, seen here, donned Peter Pan costumes and played a variety of percussion instruments. (Photograph by Raymond Hitchcock.)

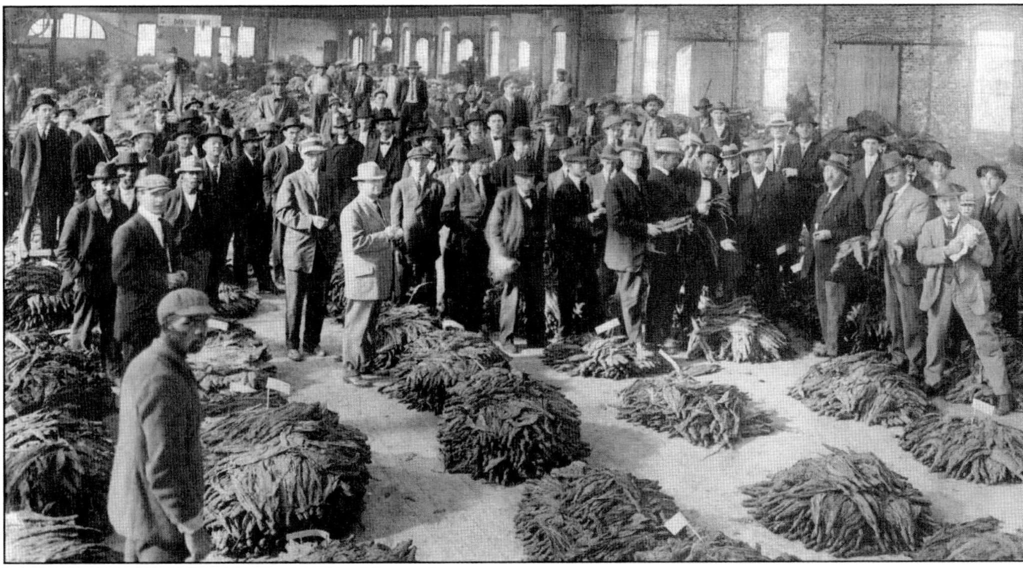

Crowded with farmers, buyers, ticket markers, an auctioneer, and warehousemen, this c. 1920 photograph reflects the heady anticipation of a big sale day in Danville's tobacco district. Auction warehouses—like Central and Exchange on North Union Street and Lee's and Acree's on Bridge Street—embraced the "Danville System" of selling loose leaf tobacco, which was introduced at Neal's Warehouse in 1858. (Courtesy of Gary Grant.)

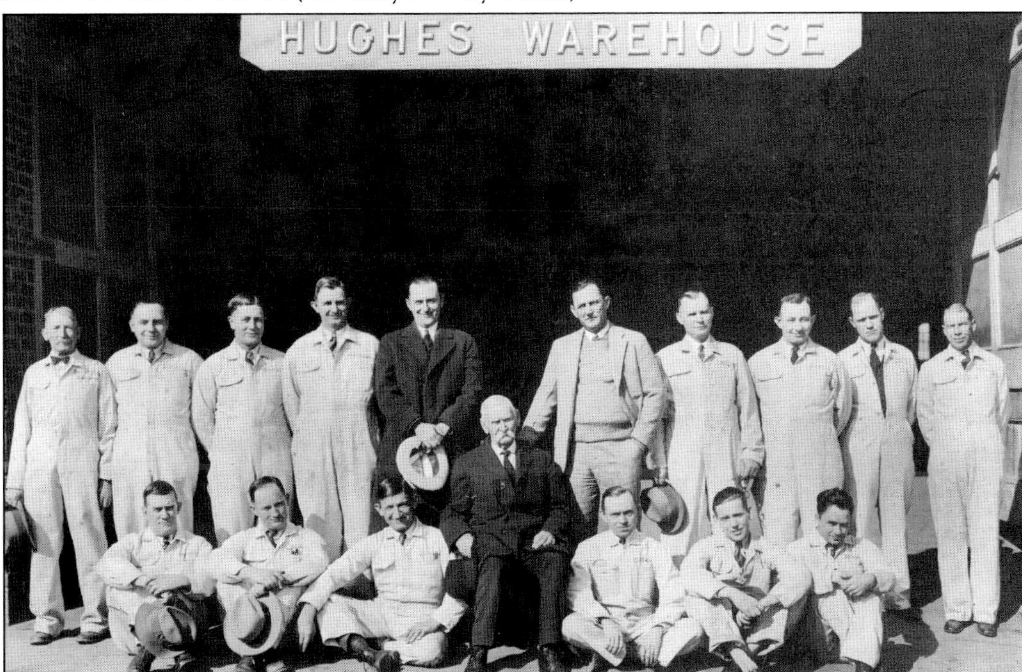

This 1927 group portrait at the W.T. Hughes tobacco auction warehouse on Loyal Street includes, from left to right, (first row) George Blair, Tom Pleasant, Ewart Collie, Capt. John G. Lea, Fred B. Holderby, Stephen McDaniel, and Hugh Moore; (second row) ? Powell, Fritz Anderson, Glen Hunt, Rosser Bradley, Harry Lea, Gorgon Tuggle, E.K. Barker, Jack Neal, Frank Hayes, and James Slade. (Photograph by Leon Taylor.)

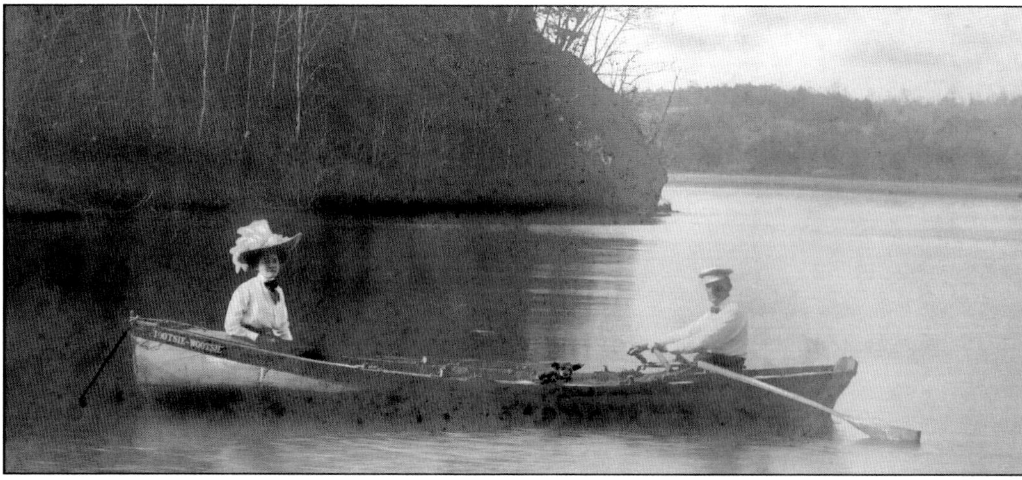

In 1908, four years after the completion of Schoolfield's hydropower dam, Harry Ficklen took advantage of the newly created lake to row his fiancée, Mary Louise Tucker, on the *Tootsie-Wootsie* in the shadow of House Rock above the Dan River. Ficklen wrote historical notes for *Art Work of Danville, Virginia*, the city's first pictorial album, published in 1903 by the Gravure Illustration Company. (Courtesy of the Langhorne House.)

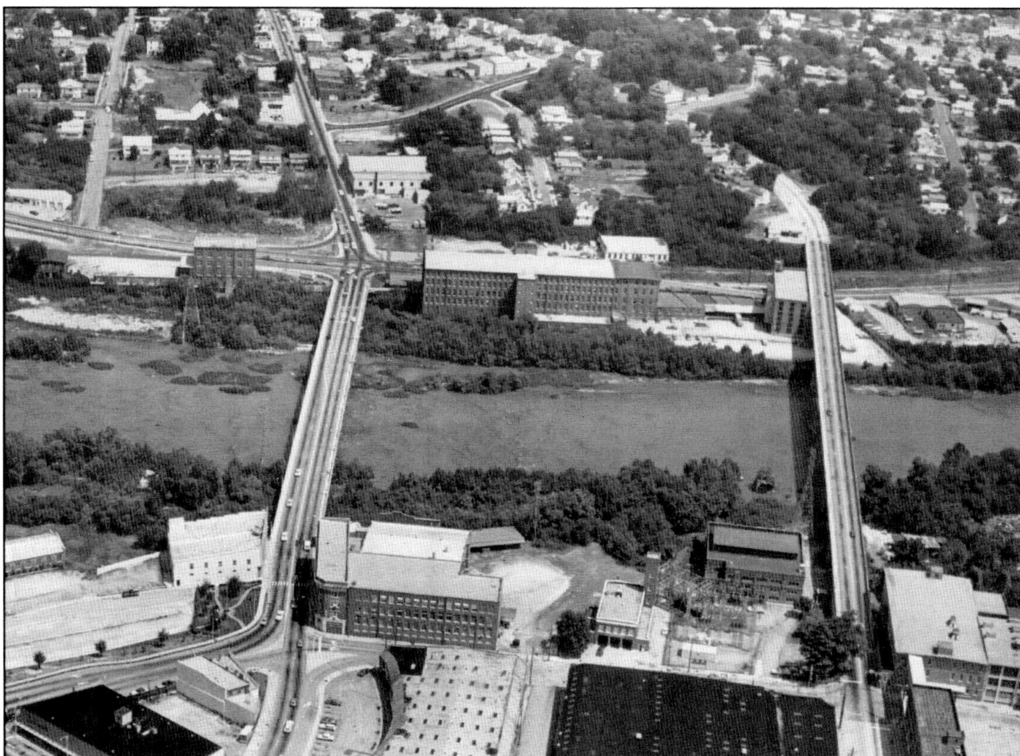

Circulating traffic for decades like blood through arteries, two bridges linked Danville's heart across the Dan River, where the city originated. Indiana-based bridge engineer Daniel B. Luten designed both the Main Street (left) and Worsham Street spans in the 1920s. The city recently dubbed Main Street's refurbished 1927 span—and its 2009 twin (at its left)—the Martin Luther King Jr. Bridge; the 1928 Worsham Bridge was then demolished. (Photograph by Richard T. Davis.)

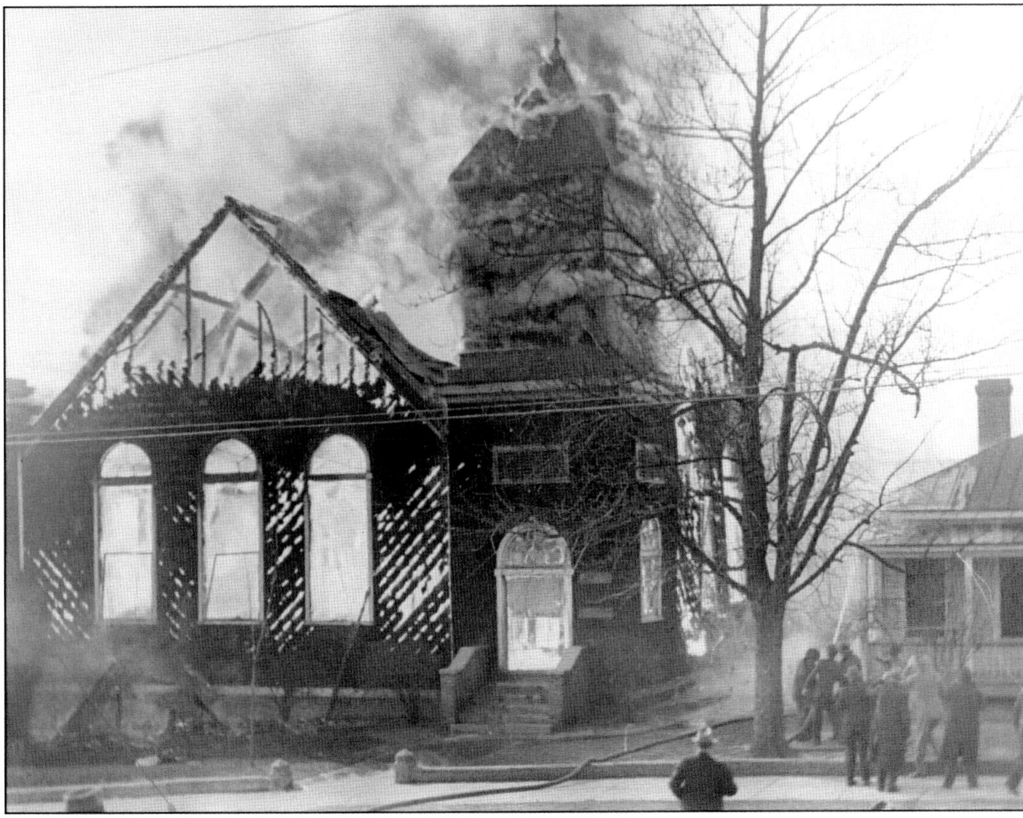

On Sunday, February 9, 1941, a fire broke out in the auditorium of Schoolfield Baptist Church. Fire units from Schoolfield and Danville tried to save the building, but a shortage of waterpower worked against them. When the fire reached the steeple, spectators said it looked like a flaming torch. Firemen saved the adjacent houses, but the church was a total loss. (Photograph by Robert Poett Garrett.)

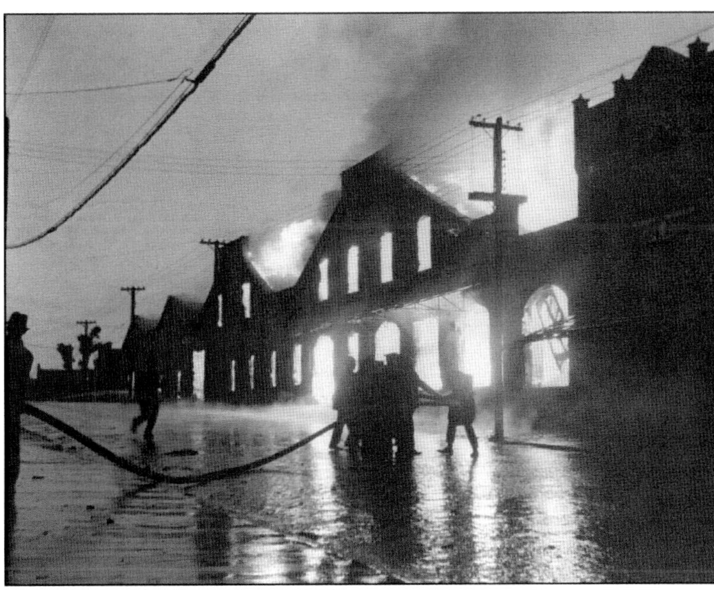

Called the worst blaze in 10 years, this May 14, 1938, fire on North Union Street gutted Holland's Warehouse and an adjoining building used by the Danville Hardware Company. Danville firemen also had to deal with high winds and heavy rain. The brick wall of the storage building collapsed onto Union Street, a further problem for firemen and police, who directed onlookers to safety. (Photograph by Julian Hoffman.)

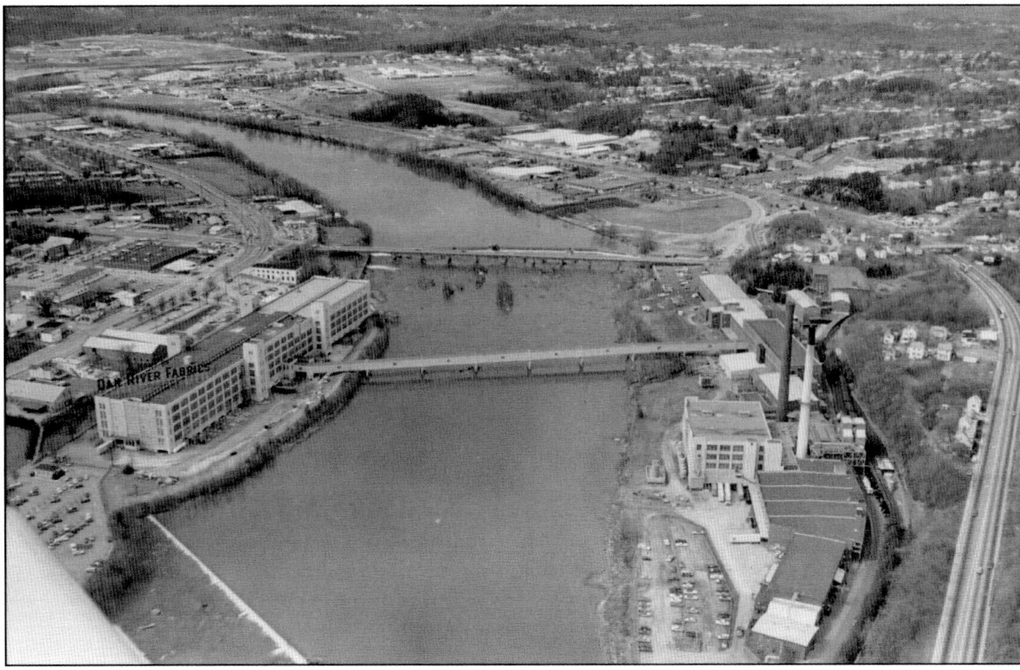

Dan River Inc. began as Riverside Cotton Mills in 1882 in a single building at the foot of the Main Street hill, the site of Danville's early tobacco inspection station. As business grew, the company added seven buildings on both sides of the river, as seen in this 1985 photograph. Dan River Inc. claimed that its c. 1920 span was the world's longest covered bridge. It linked Mill No. 8 (left) with the earlier Long Mill complex, which was destroyed in 2007. (Photograph by Richard T. Davis.)

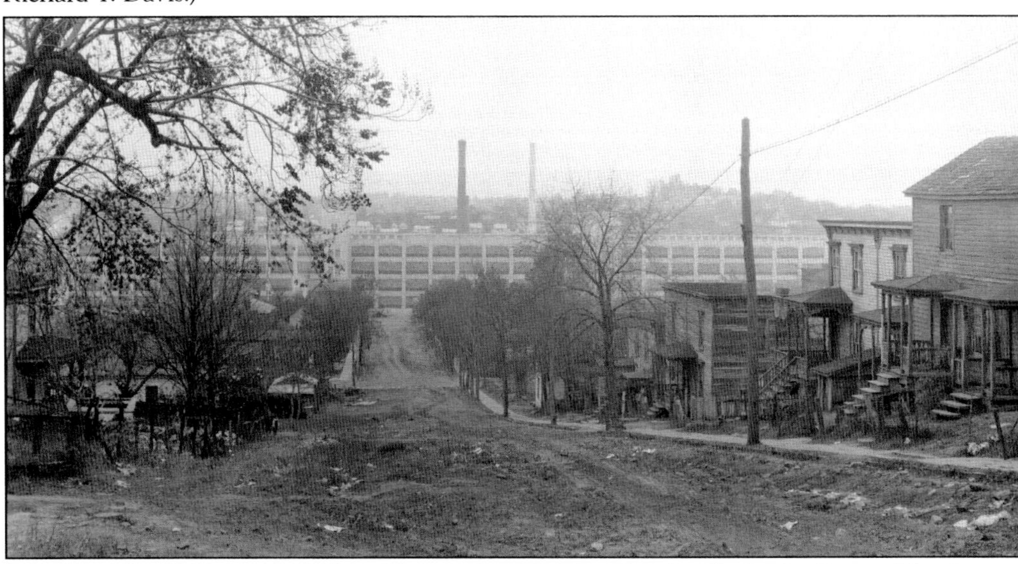

Mill No. 8 closed the river view from Monroe Street, a slope lined with the dwellings of shopkeepers and prosperous tradesmen in the area north of Ridge Street, which was sometimes called Mechanicsville. Aberthaw Construction Company, the contractor for Mill No. 8, commissioned this 1921 photograph of the mill, which had just been completed from plans created by the famed industrial engineering firm Lockwood, Greene, and Company. (Courtesy of Clara Fountain.)

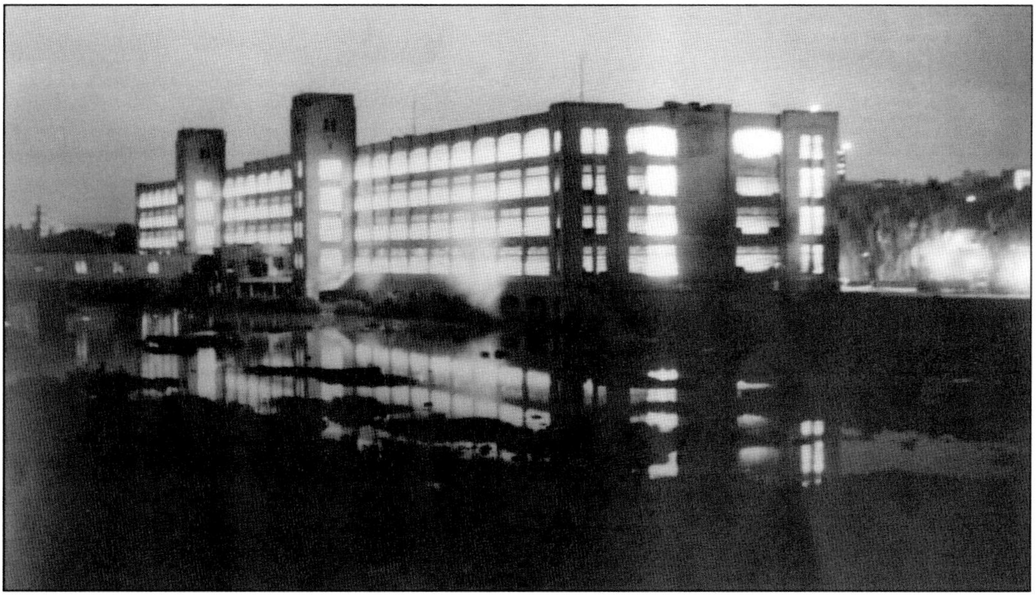

Built in 1921, Dan River Inc.'s steel-reinforced concrete monolith, Mill No. 8, completed the company's Riverside Division just upriver from where its first mill began production near the Main Street Bridge in 1882. Several years after this glowing 1937 image was created, workmen applied blue security paint to all the windows during World War II, a time when the company's fortunes soared with government orders for military fabric. (Photograph by Julian Hoffman.)

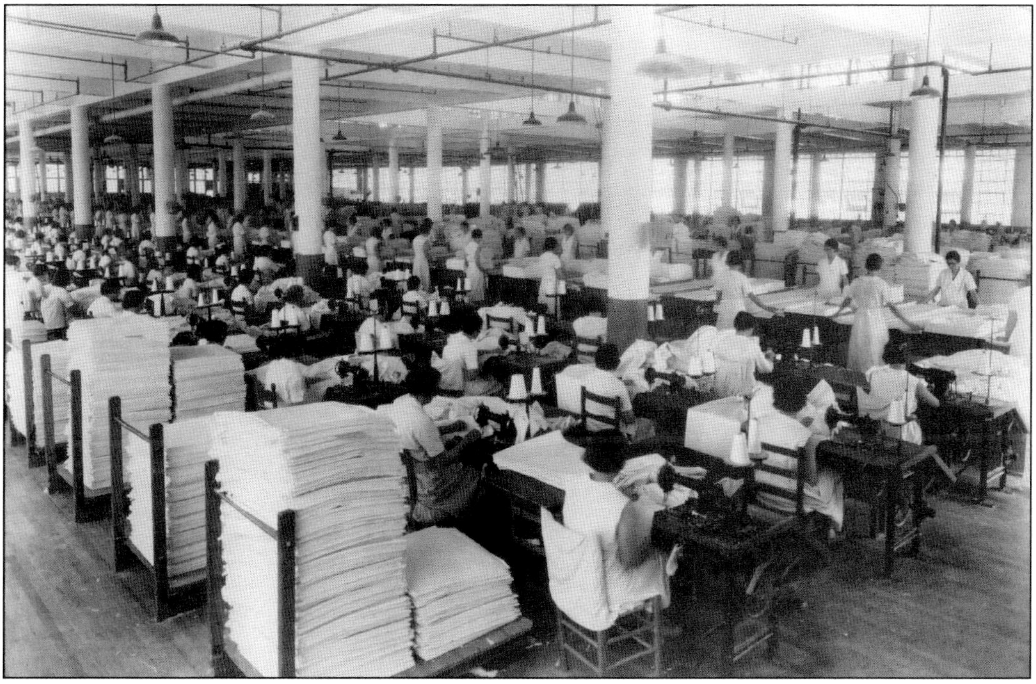

Mill No. 8's sometime nickname, the White Mill, referred not so much to its light-painted exterior but instead to the quantity of white—often called "greige" or undyed—fabrics woven inside the cavernous structure. Female employees sat at sewing tables for hours making sheets, pillowcases, and even diapers. (Courtesy of Clara Fountain.)

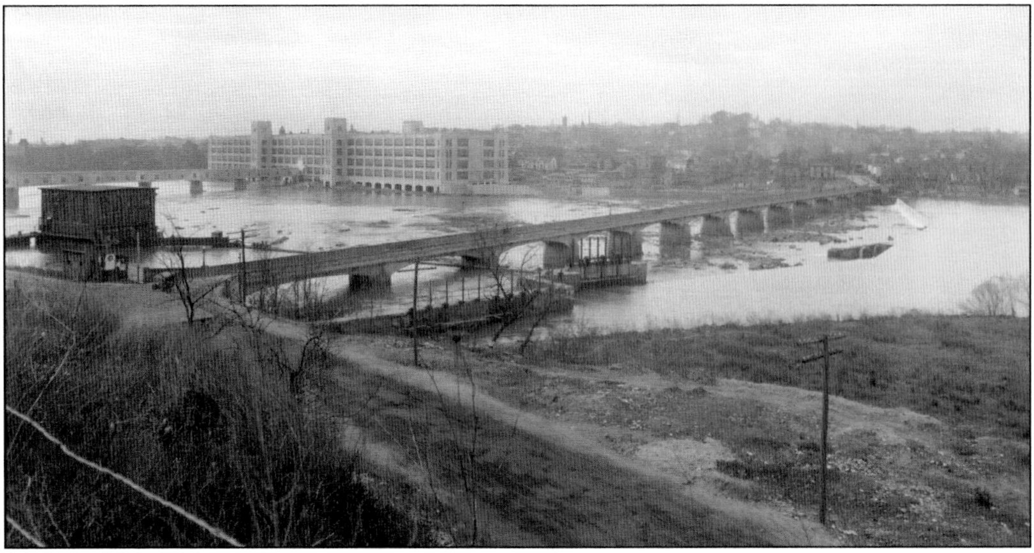

This concrete 1913 Union Street Bridge replaced a late-1800s covered wooden bridge that was a contemporary of the late-1870s Union Street dam. An earlier dam at this site was built in the early 1800s and made river transport accessible by way of a canal around Wynne's Falls. By the early 1880s, that canal was retrofitted with turbines that powered spinning frames and looms to drive production at Riverside Mills. (Courtesy of Clara Fountain.)

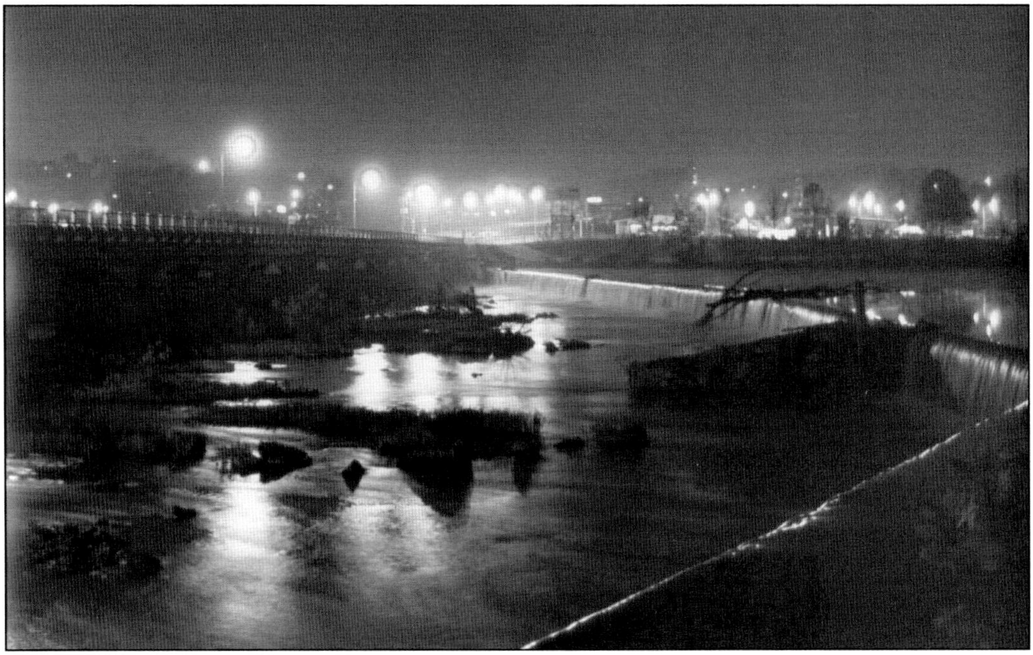

Hoping to capture the Union Street Bridge at night without cars or traffic, local photographer Bill Garrett stood beside the dam near Riverside Drive at 2:50 a.m. on a clear night in 1979 and shot this dramatic view. Garrett used his favorite roll film at the time, Kodak Panatomic-X. (Photograph by William H. Garrett.)

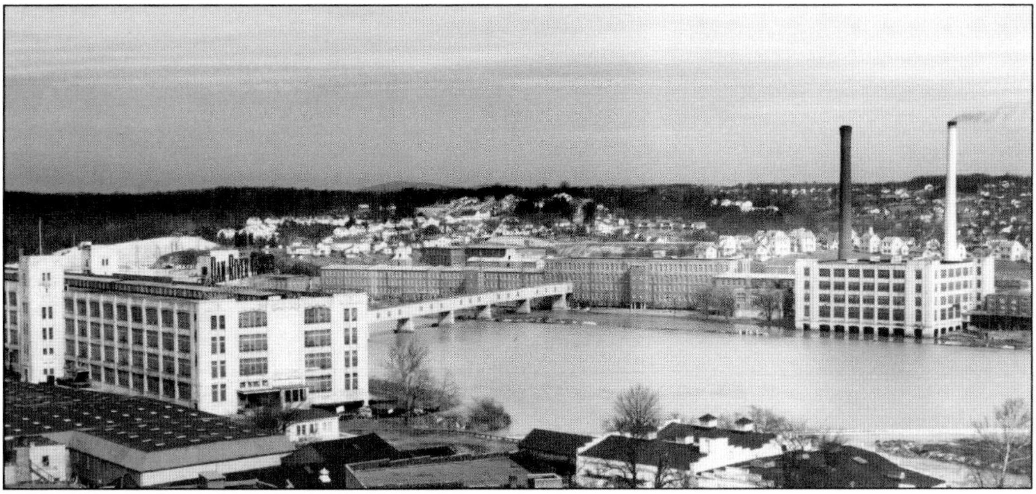

From 1885 to 1897, Riverside Cotton Mills built mills numbered two, three, five, and seven north of the Dan River between the Union Street and Main Street Bridges. The goods produced in the company's early years forged its reputation for plaid cotton fabrics, which became popular around the globe. This late-1940s photograph shows the massive Riverside division of Dan River Inc., presumably running at full tilt. (Photograph by Dempsey DeHart.)

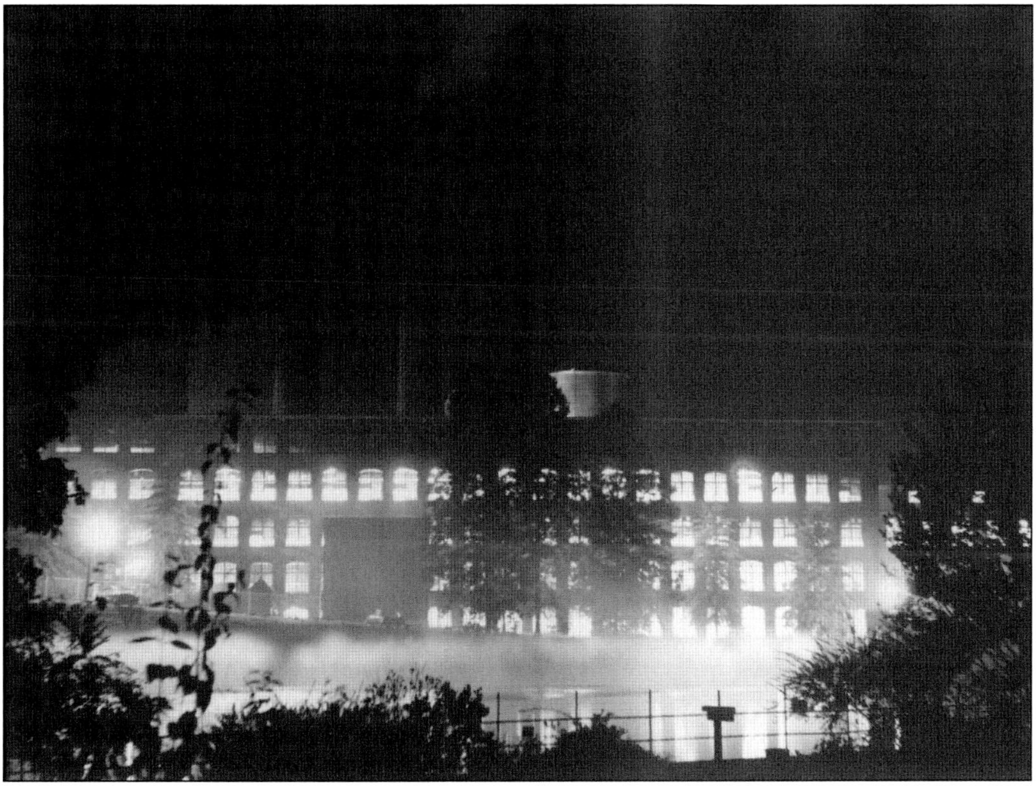

During the best of times, the Riverside and Schoolfield divisions of Dan River Inc. employed more than 14,000 people. The looms ran 24 hours a day, six days a week, with eight-hour shifts beginning at 8:00 a.m., 4:00 p.m., and 12:00 a.m. This Dan River plant at Schoolfield sounded a steam whistle to call workers to each shift. (Photograph by William E. Land.)

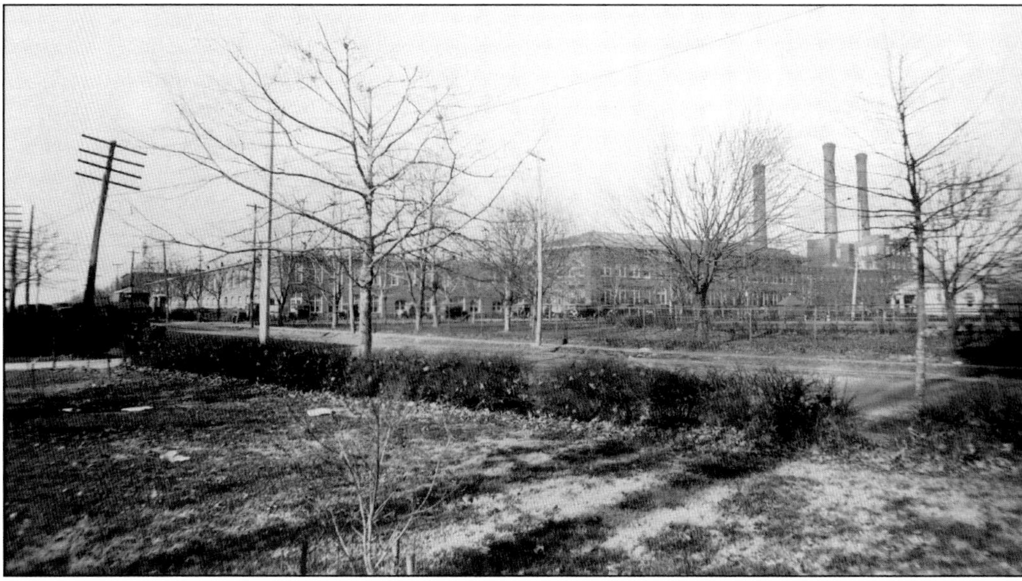

In the first decade of the 20th century, Danville investors created another cotton complex near the Dan River, and their village of Schoolfield grew up around it. By 1909, the older and newer divisions, Riverside and Schoolfield, merged to become the Riverside & Dan River Cotton Mills, the largest single-unit cotton mill in the world. In this c. 1930 image, Schoolfield's smokestacks loom behind the company's executive building (center). (Photograph by Leon Taylor.)

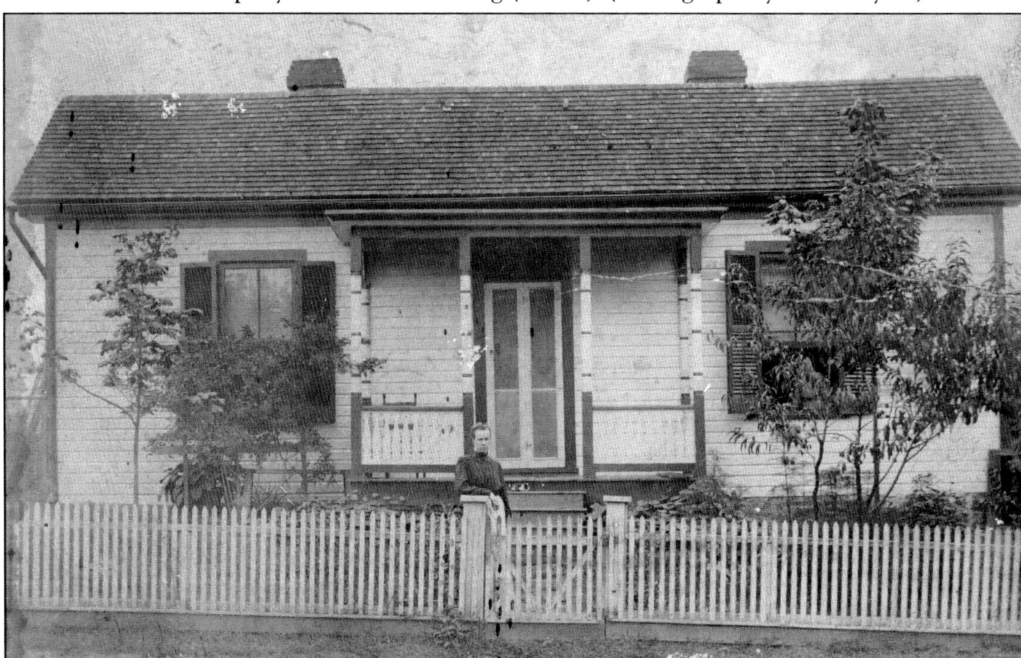

To make working in Schoolfield convenient and attractive, Dan River Cotton Mills provided the company's workforce affordable houses, completing the first 10 cottages along Park Avenue in 1903. By 1910, around 400 two-, four-, or six-room dwellings lined the streets of Schoolfield—namely Wood, Baltimore, Washington, Dallas, and Richmond Streets. Here, Elizabeth Forbes stands at the gate in front of her home at 133 Wood Avenue. (Courtesy of Dee Smith.)

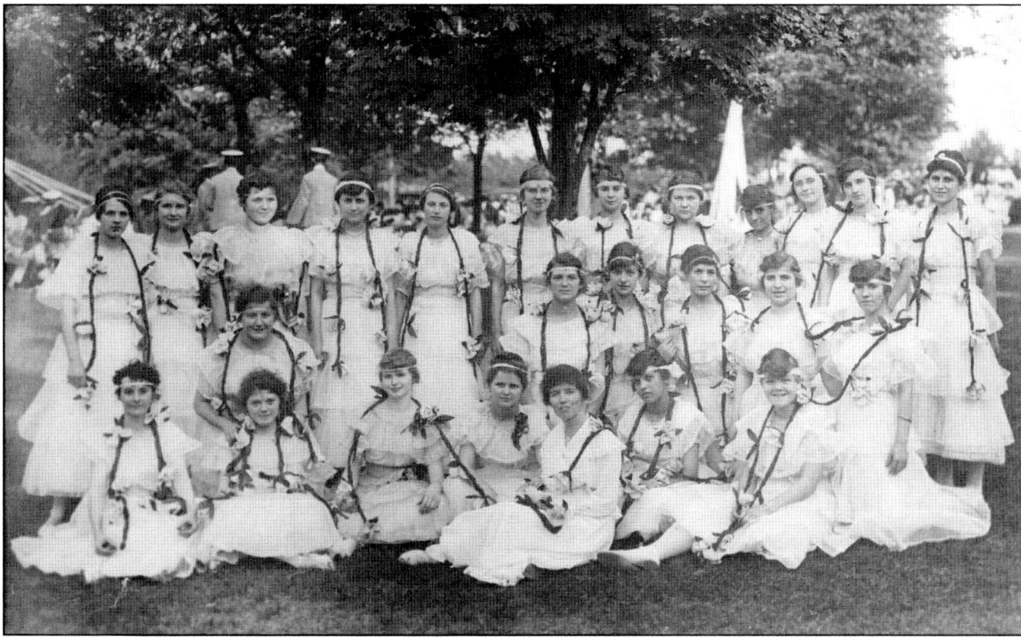

Dressed in springtime white finery and flowers, Schoolfield's young ladies adopt demure poses for this c. 1920 May Day celebration. The cotton mill encouraged such celebrations for its workers and their families. Dancing around the maypole was the high point of these springtime festivals in the park. (Courtesy of the Schoolfield Museum and Cultural Center.)

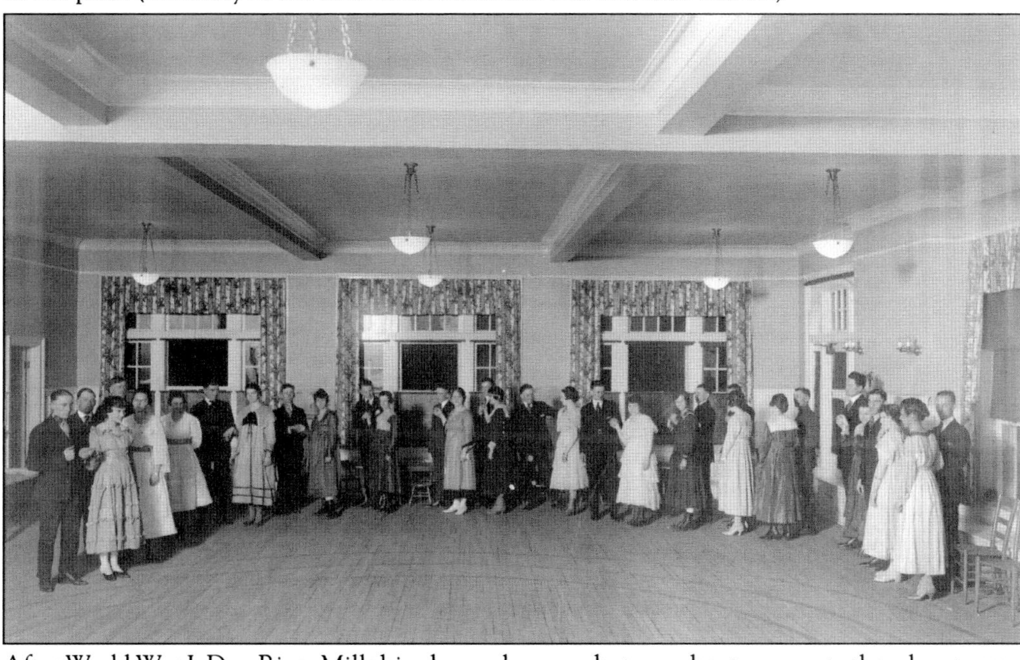

After World War I, Dan River Mills hired an unknown photographer to promote the advantages of working for the mill and living in its Schoolfield village. The Girls' Pastime Club and their escorts are shown here at a party in the Welfare Building, completed in 1917. Principally a kindergarten and clinic for mill employees and their families, this building now serves as the Schoolfield Museum and Cultural Center. (Courtesy of the Schoolfield Museum and Cultural Center.)

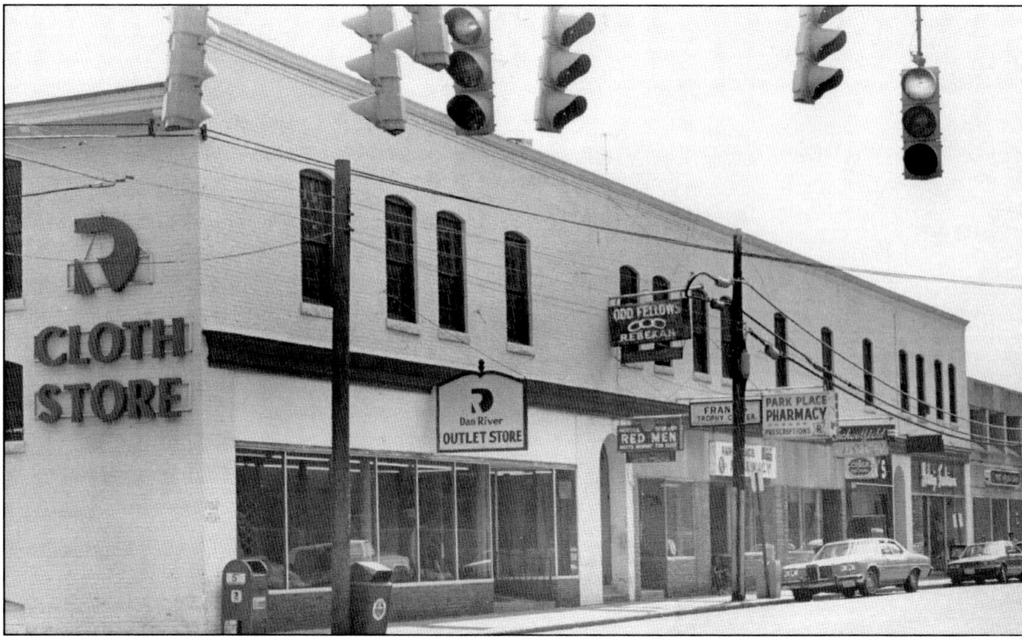

The Dan River Cloth Store occupied the corner storefront of a 1920s row on West Main Street and Wood Avenue, where generations of mill workers purchased goods with "scrip" deducted from their wages. Patrons traveled to this store to purchase defective items at bargain prices. The mill's rigorous quality control required that goods or bedding with the slightest defects be pulled and marked down. (Photograph by Richard T. Davis.)

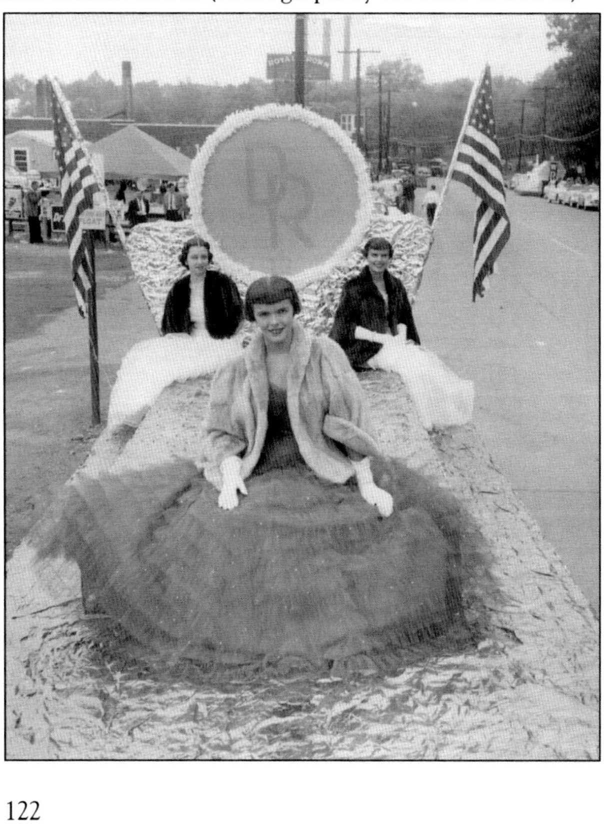

In 1956, Danville welcomed W.C. "Dan" Daniel with a homecoming parade honoring his recent appointment as the American Legion's new national commander. Waiting in line on West Main Street for the parade to begin, the float from the Dan River Cotton Mills featured a trio of Schoolfield's "daughters" led by Madeline Fisher (front), Marie Oakley (back left) and Ruby Lee Rich. (Photograph by Dempsey DeHart; courtesy of Carolyn Miles.)

Carolyn Waller (Miles) poses with her father, Chesley Richard Waller, for a 1933 portrait made by Jesse G. Seay, who ran a studio on the second floor of the mill's cloth store from 1927 to 1946. Carolyn was the third of five generations on her mother's side to work for Dan River Inc. (Photograph by Jesse G. Seay; courtesy of Carolyn Waller Miles.)

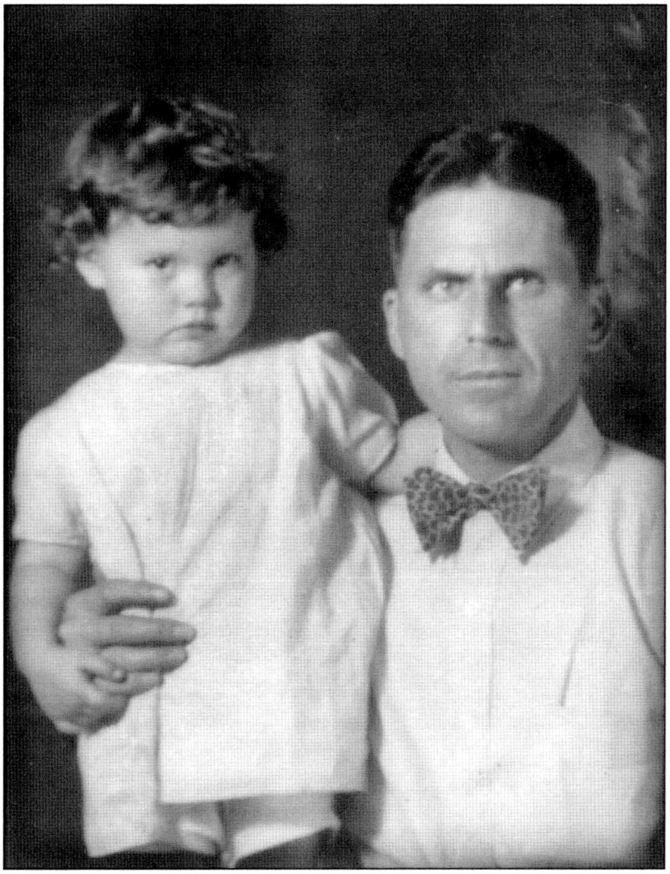

Jesse G. Seay became a household name in Schoolfield while working with his father, Edward, at the community's only photography studio, which specialized in school yearbooks. Sisters Ellen (left) and Ruth Barton posed for the photographs below while attending Schoolfield High School around 1935. (Photograph by Jesse G. Seay; courtesy of Mike Owen.)

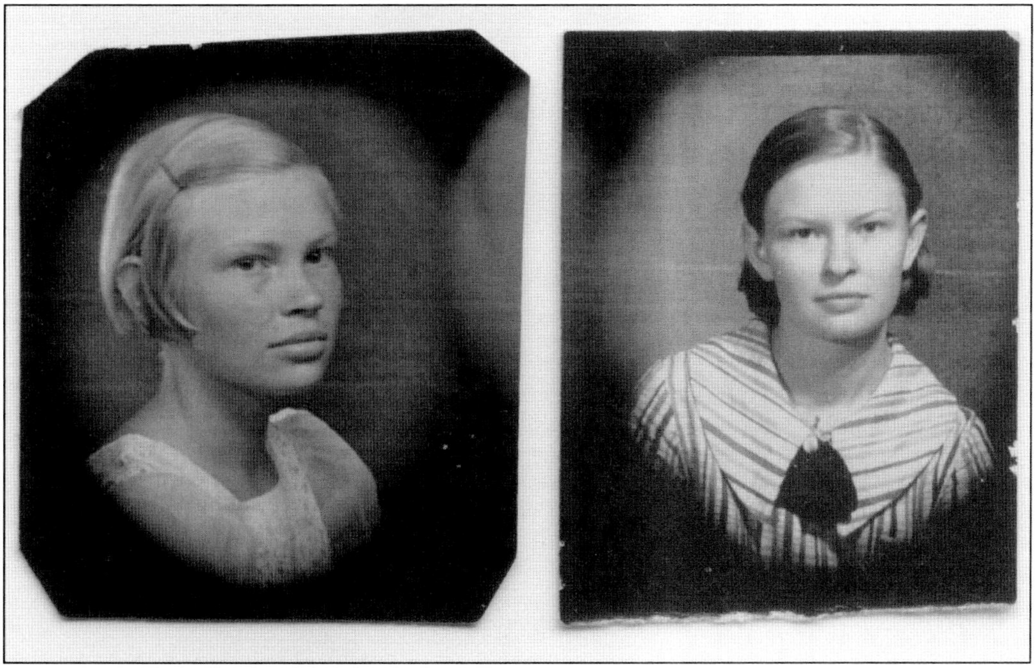

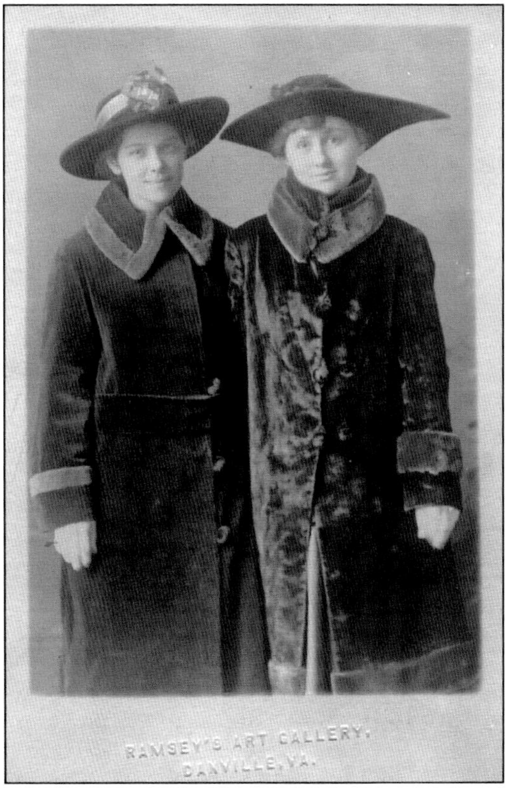

Daniel H. Ramsey was a studio photographer for just four years. Sometime between 1917 and 1921, Blanche Hamlett Forbes (left) and an unidentified friend posed in fancy winter outfits at Ramsey's Art Gallery. Forbes was a daughter of John and Lula Forbes of North Danville. (Photograph by Daniel H. Ramsey; courtesy of Dee Smith.)

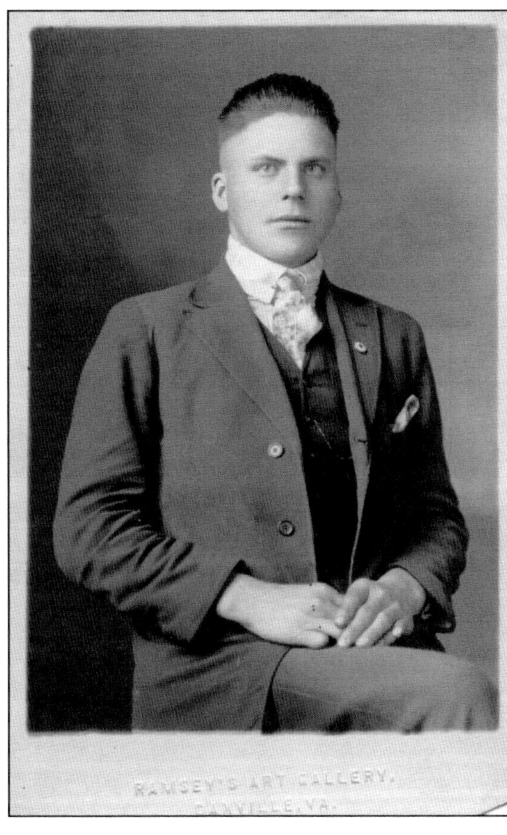

In this 1918 photograph, 18-year-old Chesley Richard Waller sits for his portrait in Ramsey's Art Gallery at 311 Main Street. Waller worked at the Schoolfield Division of Dan River Mills for more than 40 years, in the finishing department, and later, due to declining health, as a guard. A quiet person by nature, Waller served his country in World War II. (Photograph by Daniel H. Ramsey; courtesy of Carolyn Waller Miles.)

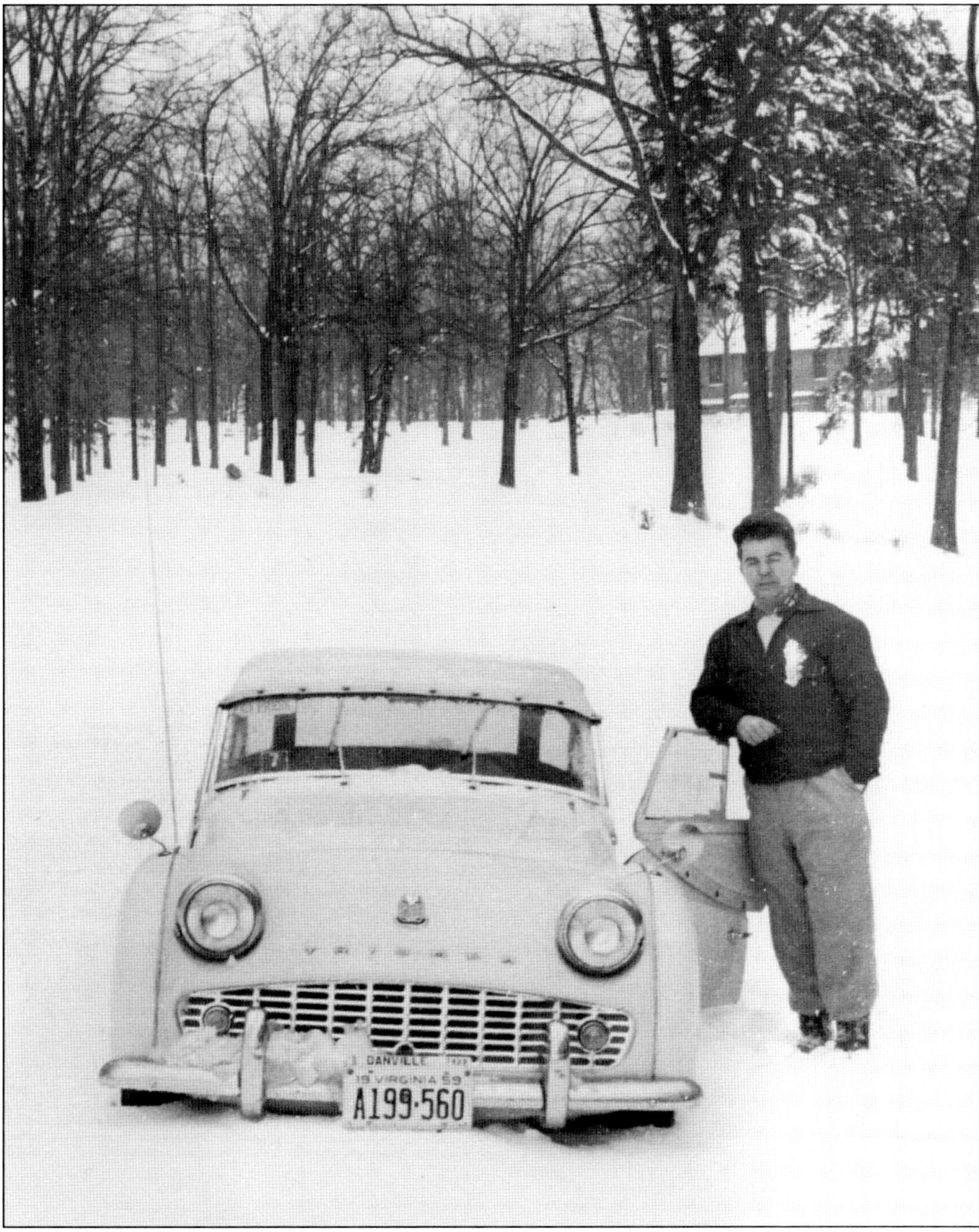

Leon Townsend stands beside his new 1958 Triumph TR3, which he used for years as his press car. Townsend worked for the *Register & Bee* from 1948 to 2002 in several positions, but mostly as the staff photographer. Townsend began his newspaper career at age 13, when his parents put a lien on their house to purchase his first paper route, a debt he managed to pay off in six months. After serving in World War II, Townsend returned to Danville and worked in the engraving department of the newspaper before he became chief photographer. At the newspaper, Townsend served as a mentor to many newcomers to the publishing world. Frequently the first photographer on the scene, Townsend had an opportunity to get to know people all over the community. Anywhere he went, he seemed to know everybody. (Courtesy of Leon Townsend.)

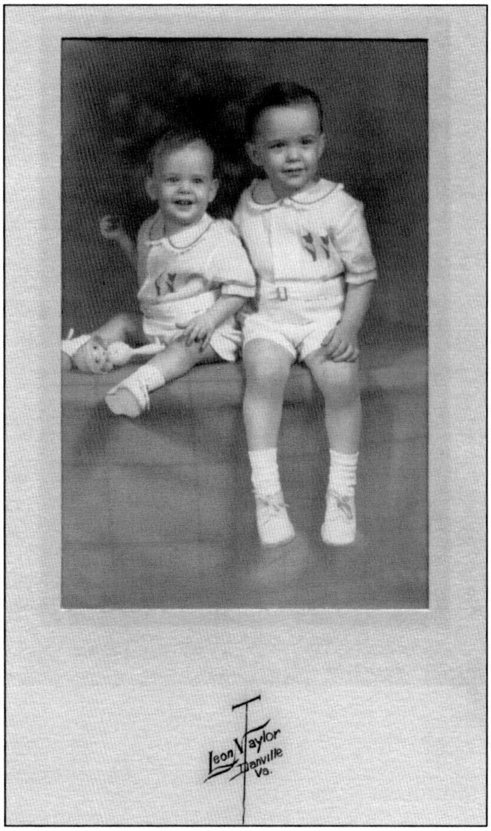

Among his many talents, Leon Taylor specialized in portraits of children. Here, Tom (left) and Earle Garrett sit in front of his camera in 1936, one year before Taylor's death. By that time, Taylor had given up his Main Street studio and was conducting business in his home at 1002 North Main Street. (Photograph by Leon Taylor; courtesy of Earle Garrett III.)

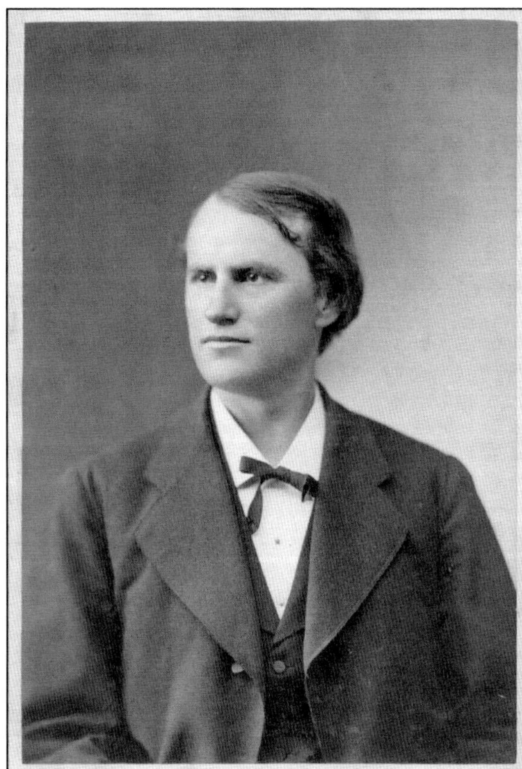

Although not from a Danville studio, this portrait of Archibald Murphy Aiken Sr. is important because of its association with an icon of American photography, famous Civil War photographer Matthew Brady. Aiken was chosen as the judge of corporation court in 1878 and sat on the Danville bench for 22 years. Aiken sat for this portrait in Brady's Washington, DC, studio. (Photograph by the Matthew Brady Studio; courtesy of the Danville Historical Society.)

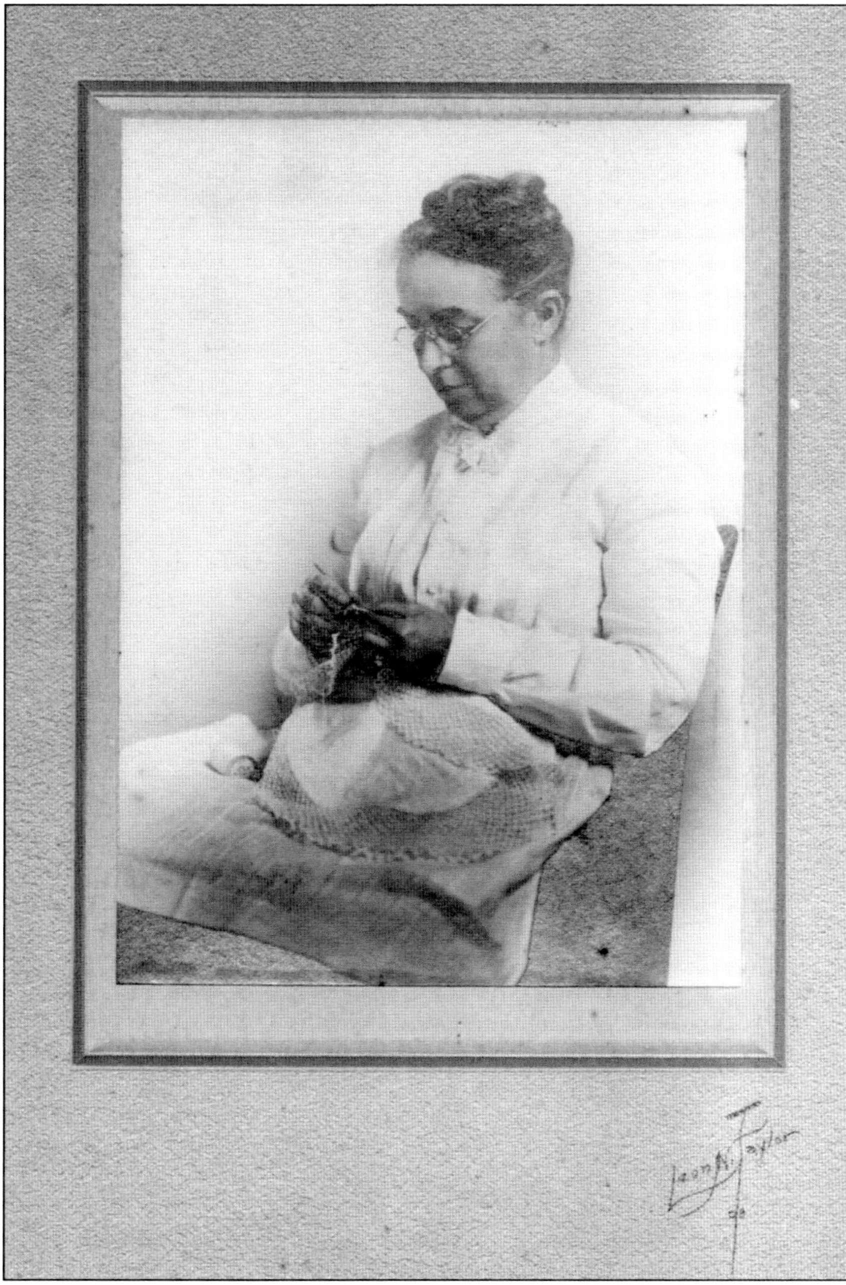

The daughter of Lewis A. and Martha R. Yates, Mary Ella Yates joined the Episcopal Church of the Epiphany early in her life. She and her sister Augusta spent their entire lives as leaders of that church. For a number of years, Mary Ella served as president of the local Ladies Memorial Association, which was founded in 1872 by Augusta to locate burial sites of all local Confederate soldiers and bring their remains home for reburial. In 1881, Mary Ella married Judge Archibald Murphy Aiken Sr. Known for her fine sewing skills, Mary Ella stitched an exquisite, crazy quilt—which now belongs to the Danville Museum of Fine Arts and History—for her hope chest. In this 1908 portrait, Leon Taylor captured the very soul of Mary Ella Aiken as she sat crocheting, still creating with her hands. (Photograph by Leon Taylor.)